Body Space Medicine

D1023925

Dr. Zhi Chen Guo

Foreword

Master, Professor and Dr. Zhi Chen Guo is my most beloved spiritual father and teacher. If I have attained a little success in acquiring healing wisdom and knowledge, and in offering and teaching healing, it is because Master Guo has trained me seriously and intensively since 1993. Through his training, I developed my physical energy, vitality and stamina, and my spiritual capabilities. I opened my spiritual channels to become a medical intuitive. As a spiritual master, I have cleansed the bad karma of thousands and enlightened the souls of hundreds. As a divine servant, vehicle and channel, I am honored to have transmitted millions of permanent divine healing and blessing treasures to humanity and souls in the universe. As an author and teacher, I am blessed to have written two best-sellers, *Power Healing* and *Soul Mind Body Medicine.*

I give the credit and the honor for my accomplishments to my beloved Master, Dr. Zhi Chen Guo. Without his delivery of sacred wisdom, knowledge and practice, I could not have built the physical and spiritual foundation to serve humanity and souls in the universe. I honor Master Guo first and foremost. Of course, I honor all of my spiritual fathers and mothers in both the physical world and the spiritual world. As a universal servant, I honor every human being and every soul in all universes. I honor the Divine totally.

I say this in order to explain the relationship between Master Guo and me, as well as to show why I would like to give my teacher the highest and greatest honor. Thank you for giving me the opportunity to share these words from the bottom of my heart. Now, I am Master Guo's worldwide representative and adoptive son. It is my duty and great honor to spread his profound and heart-touching wisdom, knowledge and practice worldwide. Millions of people are waiting for this. Millions of people will benefit from this.

Body Space Medicine reveals secret wisdom, knowledge and practice for healing, prevention of illness, rejuvenation and prolonging life. Some of these secrets are:

- Body Space Medicine introduces the concept of *body space* to medicine. There are two kinds of body space. One is the smaller space between the cells. The other is the bigger space between the organs.

- Body Space Medicine distills the essence of all other healing modalities into the revolutionary theory that there is only *one* cause of sickness: *imbalance of body fluids.* The unimpeded flow of body fluids in the smaller and bigger body spaces is the foundation of good health.

- Body Space Medicine reveals the secret of healing: *promote the Gong Zhuan,* the main vertical circle in the body, for circulation of body fluids and energy.

- For diagnosis, Body Space Medicine uses a unique and simple *tongue reading* system.

- For healing, Body Space Medicine uses a formulary of fewer than twenty herbs instead of the thousands of herbs used in traditional Chinese medicine. These herbs are further distilled to a *quantum formulary* (patents pending) consisting of a mere five herbs used in four standard herb formulas instead of the hundreds used in traditional Chinese medicine. Each of these four formulas consists of only three, four or all five herbs. For each herb, the dosage is only four or seven grams.

If you know a little about traditional Chinese medicine, you are no doubt astonished. Is this possible? Can it really be so simple? Four herb formulas with only a few herbs each can treat any illness? There is a famous Chinese saying: *If you want to know whether a pear is sweet, you need to taste it.* If you want to know whether this incredibly simple new medicine is effective, you need to experience it.

Does Body Space Medicine work? I ask you to open your heart and soul. Learn, practice and experience Body Space Medicine. Master Guo has practiced healing with herbs for more than fifty years. Even more significant is the fact that he is a spiritual leader. Throughout his entire life, spiritual inspiration has guided him to new wisdom. He has been able to experience this new wisdom, see it in action, confirm it through clinical practice and research, and finally apply it in its most distilled, essential and powerful form. He has treated hundreds of thousands of patients in his life, and from this he has assembled a massive bank of experience, case studies, clinical practice and research. Several million people in China have learned his Zhi Neng Medicine (both a precursor of and a co-creation with Body Space Medicine) and Body Space Medicine. He has healed thousands of chronic and life-threatening conditions. He is one of the most important spiritual leaders and teachers as well as one of the most exceptional healers in our time.

Throughout his eminent career, Master Guo has continually expanded, refined, simplified and distilled his theories, wisdom, knowledge and practice. Finally, he is ready to give the simplest and deepest wisdom of Body Space Medicine to the world. Although these methods are simple, they are also the most effective and most powerful. I honor Master Guo's total generosity and selflessness in sharing his entire life study, including research and practice. Ever since the day I met him, he has taught me that the purpose of life is to serve. Master Guo's generosity comes from *his* pure heart and unconditional service.

As a universal servant, I am extremely honored to introduce my teacher's Body Space Medicine worldwide. The wisdom, knowledge and practice of Body Space Medicine are too simple to believe. The power is heart-touching. The results are heart-and-soul-moving.

I am totally committed to travel worldwide to teach and spread this new medicine. This is my service to appreciate my teacher. I am honored to follow his example by offering my service to humanity and souls in the universe.

Study Body Space Medicine. Use it. Benefit from it.

I love my heart and soul.

I love all humanity.

Join hearts and souls together.

Love, peace and harmony.

Love, peace and harmony.

With love and blessing,

Zhi Gang Sha

Introduction

A Revolutionary Model for Health and Healing

Welcome to Body Space Medicine!

I am honored to present a revolutionary model for health and healing. This work is the culmination of more than five decades of clinical practice. I have conducted extensive and in-depth research on diagnosis and treatment and learned much from thousands of case studies. I have thoroughly studied the effects of emotional and spiritual factors on health. I have methodically tested and verified the theories, methodologies and efficacy of Body Space Medicine and humbly share this powerful healing science with you. I welcome feedback and guidance from my peers in the medical community and from all citizens of the world.

Body Space Medicine uses Chinese herbs, energy healing and message or spiritual healing, together with quantum medicine, to adjust and regulate the body and treat illness. Body Space Medicine offers preventive techniques as well. Regular practice of these techniques prevents illness, rejuvenates and prolongs life. Body Space Medicine develops the intelligence of the mind and soul, as well as their abilities to manifest and create. Body Space Medicine also purifies and uplifts the soul.

Body Space Medicine is so named because it deals with the *spaces* within the human body. I have defined two types of spaces — small spaces and large spaces. The small spaces are those between the cells. The large spaces are those between the organs. Energy flow in the small spaces directly affects the functions of the cells. Energy flow in the large spaces directly affects the functions of the organs.

Body Space Medicine asserts that health depends on normal functioning of the cells and organs. Consequently, the application of Body Space Medicine focuses on normal cellular function.

A typical cell contains various substances such as fluid, proteins, organelles that produce energy, a nucleus, and genetic material in the form of DNA and RNA. Body Space Medicine considers the structures and material within a cell to be *cell matter*. All living cells contract and expand as they function — expansion, contraction, expansion, contraction … When a cell contracts, cell matter converts or transforms into *energy* outside the cell. In traditional Chinese medicine, this energy is known as *qi*, and is considered to be vital energy or life force.

Expansion follows contraction. During expansion, the energy outside the cell converts or transforms back into matter within the cell. The two processes of transformation — *cell matter into energy* during cell contraction, and *energy into cell matter* during cell expansion — should be in relative balance. Imbalance results in illness. The greater the imbalance, the graver the illness. Body Space Medicine focuses on restoring and maintaining balance in the transformation between cell matter and energy.

Energy Movement

As energy radiates from the transformation of cell matter, it moves in the spaces between cells and between organs. This energy tends to move in a relatively regular pattern, with a specific direction and force.

Illness will occur if the direction of movement is abnormal or the force of movement is too weak or too strong.

During the development of Body Space Medicine, I have come to the conclusion that two principles govern energy movement in the body: Gong Zhuan (revolution) and Zi Zhuan (rotation). Body Space Medicine posits that energy from our organs, limbs, bones and cells moves in patterns of revolution and rotation. If the energy flows in the normal direction and with normal force, the body is healthy and illness is treated or prevented.

Throughout my life, I have adopted one of the major teachings given in the "Yellow Emperor's Classic of Internal Medicine" or *Huang Di Nei Jing,* the revered five-thousand-year-old canonical text of traditional Chinese medicine:

The best doctor is one who teaches people how to prevent sickness,
not one who treats sickness.

In this spirit, I offer you my expertise and understanding of the Gong Zhuan (revolution) and Zi Zhuan (rotation) so that you can use this wisdom and knowledge to help others prevent illness. If you understand the theory of Gong Zhuan and Zi Zhuan, you can prevent and heal illness regardless of its origin or whether it is physical, emotional, mental or spiritual in nature. The theory of revolution and rotation is the essence of Body Space Medicine and the most important focus of its therapeutics.

Zi Zhuan refers to the horizontal movement or *rotation* of the energy of each organ and cell. Thus, there are as many individual Zi Zhuan movements as there are cells and organs in the body. Proper horizontal rotation of energy in a specific location of the body can clear a specific blockage and treat a specific illness.

Gong Zhuan refers to the vertical movement or *revolution* of energy within the body. Gong Zhuan movement is much more important than Zi Zhuan movement because Gong Zhuan leads and drives Zi Zhuan.

If Gong Zhuan is blocked, Zi Zhuan will also be blocked. If Gong Zhuan flows freely, Zi Zhuan will follow suit and the body will be healthy.

Body Space Medicine is integrative and holistic. It emphasizes the health of the body as a whole. The function of each organ and cell in the body is closely linked to the function of the entire body. The treatment of illness should focus not on specific organs, but rather on the circulation of body fluids and energy throughout the entire body, especially through the Gong Zhuan.

Message Healing

Body Space Medicine uses *message healing.* How is this related to the matter and energy within the body? Everything is composed of matter. On the microscopic level, matter consists of molecules, atoms, neutrons, protons, electrons, quarks and even smaller units of matter as yet undiscovered by science. Quantum physics considers the quark and the lepton to be the two basic units of matter. However, future scientists will discover forms of matter smaller than quarks and leptons. Later still, the scientific community will confirm the existence of even smaller forms of matter. It will always be impossible to identify and truly understand the smallest form of matter in the universe as there will always be something smaller. I understand that matter in the universe is infinite and infinitely divisible. It can be divided into infinitely smaller and smaller units.

In Body Space Medicine we can think of the smallest unit of matter in the universe as a kind of information wave or message. Messages accumulate to form perceptible matter. We also understand that energy is the minutest form of matter. Consider Einstein's famous equation $E = mc^2$, where E is energy, m is mass (matter) and c is the velocity of light. This equation radically changed the understanding of the physical nature of matter and energy. It states that matter and energy are equivalent. Moreover, even a tiny particle of matter has a huge amount of energy (minutest matter).

Body Space Medicine is based on the Message Energy Matter Theory, which states that matter and energy are carriers of information or *message.* Think of information as a message, wave, soul or spirit. All forms of matter — animate and inanimate — carry information. This is to say that everything has a soul. The information, message or soul can directly affect matter and energy, as well as the transformation between matter inside cells and energy outside cells. Body Space Medicine treats illness by using the message or soul of herbs, of vibrational sounds and of acts or emotions such as love, forgiveness and compassion. Indeed, Body Space Medicine can use the message inherent in all entities of the universe. Thus, Body Space Medicine advances the theory and implements the practice of information, message or soul in its therapeutics.

Over the past several decades, I have used Chinese herbs (matter), energy and information (message) to treat illnesses. In 1982, I began to use energy and message to treat illnesses remotely in clients who could not consult me in person. Remote healing of the soul in Body Space Medicine is closely linked to and in accordance with quantum science. Healing with energy and message can transcend physical parameters such as time and distance. The method is flexible and creative, which means if you say *this is the method,* it is *not* the method. If you say *it has a method,* it has *no* method. This is the highest spiritual philosophy of creativity and flexibility. It is doctrine *and* non-doctrine. Doctrine is present and doctrine is absent. What is the true method? Sudden awareness is the true method. Inspiration is the true method. The method of Body Space Medicine is the doctrine of enlightenment and inspiration. I therefore regard Body Space Medicine as quantum medicine.

I developed Body Space Medicine based on my Xiu Lian journey. *Xiu* means purification of soul, mind and body. *Lian* means practice. Xiu Lian is the entire process of one's spiritual journey — spiritual training and cultivation of one's entire being — soul, heart, mind, and body, from the time your soul was created to the time it reaches its ultimate goal, which is to reach the highest realm of Heaven, the divine realm. Xiu Lian is not a journey of a single lifetime. In every lifetime we do Xiu Lian. Body Space Medicine emphasizes Xiu Lian. If you do not have a good Xiu Lian background, you will not be able to see the root blockages in the body as a medical intuitive. You will not be able to give highly precise diagnoses and treatments. The highest standard for a practitioner of Body Space Medicine requires advanced Xiu Lian training and capabilities.

I will write a separate volume to teach Xiu Lian, to guide your spiritual journey, to develop your soul potential and to enlighten your soul. This volume presents the theories, methods and secrets of Body Space Medicine to the entire healing community and beyond. I hope people will study this breakthrough healing science in earnest and use it to strengthen the body, develop the mind, cultivate and purify the soul, and, above all, elevate the soul.

Anyone can learn Body Space Medicine. Anyone can learn how to treat illness not only with Chinese herbs, but also with energy, consciousness and message. Using our consciousness is the essence of training and purification, and the key to healing with energy. Furthermore, it is my fervent wish that practitioners grasp the principles of quantum medicine, and truly master message healing.

Our journey is blessed. Innumerable messages now converging from within the boundless universe will quickly unlock many mysteries. There is infinite benevolent information in the universe, which can permeate our bodies, broaden our thoughts, cleanse our souls and develop our potentialities. Let Body Space Medicine unfold and benefit all humanity!

A Tool for the Service of Humanity

I hope with all my heart that Body Space Medicine will bring you the wisdom and knowledge to use Chinese herbs to adjust and regulate the body and mind. May it also teach you to heal using energy and message. May it further help you to unveil the eternal mysteries of the soul. You — anyone — can use the wisdom and the practices of the soul to benefit yourself and your family. If each family could live in stability, peace and harmony, why could we not achieve the same with a larger "family," such as a work team, a large corporation, a city, a country, every country, all of humanity, the entire planet or the entire universe? We *can* reach a state where all souls coexist in prosperity and peace, enjoy abundant harvests and happiness, and reach fulfillment and completion of the soul journey. May Body Space Medicine become a universal tool to serve humanity so that we can reach this ideal condition.

I am grateful to all people, to Heaven and to the universe for developing my wisdom and my potential. I will forever be a servant of the universe. I dedicate my service to humanity, Mother Earth and the universe.

1

Key Theories and Concepts

Cell Biology

The cell is the smallest independent functional unit of all living organisms. Some organisms are single-celled, such as bacteria; others are multi-celled. The adult human body is estimated to have at least thirty trillion or 3×10^{13} cells. Groups of similar cells make up each of the various organs and tissues in the body.

Each cell is a self-contained unit of life. Like all living things, cells eat, breathe, produce energy, carry out specialized functions and excrete waste. A typical cell contains various substances such as fluid, protein, organelles with different functions, and the genetic material that regulates cell functions and contains hereditary information.

A cell generates energy through its constant activity, dissipating and radiating it outward through the cell membrane. At the same time, this constant activity requires the absorption of nutrients and other matter into the cell. The functions of a cell include digesting, absorbing and storing nutrients.

Body Space Medicine recognizes the critical importance of understanding cell functions in Western medicine. However, Body Space Medicine recognizes how much more important it is that the energy radiated by and from the cells be able to circulate smoothly and unimpeded in the body space, both the smaller spaces between the cells and the larger spaces between the organs.

Highly developed systems of medicine have their own theories on the causes of illness. For example, Western medicine operates on the premise that bacteria and viruses can affect cell functions and cause illness. Traditional Chinese medicine recognizes three groups of factors that can lead to illness:

- external factors (i.e., environmental), known as the Six Excesses: wind, cold, summer heat, dampness, dryness and fire

- internal factors, known as the Seven Emotions: overexcitement, anger, anxiety, worry, grief, fear and fright

- other factors: parasites, epidemics, diet, stress, injury, etc.

The perspective of Body Space Medicine is that all illnesses, regardless of cause or origin, ultimately affect the body at the cellular level. The changes in cellular activity in turn affect the circulation of energy in the body space. This concept was already understood thousands of years ago by ancient Chinese healers in their adjustments of *qi* or vital energy. The guiding principle used five thousand years ago was that energy must flow freely in the body for one to be healthy.

Body Space Medicine, however, looks beyond *qi*, energy and cell matter. *Fluid* is the important medium. Fluid is both energy and matter. If one understands "fluid" in Body Space Medicine, one will have mastered Body Space Medicine and be a powerful healer. The concept of fluid in Body Space Medicine will be explained further in this and subsequent chapters.

There is much wisdom in ancient healing systems. Body Space Medicine is built on the foundation of ancient theories. Yet, Body Space Medicine also incorporates modern concepts such as cell theory. Regardless of the cause of illness, Body Space Medicine teaches one to focus on the cells. The transformation between cell matter and energy, the flow of fluid and energy in the body space, Xiu Lian (spiritual training and cultivation, which I will explain fully in a separate book) and message healing are the core of Body Space Medicine.

Cell Theory

A cell is the smallest functioning unit of the body. Cells consist of matter. A cell contains various units, such as the nucleus, DNA and RNA. Biochemical changes occur within the cell. These changes are observed and measured in laboratory studies by Western medicine. For example, certain proteins control specific cell functions. Each type of protein is typically sent to a specific part of the cell.

Cells constantly vibrate, expanding and contracting. Body Space Medicine understands that when cells contract, matter inside the cells transforms to energy or *qi* outside the cells. When cells expand, energy or *qi* around the cells transforms back to matter inside the cells. For health, this transformation between matter inside the cells and energy outside the cells must be in relative balance.

Body Space

In 1982, I developed my medical intuitive abilities and began to observe spiritual images in my patients' bodies during clinical practice. I attribute this ability to my many years of Xiu Lian (spiritual training and cultivation). It was during my Xiu Lian and my clinical observations that I suddenly grasped the concept of body space or the spaces in the body.

Body space can be classified as two types:

• the small space, which is the space between cells

• the large space, which is the space between organs

There is space even within each cell. We can even classify infinitesimally smaller spaces but, for simplicity, Body Space Medicine considers the small space to be the space between cells, and the large space to be the space between organs.

Traditional Chinese medicine considers the flow of *qi* (vital energy or life force) within the body. *Qi* flows in the spaces between the cells and between the organs. To heal is to promote the flow of *qi*. As the Yellow Emperor's Classic stated 5,000 years ago: *If* qi *flows, one is healthy.*

To broaden the theory, the universe is the big space and the human organism is the small space. All things in the universe contain space, even "solid" matter such as a steel rod. Space is everywhere. There is nowhere without space. Man lives in the universe and it is the space in the universe that has brought into being all things and all matter.

Consider the weather. When skies are overcast, it brings on a gloomy feeling. Sustained rain dampens the spirits. A bright and clear sky makes you feel limber, active and happy. An expanse of ocean makes you comfortable and opens your heart. When the weather is overcast, the space is dense due to the cloud cover, causing discomfort. When the environment is polluted, the space is dense with pollutants, making you feel even worse. The density and pressure of the bigger space of our environment directly affect the body space. The sky is a big universe; the body is a small universe. Man and sky are one.

If you want to know about the big universe, you need to study the mysteries of the small universe. If you unlock the mysteries of the small universe, you will understand the mysteries of the big universe. The converse is also true. To unlock the mysteries of the small universe, study the mysteries and mechanisms of the large universe and apply this knowledge to the small universe.

The ancient Chinese knew about the importance of space in their practice of feng shui, which literally means "wind and water." Feng shui has deep Taoist and Confucian roots and its practice emphasizes arranging the space of one's home or facilities in harmony with the environment. The most important point of feng shui is to keep the space clear and uncluttered. Good feng shui is of utmost importance to the harmony and success of the home, office, clinic, factory or any other facility.

The benefits of a clear and uncluttered space can be likened to the experience of a bright clear sky, an expansive ocean, a deep forest, a field of blooming flowers, a flock of birds chirping – all of which have the effect of uplifting the spirit and clearing the mind. If you understand the importance of feng shui in the big universe of nature, you will understand its importance in the body space. As in nature, good feng shui in the human body will make one feel unburdened, comfortable and happy. When the body space is uncluttered, people enjoy good health, have clarity of mind and power of wisdom, and can develop their potential.

San Jiao and Wai Jiao

Body Space Medicine teaches how to adjust and regulate the small space between the cells and the big space between the organs. Within the body there are four big spaces between the organs:

- Upper Jiao (the upper visceral cavity)

- Middle Jiao (the middle visceral cavity)

- Lower Jiao (the lower visceral cavity)

- Wai Jiao (the "external" cavity)

The Upper Jiao is the body space above the diaphragm, including the neck and head. The Middle Jiao is the body space between the diaphragm and the level of the navel. The Lower Jiao is the body space below the navel down through the genitals. The upper, middle and lower visceral cavities are collectively called the San Jiao ("three areas"), a term from traditional Chinese medicine, where it is also known as the Triple Warmer. The visceral cavities are the channels in which the body's vital energy or *qi*, blood and fluid circulate. An uncluttered and clear San Jiao will bring one health, good spirits, comfort and vigor.

During clinical observations in 1988, I suddenly realized that the biggest space in the human body is not the San Jiao, but something much larger. The large space I observed is located in front of the entire back. It encompasses the space in front of the spine and the back ribs, and includes the space in the brain, the chest cavity, the cavity in front of the spine and the abdominal cavity. I have named this largest space of the body the Wai Jiao ("external area").

To understand the relationships among the large body spaces, think of the Wai Jiao as the sea and of the San Jiao as the lakes and rivers which flow to the sea. If the sea is unblocked, the waters of the lakes and rivers can flow unimpeded. If the sea is blocked, passage of the waters of the lakes and rivers will be blocked. A clear and unblocked sea, or Wai Jiao, is a requisite for an uncluttered San Jiao. Consequently, Body Space Medicine recognizes the importance of the smooth flow of energy in the San Jiao, but places even greater emphasis on the unimpeded flow of energy in the Wai Jiao.

The Wai Jiao and San Jiao constitute the big spaces of the body. When body fluids and energy flow smoothly in the big space, energy will likewise flow smoothly between cells, that is, in the small space. The small space between cells constitutes the brooks and streams that feed the rivers and oceans. Like the rivers and oceans in nature, we want the fluid and energy passageways in our body to flow smoothly. To keep the body's passageways open, first adjust and regulate the Wai Jiao. Then, the small space between the cells will be open and clear. An open and uncluttered body space brings health, develops wisdom and uplifts the spirit.

The whole focus of Body Space Medicine is to promote and maintain the smooth and unimpeded flow of fluid and energy in the body space. An open and uncluttered body space is the key to treating illnesses. Purifying the fluid and energy in the body space is also the key to the soul's cultivation and purification, which I will discuss in depth in a separate book on Xiu Lian and Body Space Medicine. Without a purified space, neither the wisdom of the soul nor the latent capabilities of the human body can develop. Therefore, to apply and practice Body Space Medicine, first unblock the body space. Then, more importantly, purify the body space. Both steps are crucial in order to adjust and regulate the body and its fluids and energies; treat illnesses; develop intelligence, capabilities and latent powers; elevate the standing of one's soul; and complete the soul's journey.

Matter Inside Cells and Energy Outside Cells

A cell is a self-contained unit of life. This containment is provided by the cell wall and cell membrane, which separate the cell's internal components from the surrounding environment and control what moves in and out. Within the cell, there are fluids, genetic material (DNA, RNA) with hereditary messages and other information, and many little organelles that carry out specialized functions such as reproduction, control, protein synthesis, digestion, energy production and management of water and waste. Body Space Medicine defines everything inside a cell as "matter."

Matter moves, expands and contracts, collides with and stimulates other matter. This activity of cell matter produces energy. When the cell contracts, matter inside the cell transforms to energy that is radiated out of the cell into the small space (the space between the cells). When the cell expands, energy from outside the cell transforms to matter inside the cell. There is a continuous transformation between matter and energy as cells contract and expand.

All illnesses stem from an imbalance between the transformation of matter inside the cell and energy outside the cell. We are speaking of a relative balance, not an absolute, fixed balance. To treat illnesses ultimately is to restore and maintain this relative balance. This is the

key for treating and preventing illnesses. This principle is also the key
for rejuvenation.

Body Fluids

Water is essential for a human being. About 70% of a typical adult's
body consists of water or fluid. Babies are as much as 80 or 90% water
or fluid. Body Space Medicine introduces a revolutionary theory of
the role and function of fluid in the body. It states that fluid balance is
vital for restoring and maintaining health. Body Space Medicine views
matter as fluid and energy (or *qi*) as "steam" or fluid vapor. This is yet
another way in which Body Space Medicine goes beyond and apart
from traditional Chinese medicine, which focuses on *qi*.

How does Body Space Medicine understand that fluid imbalance is the root cause of all illnesses? Take blood clots, for example.
Blood clots in the brain block the blood vessels in the brain, causing
stroke. Blood clots are body fluids sticking together to create high density fluid. That is a fluid imbalance. Cancer patients often have many
blood vessels blocked. I have observed that many cancer patients have
heavy, high density fluid outside the cells. We know that exposure to
some chemicals (carcinogens) can cause cancer. Whatever the reason,
chemical or other, cells can become overactive. They radiate out lots
of energy, increasing the energy density and pressure around the cells.
This high density and high pressure energy acts on the cells, causing
them to become irregular or precancerous, and then cancerous. This is
how normal cells become cancer cells. Western medicine does not think
that cancer cells can revert to normal cells. In Body Space Medicine, so
long as the high density and pressure can be released, fluid balance will
be restored, the accumulated energy will dissipate, and cancer cells will
transform back to normal cells. In Body Space Medicine, we can also
use the power of soul, together with the power of energy and the power
of the quantum herb formulas to be presented in Chapter 3, to release
the high density and pressure, creating a solution for cancer.

In summary, blood clots are caused by fluid becoming sticky and high in density, blocking the "tubes" of the blood vessels. Similarly, tumors are due to high fluid density *inside* the cells, while cancer is due to high fluid density *outside* the cells. You will see that my theory of body fluids is very simple, and yet it explains all illnesses *and* how they can be healed. In two words: *balance fluids.* I have reached this theory as the culmination of my life's work with hundreds of thousands of patients. It has empowered me to diagnose and treat a patient in thirty seconds. I will explain my theory of body fluids and its application in Body Space Medicine in depth in Chapter 3.

Message Energy Matter Theory

Inspiration is the best teacher. Who gives me inspiration? Heaven gives me inspiration. The universe and people give me inspiration. Suddenly, I understand the truth and laws of the universe. Suddenly, I can see the creation, development and progress of the universe, and comprehend what the future will hold.

In 1988, I was inspired by Heaven as I was teaching my training method, Dong Yi Gong, to a group of students. Dong Yi Gong translates as "using thinking exercise." This Zhi Neng Medicine style of qi gong uses creative visualization exercises to quickly develop and balance the soul, mind and body. I suddenly understood that my combined concept of message, energy and matter *is* the *Tao,*[1] and an indisputable law of nature. In other words, the theory is applicable and valid in any kind of space, in any universe and in any facet of human life, down to every action and even every intention. Thus was born the Message Energy Matter Theory, which states:

Message is soul or spirit.

Matter and energy are carriers of message.

Message can directly affect the transformation between matter inside the cell and energy outside the cell.

All things in the universe are comprised of matter. Matter is infinitely divisible. The smallest unit of matter is the information wave or message. The accumulation of messages forms energy, so that energy can also be considered to be matter. When a volcano erupts, matter converts to energy. In an earthquake, the vibration of matter also explodes into energy. In the body, cells consist of matter. When a cell contracts, cell matter becomes energy, which moves out of the cell. Energy, in turn, can turn into matter. In fact, energy in the body space constantly returns to the cell to become matter. Let me give an example of energy transforming to matter inside the body. There is a famous statement in the "Yellow Emperor's Classic of Internal Medicine": *Ju zhe cheng xing, san zhe cheng feng.* The literal meaning of the words is accumulation (*ju*), thing (*zhe*), becomes (*cheng*), shape (*xing*), dissipation (*san*), thing (*zhe*), becomes (*cheng*), wind (*feng*), but the statement translates as:

When energy accumulates, it becomes a form.

When energy dissipates, the form disappears, just like the wind flowing away.

This is an energy and spiritual secret which explains how a tumor or cancer is formed. When energy accumulates in a specific part of the body, a form is produced. This form is a tumor or cancer. Dissipate the energy and this form will disappear. Tumors and cancers will disappear. This is an example of how energy (tiny matter) accumulates to transform to matter and how matter dissipates to transform to energy.

As I have previously indicated, energy is also matter. Energy is minute particles of matter. When matter gets even smaller, it becomes an information wave or a message. Message, energy and matter in the usual sense are all forms of matter.

The division of matter becomes energy. The division of energy becomes message. The division of message becomes matter. The accumulation of matter becomes energy. The accumulation of energy becomes message. The accumulation of message becomes matter. Message, energy and matter are interchangeable. Matter and energy are carriers of message. Matter and energy *are* message.

Most healing systems, including Western medicine, traditional Chinese medicine, Ayurvedic medicine and naturopathic medicine, use matter such as drugs, herbs and foods to treat illness and disease. Matter is used to adjust and regulate the body's fluids, energies and messages.

Body Space Medicine carries the use of message one step further. It knows that matter carries message, that matter can transform into energy, and that message can influence both matter and energy. Body Space Medicine therefore uses matter, energy *and* message for healing. Message leads and drives energy. Energy transforms and drives matter. Message, energy and matter meld in harmony.

Message can directly adjust and regulate cell and organ functions, treat and prevent illnesses, rejuvenate soul, mind and body, improve longevity, and develop the intelligence of the brain and the latent power of the soul. Message can elevate the quality of the soul and complete the soul's journey. In the end, all souls will join as one to become harmonized. There will be peace in the world and the universe.

Gong Zhuan (Revolution) and Zi Zhuan (Rotation)

Man is the small universe. Nature is the big universe. Understand the big universe to understand the small universe.

Consider Mother Earth. This planetary body rotates constantly as it revolves around the sun. Now consider the human body. Every cell, organ and organ system radiates energy. This energy outside the cells, organs and systems (i.e., in the body space) moves in a spiral fashion, like the rotation of the Earth. The movement of the energy around the cells differs from the movement of the energy around the organs, which in turn is different from the large-scale movement of energy about the body. The differences are in the direction of, force of and light emitted by each movement.

Energy movement in the body falls into only two categories: (1) Gong Zhuan (revolution) and (2) Zi Zhuan (rotation). The energies from our organs, limbs and cells all move in patterns of revolution (orbits) and rotation (spin). So long as there is life, these patterns of energy movement are continuous. The Gong Zhuan and Zi Zhuan pathways of energy in the body are shown in Figure 1.

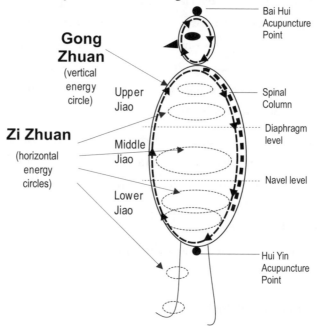

Figure 1. Gong Zhuan and Zi Zhuan Energy Circles of the Body

Zi Zhuan "rotation" refers to the continuous horizontal spinning movements of the energy of each system, organ and cell. Each spin is different in direction, force and light emitted. There are as many individual Zi Zhuan rotations or spins as there are cells and organs in the body. Collectively, this category of rotational movements of the energy about the body's systems, organs and cells is known as the Zi Zhuan or Horizontal Energy Circle. A smooth and unimpeded Zi Zhuan will regulate the body and mind, develop wisdom, clear specific blockages and treat specific illnesses. However, an unimpeded Zi Zhuan by itself is not enough. It is more important to achieve unimpeded energy flow within the Gong Zhuan.

Gong Zhuan "revolution" refers to the large-scale movement of energy as it continuously circulates or orbits vertically about the body. The Gong Zhuan is also known as the Vertical Energy Circle. Gong Zhuan revolution is much more important as it drives Zi Zhuan rotation or spin. If revolution of the body's Vertical Energy Circle is unimpeded, it follows naturally that the horizontal rotation of energy within the Zi Zhuan will also be unimpeded. If energy flows freely through the Gong Zhuan, the Zi Zhuan will follow suit and the body will be healthy.

The path of the Gong Zhuan is shown in Figure 1. The flow of energy in the Vertical Energy Circle starts from the Hui Yin (Meeting of Yin), the acupuncture point between the external genitalia and the anus. It rises up the anterior midline of the body, traversing the acupuncture points of Guan Yuan (Origin Gate) in the pubic region and Qi Hai (Sea of *Qi*) on the lower abdomen. It continues to rise through the navel, the central gastric cavity and the diaphragm, passing the Shan Zhong (Chest Center) acupuncture point centered between the nipples. The flow of energy continues onward and upward, through the throat and brain, finally reaching the Bai Hui (Hundred Meetings) acupuncture point at the top of the head. From there, it travels down the posterior in front of the entire spinal column, past the acupuncture points of Ya Men (Mute's Gate) on the back of the neck below the first cervical vertebra and Da Zhui (Great Hammer) below the seventh cervical vertebra between the shoulders. The Gong Zhuan continues down the back in front of the spine through the Wai Jiao, the external cavity, in front of the cervical, thoracic and lumbar vertebrae, returning finally to the Hui Yin acupuncture point.

The Gong Zhuan pathway is not the same as that used by Taoists in their practice of *Xiao Zhou Tian* (the Small Circle or Microcosmic Orbit) to enhance internal *qi* in their quest for longevity. The upward path of the *Xiao Zhou Tian* is the same as that of the Gong Zhuan, but its downward path follows the Du, or Governor, meridian, which is *inside* the spinal column, whereas the Gong Zhuan travels down *in front of* the spine. Moreover, the Gong Zhuan is a much wider pathway, as it extends two inches to the left and two inches to the right of the midline, on both its upward and downward segments. In contrast, the Du meridian is a mere filament, approximately four-tenths to seven-tenths of a millimeter wide, or roughly two to three-hundredths of an inch.

The goal of promoting unimpeded fluid and energy flow in the Gong Zhuan is to thoroughly unblock the body's biggest space, the Wai Jiao. As Gong Zhuan drives Zi Zhuan, purification of the big space leads to purification of the small space. Energy flow will be smooth and unimpeded in both the big space and the small space, purifying and unblocking both. With all spaces unblocked, all illnesses vanish. Free flow in the Gong Zhuan also helps to purify the soul and heart.

If you truly understand Gong Zhuan and Zi Zhuan fluid and energy flow in Body Space Medicine, you can prevent and heal any illness regardless of its origin, whether physical, emotional, mental or spiritual. Remember the following principles:

- If the energy flow is too weak, too strong or abnormal in direction, illness occurs.

- If the energy flow is normal in force and direction, illness can be treated, or the body is already healthy and illness can be prevented.

- Consider the health of the body as a whole. Do not focus on specific organs, but rather on the fluid and energy circulation in the whole body. Heal by ensuring free flow of the Gong Zhuan and the Zi Zhuan.

Gong Zhuan (revolution) and Zi Zhuan (rotation) are the essence of Body Space Medicine and the focus of its therapeutics. Body Space Medicine utilizes Chinese herbs, message and various Xiu Lian training methods to enable an unimpeded and purified Gong Zhuan and Zi Zhuan, to return the body to health, to prevent illness and to develop intelligence and capabilities.

Body Space Medicine Is Quantum Medicine

Body Space Medicine regards the universe as infinitely big and yet infinitely small at the same time. In the vast universe, all wondrous and magical things are possible. Nothing is so wondrous and magical that it cannot be created. Nothing is so wondrous and magical that it cannot be destroyed.

In Body Space Medicine, healing transcends space and time. You are most familiar with healing in the healer's physical presence. Body Space Medicine also teaches you *remote* or distant healing, which is one aspect of quantum medicine. The healer can be in one location and the patient in a totally different location. The patient may not even know that he is being treated. Remote healing can be done via a physical link, such as the telephone, or without any physical links at all. There are many techniques of remote healing.

This section introduces the use of remote healing in Body Space Medicine. In doing so, I reveal some of the secrets of transcending space and time. Body Space Medicine regulates spiritual messages to treat illnesses caused by spiritual blockages[2]. Its methods can treat illnesses that are caused by spiritual blockages, whether the blockage originated in this lifetime or a previous one. If we can successfully treat the message issues of previous lives, those pertaining to this life will be resolved easily. In fact, message issues related to future lives can be handled in a similar way. When your training has reached a certain level, your spiritual channels will open and you will be able to see your patients' future illnesses. If you do not resolve them now, these illnesses *will* occur. The messages you receive from your open spiritual channels will help you treat future illnesses. Adjust the message and you can prevent future illnesses.

Body Space Medicine can treat current sicknesses physically and remotely, whether they are physical, emotional, mental or spiritual. Body Space Medicine also can adjust message issues in previous lives and future lives. There is no time, no space. Treatment is the same for all souls, human or other. This is quantum medicine for our time. When your spiritual abilities are developed, your spiritual wisdom expanded and your inspiration initiated, you will better understand the significance of the ability of Body Space Medicine to transcend space and time. You will more fully appreciate its adaptability and universal and limitless possibilities.

Soul Wisdom

Everything has a soul. Human beings have souls. Animals have souls. Plants have souls. Mountains and rivers all have souls. Animate objects have souls. Inanimate objects also have souls. The soul is spirit. The soul is *message*. The soul is the essence of life.

A human being is made up of body and spirit. The body is the physical aspect, which includes the organs and cells. However, the brain has its own consciousness, the heart has its own consciousness, the liver has its own consciousness, and so on. Every cell, every organ, every bodily system and every energy center has its own matter and form (body), consciousness and intelligence (mind) and message (soul). Collectively, the body's physical components do not make up a person. Only when the body's soul is added do we become a human being. Similarly, each organ has its own internal matter and consciousness, yet they do not make up the organ. The organ is complete only when the soul of the organ is added.

For example, the soul of the liver is called the liver *hun*. The soul of the heart is called the heart *shen*. The soul of the spleen is called the spleen *yi*. The soul of the lungs is called the lung *po*. The soul of the kidneys is called the kidney *zhi*. Cells have souls, internal organs have souls, the brain has a soul, each energy center has a soul, the whole body has a "whole body" soul — every physical aspect of the body has a soul. Each soul is a source of untapped potential, which is why I am introducing the wisdom of the soul.

To summarize, every person has a soul. Every system has a soul. Every organ has a soul. Every cell has a soul. Every DNA and every RNA has a soul. Soul, mind and body unite to become a single entity as a complete and healthy being.

Soul Power

Body Space Medicine teaches you how to adjust and regulate not only your body, but also your mind and soul. Which is most important — body, mind or soul? Each is important. Let me answer by revealing the secret for treating illness.

In the treatment of illness, traditional Chinese medicine states that if *qi* flows, blood follows; if *qi* is blocked, blood stagnates. Body Space Medicine, however, emphasizes treatment of the soul first. Heal the soul first; then healing of the mind and body will follow. My specific guidance for healing is: *Treat the soul first; then regulate the Gong Zhuan.* Follow this principle and all problems can be solved. Ignore this principle and your capabilities as a practitioner of Body Space Medicine will be limited.

Anyone can regulate the soul. Simply call upon the soul to act. Later in this book, I will teach you how to invoke the *soul* of the herbs to heal. My worldwide representative, Zhi Gang Sha, calls this Say Hello Healing. However, the results depend on the soul's capabilities and your capabilities. Has Heaven given you, the requestor, high-level capabilities to treat the soul? To develop these capabilities, you need to work hard at Xiu Lian, to enlighten your heart and to see your soul. Even if you have seen your soul, you must continue to train, to transform and enlighten your soul. Finally, uplift your soul in Heaven's Realm. The higher you stand in Heaven's Realm, the more power and abilities you are given to serve.

Transcending Space and Time

To master the skill of remote healing and to effectively transcend space and time, you must train diligently to open your spiritual channels and your soul's warehouse of latent wisdom. Strive to open your mind and every system, organ and cell in your body. Most people have no idea of their potential. Do not underestimate the latent powers, the infinite wisdom and the longevity that can be yours.

Body Space Medicine stresses that the most highly skilled healer, one who can truly rid people of illness and pain, or possibly revive the dead, must Xiu Lian to the highest degree. Although I will focus on Xiu Lian in Body Space Medicine in my next book on Body Space Medicine, you must know that when the soul reaches a high level, the power conferred by Heaven is great. What the healer says will happen and the results of his treatment will be miraculous. This is the truth I have understood and observed from more than fifty years of hard training. I share this with you to emphasize the importance of one's soul power. Soul power is immeasurable, unlimited and invaluable.

You need to practice the methods of Body Space Medicine that I teach in earnest and test them repeatedly. You must respect the rules of training. Just as there are rules in the physical universe, there are also rules and regulations in the spiritual world. Respect and adhere to the rules of the spiritual world. Contravening them can be costly, not necessarily in the physical world, but certainly in the spiritual world. Work hard and pledge your heart to Xiu Lian.

When Heaven is ready to confer blessings to you, special abilities, power and success can be yours in an instant. You will then have arrived at the transcendent and divine realm. Stay within its graces and fortune, and prosperity and longevity will always be yours. I wholeheartedly wish every Xiu Lian practitioner and Body Space Medicine practitioner success in this training to become transcendent and divine. I wish you will receive the highest abilities and wisdom. I wish you will fulfill the potential power of your soul to serve and benefit humanity and the universe.

Serve humanity. Serve others. Serve all souls. Science should advance, so progress will be made. Society should develop and people should be happy. Throughout history, science and technology have developed step by step. People's intelligence and wisdom have also increased step by step. We must always continue to progress. Science is boundless. Wisdom is infinite. The wisdom and service of the soul will promote scientific development, advance the progress of humanity, improve health conditions, and unite the world in harmony. As you continue to serve humanity and the universe tirelessly, Heaven will bless you and elevate your soul's standing.

Imagine climbing a set of stairs. If the stairs are long and steep, you must exert yourself going up each step. For your soul's journey up the heavenly ladder, you need to go up step by step, and you will need to exert yourself. The effort is your service to humanity and the universe. The record of your service is your virtue, which shines brightly in your spiritual journey. In due time, Heaven will bless you for your exertions. Your soul will continue to ascend to higher and higher levels until it reaches the first or highest level of Jiu Tian, the nine layers of Heaven.

Does the soul's journey end there? Far from it, for beyond the Jiu Tian is Tian Wai Tian[3], the Heaven beyond the nine layers. The soul's journey must continue upward infinitely. The more the soul ascends, the greater its virtue and the higher its standing in Heaven. The only goal to strive for is to continue to uplift one's soul. If you think your soul has reached a high level, there will be still higher levels to attain. If you think it has reached a higher level, there will be levels beyond that are even higher. As the Chinese sages taught, "There are men beyond men. There is Heaven beyond Heaven."

I urge you always to be humble. Only with humility and unconditional service to humanity and the universe will you be able to achieve *the great completeness after the great completeness.* The great completeness is the highest enlightenment for the soul, which means the highest soul standing in the Jiu Tian. May you achieve the great completeness time after time.

I call on all Xiu Lian practitioners to unite, train hard, and use love, compassion and dedication to attain completeness and fulfillment of the yin and yang universes (the soul or spiritual world and the physical world, respectively), as well as the happiness, health and completeness of all souls. Lastly, I wholeheartedly wish humanity and all souls health, happiness and harmony. May there be health, happiness and completeness in the realms of the yin and yang.

2

Tongue Reading

I offer without reservations to healthcare practitioners and all people of the world the new tongue reading, herb formulas and methodology of Body Space Medicine. This wisdom and knowledge are the culmination of over fifty years of clinical practice, study and Xiu Lian training. These theories, methods and applications are for the benefit of the healthcare community and all of humanity. They have proven to be life-saving.

At the peak of my medical practice, I wrote more than one thousand patient prescriptions a day. I have literally seen hundreds of thousands of patients and given as many prescriptions in my lifetime. No matter how many patients I saw, each one was diagnosed and prescribed with focus. Most of my patients have been blessed to recover their health quickly.

I ask that each practitioner of Body Space Medicine treat patients with the same focus and diligence. Help them recover their health as quickly, as humanely and as compassionately as possible. The heart of my service has been unconditional love, compassion and kindness. Only with this intent can one diagnose clearly and concisely, apply herbs correctly and see fast and effective results. Only with this intent can one develop abilities to receive the information in messages — messages about the patient's condition, messages from the universe and messages from Heaven — that will help deliver the most effective treatment for the patient.

Body Space Medicine has two aspects — a medical aspect and a Xiu Lian aspect — both of which must be practiced diligently and with heart in order to become an exceptional healer and a true Body Space Medicine practitioner. This book focuses on the medical aspect of Body Space Medicine[1]. In this chapter and the next, I teach all practitioners the key points of Body Space Medicine's tongue reading, herb formulas, treatment approach and applications.

The knowledge presented here has been distilled from decades of proven clinical practice, research and my personal Xiu Lian training. The information is highly summarized. Theory, methodology and techniques are explained step by step in simple and practical terms. Key points are emphasized. My intent is that anyone studying this material will quickly understand the key principles, wisdom and knowledge and immediately be able to apply them to benefit others.

This chapter deals with tongue reading in Body Space Medicine. In the following chapters, I will discuss the herb formulas of Body Space Medicine, treatment strategies and applications, and case studies.

My wish is for all readers to learn well the medical aspects and applications of Body Space Medicine. Apply the techniques and principles with a heart full of love and compassion. Be a good Body Space Medicine practitioner. Be a good universal servant. I wish all practitioners much success.

Key Points

Diagnosis in Body Space Medicine is based primarily on an evaluation of the conditions of the patient's tongue. Other factors that are considered are the conditions of the patient's stool and urine, as well as other physical symptoms.

After over fifty years of study and research, clinical practice, testing and application of traditional Chinese medicine theories and testing and practice of many different methods of Xiu Lian, I have finally come to understand that there are no schools or divisions in the practice of Xiu Lian. There is no limit to the new wisdom and knowledge that can be brought forth by continuous and advanced practice of Xiu Lian.

For example, this book introduces the Message Energy Matter Theory of Body Space Medicine to the West. The unique relationship among these three entities revealed itself to me many years ago during my ongoing practice of Xiu Lian, and I immediately understood how it could be used to transform any aspect of life.

To apply the Message Energy Matter Theory in healing, the practitioner would simply adjust the message or messages causing the illness. The new, adjusted message activates energy movement in the patient's body. This energy then collides with the matter in the body, adjusting the balance of matter inside the cells, of energy outside the cells, and of body fluids both inside and outside the cells.

Having already acquired a solid foundation in traditional Chinese medicine tongue diagnosis, I developed new methods for reading the tongue as my evolution of Body Space Medicine unfolded. Over the last decade, these new methods have been extensively tested, refined and proven in my clinic with thousands of successful patient evaluations and treatments.

In this section I present the proven theories, observations and methodologies of Body Space Medicine tongue reading. This new system of tongue reading is based on the concept that the conditions of an individual's tongue, including the tongue coating, reflect the physical health and conditions within the body. The key points of this new tongue reading system can be summarized as follows:

• Diagnosis is simple, quick and powerful.

- The *form* of the tongue shows the conditions of the main organs and of the matter in the cells.

- The *coating* of the tongue shows the condition of energy in the body space.

- The system identifies the location of the root of illness.

The tongue reading system of Body Space Medicine is presented in three parts:

1. Distribution of Organs in Tongue Reading
    Different parts of the tongue represent different parts of the body.

2. Reading the Form of the Tongue
    The form of the tongue represents the matter inside the body's cells. Various physical characteristics of the tongue such as size, color, shape, texture, firmness, ulcers, pits and bumps reflect the conditions of the matter in the cells.

3. Reading the Coating of the Tongue
    The coating of the tongue represents the energy in the body space. For example, tongue coatings that are wet, sticky, greasy, colored, thick or thin indicate different conditions of energy in the space.

Important Note:

Before proceeding further, all practitioners and readers should understand that the standard tongue diagnosis of traditional Chinese medicine does not apply in Body Space Medicine. Practitioners are urged not to combine or confuse the two systems of tongue diagnosis in the practice and application of Body Space Medicine. They are different systems. The simplicity of the tongue reading system of Body Space Medicine makes it completely and readily accessible to lay persons.

DISTRIBUTION OF ORGANS IN TONGUE READING

The Body Space Medicine system of tongue reading is based on the finding that the condition of the organs and other parts of the body is reflected in the condition and appearance of the tongue and the tongue coating. There is most definitely a direct correlation between the body organs and their representative locations on the tongue.

The appearance of the tongue and characteristics in different areas of the tongue are indicative of the conditions in the organs or parts of the body they represent. Tongue conditions show the location of root blockages and identify the nature of the blockages, giving the practitioner invaluable information on how to treat the conditions presented, and where to target the treatment.

Consequently, the serious Body Space Medicine practitioner is advised to familiarize himself with the Tongue Map of the Body (Figure 2 below) and the locations of the organs and key body points, as listed in Table 1. It is important for practitioners to know the tongue landscape and what the different regions represent so that they can implement Body Space Medicine's First Glance Tongue Reading and One-Minute Tongue Reading Prescription Method.

Tongue Map of the Body

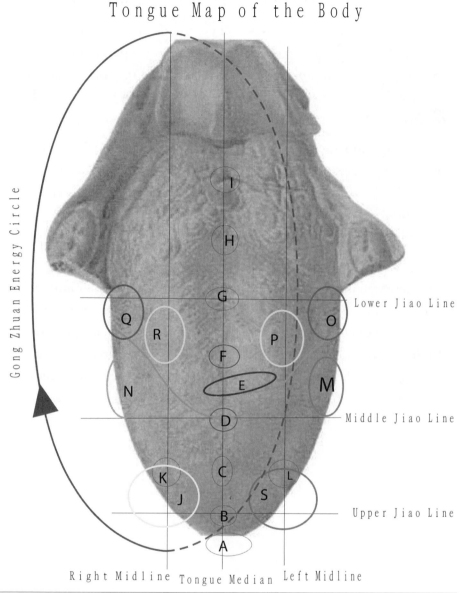

A: The tip of the Heart   B: Tian Tu   C: Shan Zhong   D: Ju Que
E: Pancreas   F: Zhong Wan   G: Navel   H: Dan Tian
I: Coccyx   J: Lungs   K: Right Breast   L: Left Breast   Q: Right Kidney
O: Left Kidney   S: Heart   P: Stomach   R: Stomach Function
N: Liver/Gall Bladder   M: Liver/Gall Bladder Function

Figure 2. Tongue Map of the Body

Figure 2 identifies the correlations between areas of the tongue and parts of the body. Horizontal and vertical lines divide the tongue into easily identifiable sections that represent different areas of the body. The areas of the tongue corresponding to the main organs and their functions are also identified. An explanation of the Tongue Map follows. All directional indicators refer to Figure 2.

1. Three Horizontal Lines

   • Bottom line — Upper Jiao

   • Middle line — Middle Jiao

   • Top line — Lower Jiao

2. San Jiao

   The Upper Jiao, Middle Jiao and Lower Jiao are three of the largest spaces in the body. Together, they comprise the San Jiao.

   • Upper Jiao
     The Upper Jiao body space is represented by the area of the tongue between the Upper Jiao line and the Middle Jiao line. The Upper Jiao is the area of the body above the diaphragm. Organs in the Upper Jiao include the heart, lungs and brain.

   • Middle Jiao
     The Middle Jiao body space is represented by the area of the tongue between the Middle Jiao line and the Lower Jiao line. The Middle Jiao is the area of the body between the level of the diaphragm and the level of the navel. Organs in the Middle Jiao include the spleen, stomach, liver, gallbladder and pancreas.

   • Lower Jiao
     The Lower Jiao body space is represented by the area of the tongue above the Lower Jiao line. The Lower Jiao is the area of the body from the level of the navel to the genitals. Organs

in the Lower Jiao include the kidneys, small intestine, large intestine, urinary bladder and the reproductive organs.

3. Front and Back

    • The tongue is further divided into an anterior (front) section and a posterior (back) section by the blue curved line that goes through Points Q, D and O.

4. Three Vertical Lines

    • The center line represents the midline of the whole body.

    • The line right of center represents the midline of the left side of the body.

    • The line left of center represents the midline of the right side of the body.

5. The Gong Zhuan or Vertical Energy Circle

    The Gong Zhuan energy pathway or Vertical Energy Circle in the body is indicated by the large red oval line in Figure 2 that runs through the entire tongue. Energy revolves through the Gong Zhuan as follows (see Figure 4 on page 91):

    a. *Starting Point* — The Gong Zhuan starts from the Hui Yin acupuncture point, which is located in the perineum, between the anus and the genitals.

    b. *Flows Up the Anterior* — The Gong Zhuan runs up inside the body along the front midline. It goes through the Lower Dan Tian and several acupuncture points, including the Shan Zhong (midpoint between the nipples) and Yin Tang (midpoint between the eyebrows), to the Bai Hui (at the top of the head).

    c. *Flows Down the Posterior* — From the Bai Hui, the Gong Zhuan runs down the posterior aspect of the body in the body space of the Wai Jiao, which is in front of the spinal column. (The Wai Jiao begins in the head and extends down to the tailbone and genitals. It is the largest space in the body.) It continues to flow down through the Ming Men area (waist level in the back) and Wei Lu (tailbone), and returns to the Hui Yin in the perineum.

d. *Continuous Energy Flow* — Energy in the Gong Zhuan circulates nonstop in the body as described — up the front and down the back, up the front and down the back, up the front and down the back.

6. Location of the Organs and Key Points

- Table 1 below identifies the tongue location of the body's main internal organs and key acupuncture points that are shown in Figure 2.

TONGUE MAP OF THE BODY		
Key	**Caption**	**Corresponding Body Part of Acupuncture Point**
A	Heart Tip	• The pointed tip of the heart (the inferior or lower part of the heart)
B	Tian Tu	• CV 22 or Ren 22 • An acupuncture point just above the jugular notch (the hollow where the neck joins the sternum)
C	Shan Zhong	• CV 17 or Ren 17 • An acupuncture point midway between the nipples on the midline of the sternum
D	Ju Que	• CV 14 or Ren 14 • An acupuncture point on the front midline, slightly below the sternum
E	Pancreas	• A small elongated organ behind the stomach in the upper middle of the abdominal cavity
F	Zhong Wan	• CV 12 or Ren 12 • An acupuncture point 4 *cun²* above the navel
G	Navel	• CV 8 or Ren 8 • The umbilicus or bellybutton

TONGUE MAP OF THE BODY		
Key	**Caption**	**Corresponding Body Part of Acupuncture Point**
H	(Lower) Dan Tian	• A fist-sized foundational energy center in the front middle lower abdomen, centered 1.5 *cun* below the navel and 2.5 *cun* inside the body
I	Wei Lu	• The tip of the coccyx or tailbone
J	Lungs	• The respiratory organs located on either side of the upper chest area or thoracic cavity
K	Right breast	• Right breast area (the right area of the chest)
L	Left breast	• Left breast area (the left area of the chest)
M	Liver / gallbladder function	• See N (liver and gallbladder) below
N	Liver / gallbladder	• A pair of organs located under the diaphragm on the upper right side of the abdominal cavity
O	Left kidney	• One of a pair of excretory organs located in the backside of the abdomen, at the level of the waist • The left kidney lies slightly higher than the right kidney
P	Stomach	• A digestive organ located under the diaphragm on the upper left side of the abdominal cavity
Q	Right kidney	• One of a pair of excretory organs located just below the liver in the backside of the abdomen, at the level of the waist • The right kidney lies slightly lower than the left kidney
R	Stomach function	• See P (stomach) above
S	Heart	• An organ located in the thoracic cavity between the lungs, under the sternum and slightly left of center

Table 1. Tongue Map of the Body

LOOKING AT THE TONGUE

Body Space Medicine tongue reading is best performed by studying the tongue the moment it is extended. The appearance of the tongue in the first few seconds is most indicative of the conditions in the body. Practitioners may find the use of a digital camera invaluable in capturing the appearance of the patient's tongue at its first extension. The digital images produced are especially useful for further study, analysis and more accurate tongue reading.

An experienced practitioner can determine the patient's main blockage areas with just a glance at the entire tongue. This first glance at the patient's tongue is known as the Body Space Medicine First Glance Tongue Reading. The tongue reading can then immediately be used (with knowledge of the physical conditions and symptoms) to determine an herb formula for the patient — the Body Space Medicine Instant Prescription Method.

On average, the whole process from beginning to end — from tongue reading to prescription — takes no more than one minute for an experienced practitioner. The entire process is referred to as the Body Space Medicine One-Minute Tongue Reading Prescription Method.

In the pages that follow, clear guidelines are presented to help the practitioner quickly learn and apply Body Space Medicine's First Glance Tongue Reading and Instant Prescription Method. It is strongly suggested that the practitioner first become completely familiar with the Tongue Map of the Body (the areas of the tongue and the parts of the body they represent) in Figure 2, learn how to read the tongue body and tongue coating, and understand the significance of the stool, urine and other factors. Practitioners will want to know this background information intimately to be able to quickly identify the root sources of illness when looking at a tongue.

With time and practice, practitioners will become increasingly proficient and will eventually be able to implement in full the One-Minute Tongue Reading Prescription Method of Body Space Medicine.

Reading the Form of the Tongue
(the Tongue Body)

In Body Space Medicine tongue reading, **the physical characteristics of the form of the tongue (the "tongue body") reflect the conditions of the matter inside cells.** The characteristics of various regions of the tongue indicate matter conditions in the corresponding parts of the body.

To read the tongue body, look for physical parameters such as size, shape, height, rigidity, mountains, valleys and trenches, bumps and dents, tooth marks and water content. *Where* these characteristics appear on the tongue reflects the state of the matter in the corresponding parts of the body.

Additional detail on tongue body size, color and other physical characteristics follows. Study each section thoroughly but be aware that tongue characteristics overlap, so interpret accordingly.

Tongue Size

The size of the tongue indicates the relative balance of matter inside the cells. In particular, the size of the tongue indicates the relative balance of *fluid* inside the cells. For example, a large tongue indicates excessive matter or water inside the cells. Furthermore, if the tongue is large and soft, it has dampness or too much water. If the tongue is large and hard, there is very dense accumulation of matter and blood in the cells (blood stagnation). If the tongue is small and soft, there is not enough matter in the cells. If the tongue is small and hard, there is not enough matter together with blood stagnation in the cells. The main tongue size characteristics and accompanying secondary characteristics are summarized in Table 2.

TONGUE BODY: SIZE CHARACTERISTICS			
Size	2nd Feature	3rd Feature	Significance
large			• too much matter (fluid)
large	soft		• too much water • this is a damp, watery tongue
large	hard		• high density of matter • blood stagnation
large	hard	thick	• extreme matter blockage • blood stagnation
small	soft		• not enough matter
small	hard		• not enough matter • blood stagnation
small	soft	trembling	• not enough matter • not enough blood

Table 2. Tongue Body: Size Characteristics

Tongue Body Color

When assessing the color of the tongue body, be careful to differentiate between the color of the tongue organ itself (the muscle) and the color of the tongue coating. This section considers the color of the tongue body only; the color characteristics of the tongue coating are described in a subsequent section.

In general, the normal color of the tongue body is light pink. A red tongue indicates heat or fire characteristics in the cells. A dull purple tongue indicates blood stagnation. If the tongue is pale and white, the patient has blood deficiency – not enough blood. Dark or purple spots on the tongue indicate blood stagnation. The main colors of the tongue and their interpretations are summarized in Table 3.

TONGUE BODY: COLOR CHARACTERISTICS	
Color	**Significance**
Pink	• normal
Red	• heat
Dull purple	• blood stagnation
Pale	• not enough matter
Pale and white	• not enough blood
Dark or purple spots	• blood stagnation
Dull purple, large, thick and hard	• excess matter • blood stagnation

Table 3. Tongue Body: Color Characteristics

Other Physical Characteristics of the Tongue

Other physical characteristics of the tongue body include its shape, firmness, angle of direction, stability, and the appearance of dents, bumps, cracks and other features. The locations of these characteristics on the tongue show the organs or areas which have the indicated matter conditions inside the cells.

For example, some tongues are shaped like a rod – thin and stick-like, which indicates extreme matter accumulation and blockage. Some tongues are large, thick and hard, which also indicates extreme matter blockage. Tongues with clear tooth marks on the outer edge indicate a water metabolism imbalance in the body. If the tongue appears watery, there is dampness or too much water in the cells.

Pay particular attention to tongue surfaces that show bumps and dents. Bumps or raised areas indicate excess matter in the cells. Dents or pits indicate inadequate matter in the cells. With regards to bumps and dents, remember only one rule: **Pay attention to bumps; ignore the dents.** This statement is a major secret of Body Space Medicine tongue reading and treatment.

Bumps, or raised areas, are like mountains. Level the mountains to fill the dents and pits. Once the bumps are leveled, the body will regain health. The location of the bumps or raised areas on the tongue indicates where treatment should be focused. For example, a tongue that is raised at the tip or in the front generally indicates blocked energy in the lungs; lung energy cannot move up.

I repeat this guidance once more. **Pay attention to bumps on the tongue; ignore the dents.** Some tongues may have chunks of matter missing here or there. The missing chunks can be interpreted as matter deficiency for the indicated organ or area. If the tip of the tongue is missing, as in an indented or notched tip, this indicates that heart blood and heart matter are deficient. The associated clinical symptoms can include apprehension, fatigue and dizziness. In general, be aware of missing chunks on the tongue as they indicate matter deficiency in specific areas of the body. The prudent practitioner would therefore adjust the patient's treatment and herb formula accordingly.

Watch out for a tongue that is angled, skewed or pointed to one side as this signifies potentially dangerous blood problems in the brain, whether pre-existing or as yet undiagnosed or unmanifest. Such a situation requires attention as there are blockages in the micro-circulation or blood capillary system in the brain. This type of tongue indicates a risk of cerebral embolism and/or brain hemorrhage.

More commonly, tongues will show a variety of physical characteristics. For example, a tongue that is large, thick, hard and dull purple in color indicates excess matter and blood stagnation in the cells. A small tongue that is soft and trembling indicates deficiency of matter and blood in the cells.

However the tongue presents itself, remember that all physical characteristics of the tongue indicate the condition of *matter* in the cells. Therefore, when looking at a tongue body for size, shape, color and other physical characteristics, it should be very clear whether the patient has too much matter or not enough matter in the cells. Reading a

tongue body is really this simple. Some of the other physical characteristics of the tongue body are summarized in Table 4 below.

TONGUE BODY: OTHER PHYSICAL CHARACTERISTICS	
Main Feature	**Condition of the Matter Inside the Cells**
rod-shaped	• extreme matter accumulation and blockage
large, thick, hard	• extreme matter blockage and blood stagnation
tooth marks	• water metabolism imbalance
watery	• too much water; dampness
bumps (raised areas)	• excess matter in the area
dents (pits)	• inadequate matter; deficiency in the area
angled (tongue points to one side)	• capillary system blockage in brain • beware of cerebral embolism and brain hemorrhage
indented tip	• insufficient heart energy and blood
vertical cracks	• Vertical Energy Circle (Gong Zhuan) blockage
horizontal cracks	• Horizontal Energy Circle (Zi Zhuan) blockage
dark spots	• excess matter in the area
soft, trembling	• deficiency of matter
soft, small or thin	• insufficient matter
rigid or stiff	• extreme matter blockage

Table 4. Tongue Body: Other Physical Characteristics

READING THE COATING OF THE TONGUE

In Body Space Medicine tongue diagnosis, **the coating of the tongue indicates the conditions of the energy in the space surrounding the cells.** The tongue coating also shows the changes in the moisture and fluid in the space. The concept of *fluid* in Body Space Medicine can be likened to the traditional Chinese medicine concept of *qi.*

The coating of the tongue is the matter on the surface of the tongue body. The normal tongue coating is generally light white in color. When the coating is yellow, damp and greasy, it indicates damp heat. When the coating is yellow, dry and greasy, it indicates dry heat. When the coating is black and damp, it indicates extreme cold in the area (use the herb Rou Gui to warm and nourish the Ming Men fire; herbs will be discussed in depth in the next chapter). When the coating is black and dry, it indicates extreme heat (use the herbs Gui Zhi and Lian Qiao to reduce the heat).

Every pathological condition of the body is reflected in the tongue coating at the corresponding regions on the surface of the tongue. Too much energy in the space can result in fluid blockage (too much matter in the cells). Conversely, when the tongue has no coating, it indicates lack of fluid in the space.

The key herb for treating the conditions indicated by the tongue coating is determined by whether the coating is wet or dry:

1. **When the coating is wet, use the herb Pei Lan.**

2. **When the coating is dry, use the herb Dang Gui.**

Several common types of tongue coatings and their significance in Body Space Medicine are listed in Table 5 below. The herb information will be discussed in depth in the next chapter.

TONGUE COATING CHARACTERISTICS		
Tongue Coating	**Condition of the Energy in the Space**	**Herbs to Use**
Thin, light, white	Normal	
Yellow, greasy, damp	Damp heat	
Yellow, greasy, dry	Dry heat	
Black, damp	Extreme cold	Use Rou Gui to warm and nourish Ming Men fire
Black, dry	Extreme heat	Use Gui Zhi and Lian Qiao to reduce the heat
Thick	Energy blockage	

TONGUE COATING CHARACTERISTICS, cont.		
Tongue Coating	Condition of the Energy in the Space	Herbs to Use
Wet / watery		Use Pei Lan
Dry		Use Dang Gui
Thick, greasy, yellow	Wai Jiao blockage; energy cannnot dissipate	Use Gui Zhi, Lian Qiao, Du Huo and Bai Tou Weng
No coating	Lack of fluid in the space	

Table 5. Tongue Coating Characteristics

FIRST GLANCE TONGUE READING — A SUMMARY

The human body can be afflicted by many kinds of illnesses and diseases. Some are unknown. Others can be misdiagnosed. The beauty of Body Space Medicine and its revolutionary nature is that the practitioner need not rely on a name or identification of the disease or illness to treat it effectively. Instead, application of Body Space Medicine is totally symptom-based. This is one reason why Body Space Medicine is very powerful.

Using tongue reading, the Body Space Medicine practitioner can determine the areas of the body that have matter and/or energy blockages and whether there are fluid imbalance issues in those areas. He can then give an herb formula as treatment after taking into consideration the conditions of bowel movement and urination. The patient can be assessed and given a prescription all within a few minutes based solely on the symptoms he displays. Thus, Body Space Medicine can be applied without waiting for biopsies, laboratory test results, MRI, CAT or other high-tech scans or tests.

In determining the root cause of illness and ensuing treatment, Body Space Medicine completely disregards the names of diseases or the diagnoses given by other healing modalities. While respecting the science, perspectives, assessments and diagnoses of Western medicine, traditional Chinese medicine, Ayurvedic medicine, naturopathy and other healing modalities, Body Space Medicine does not rely on them but uses such information only as a reference. Whatever the name of the illness or whatever the diagnosis in other healing modalities, Body Space Medicine uses its own methods and techniques, which are entirely symptom-based, to assess a patient's condition and determine treatment.

Herb formulas in Body Space Medicine consider only four factors:

1. tongue reading

2. stool conditions

3. urine conditions

4. other symptoms

To reiterate, **Body Space Medicine treatment is entirely symptom-based,** regardless of the name of the illness or disease. For any illness, Body Space Medicine determines treatment based only on the information displayed by the body as manifested through the tongue, stool, urine and body symptoms. The practitioner must therefore be familiar with the principles of tongue reading, know what to look for, and be able to discern the key points to make an accurate assessment of the patient's condition. So long as the tongue reading is correct and the stool, urine and other conditions have been taken into consideration, an effective herb formula can be prescribed.

The following section provides a summary of each prescriptive factor with an emphasis on what is most important. The practitioner who can grasp these principles will become proficient over time with Body Space Medicine's First Glance Tongue Reading. With the tongue reading in hand, the practitioner can then implement the next step of treatment: Body Space Medicine's Instant Prescription Method.

Tongue Reading Step By Step

The practitioner should first familiarize himself with the information presented in the previous sections, *Distribution of Organs in Tongue Reading*, which describes the correlation between the organs in the body and their locations on the tongue, *Reading the Form of the Tongue (the Tongue Body)* and *Reading the Coating of the Tongue*. The key points to follow for the First Glance Tongue Reading are:

- Look at the appearance of the tongue when it is first extended. The first moment is most important because the appearance of the tongue at this time most accurately reflects the conditions within the body. Tongues that are displayed for an extended length of time will change shape and appearance as the muscle tires. The coating may also change with exposure to air. Also, the tongue should not have been brushed recently. If possible, use a digital camera to capture the image of the tongue when it is first displayed.

- Look for distinguishing physical characteristics such as the color and size of the tongue, whether it is hard or soft, etc. Determine whether there is too much matter or not enough matter in the cells.

- Look for raised and depressed areas on the surface of the tongue. The locations of bumps or raised areas indicate where treatment should focus. An area where the tongue surface is raised indicates a matter blockage in the corresponding part of the body. Focus treatment on leveling the raised parts; i.e., on removing the matter blockages in the corresponding parts of the body.

- Look at the tongue coating and determine how the body space is affected. Where is there an energy blockage or deficient energy? Are there issues with water imbalance?

The above is a simple summary of Body Space Medicine tongue reading. Identify the source of the problems; then tailor treatment to tackle the key points first. Treatment is effective when the symptoms dissipate and when the tongue conditions improve.

Essence of Tongue Reading

Pay attention to the raised areas. Sometimes the raised areas are on the edges, sometimes in the middle of the tongue. The part of the tongue which is raised indicates the part of the body where there is a blockage.

For example, I may give you a formula of the herbs Du Huo, Chi Shao and Jie Geng. If there is a raised area in one spot, I may give you a particular herb for that spot. The area where the tongue is raised determines the herb. By reading the tongue, you can see where the blockage is, so simply give the appropriate herb for that area. This is a very simple principle, yet it is essential. You will use the herbs for the location of the body corresponding to the raised area. It doesn't matter if the person suffers from twenty conditions. Just make sure the energy circle flows. That is how profound this system is.

STOOL CONDITIONS

In the application of Body Space Medicine, pay particular attention to the patient's bowel movements and stool conditions. The stool is one of the main exits for matter and energy in the body, so normalizing bowel movements is important. **When first assessing the patient, make sure to ask whether he has constipation or not.** Ask about the condition of the stool – whether it is dry, soft or wet; has form or no form; its frequency and color; if there is pain, blood, parasites or any other unusual observations. All of these conditions give clues about the body's health and the conditions within.

• Dry Stool or Constipation

If the stool is dry or the patient is constipated, there is matter blockage in the intestines. The intestines can be thought of as one large cell. Dry stools therefore indicate matter blockage inside this "cell." Do not let constipation persist as it blocks the essential exit of matter and energy from the body, affecting normal bodily functions and leading to the development of serious conditions. For dry stool or constipation, the practitioner would use the herbs Dang Gui and/or Rou Cong Rong. More details will be provided in the next chapter.

• Loose and Frequent Stool or Diarrhea

If the stools are loose and frequent or the patient has diarrhea-like symptoms, there is inadequate matter inside the cells. Ongoing diarrhea should be arrested as continued depletion of matter and energy can weaken the body. For such situations, use Pei Lan, Chao Zao Ren and/or Chao Bai Zhu. More details will be provided in the next chapter.

URINE CONDITIONS

Urine provides another major exit for matter and energy in the body, so its proper functioning is crucial to good health. For urination issues, the key is night trips —how often does the patient urinate during the night after going to bed?

• Frequent Night Urination

If the patient urinates more than three times a night, the kidneys are deficient. In other words, kidney function and kidney energy are weak. For this condition, you may use Wu Wei Zi 7 g.

• Scanty or Infrequent Urination

If urine flow is scanty or urination is infrequent, the cells in the kidney area are not active enough (assuming proper hydration).

For this condition, you may use the following combination of herbs: Zhe Bei 30 g, Du Huo 30 g.

Zhe Bei reduces the pressure in the Upper Jiao space by dissipating stagnation in the lungs and chest. Du Huo clears the Wai Jiao space and moves energy. This herb combination causes lung energy from the upper part of the Wai Jiao body space to charge down into the kidney region and stimulate the kidney cells into greater action, thereby helping the kidneys regain a healthy balance.

This Body Space Medicine treatment for scanty urine is a classic application of the Five Elements mother-son generating relationship, where the lung (metal) generates or is mother to the kidney (water). In other words, lung energy is used to nourish the kidneys and restore their function.

OTHER CONDITIONS

As the methods of Body Space Medicine treatment and prescription are totally symptom-based, pay attention to other symptoms the patient may report. If the patient does not volunteer this information, ask some leading questions to determine if there are any symptoms that need to be considered in addition to the tongue, stool and urine conditions.

For example, the patient may complain of fullness on the right side of the abdomen, heaviness in the head, tightness in the shoulders, chest pain, night sweats or craving sweets. All symptoms experienced by the patient are signs of the body's healthy ease or dis-ease and can provide valuable clues in the final consideration of treatment.

The patient may also share the names of the illnesses or diagnosis he has been given; however, the practitioner should use this information only as a reference, not as the basis of treatment.

3

Herbs in
Body Space Medicine

The Chinese herbs used in Body Space Medicine are very safe as they have very little known toxicity when used in the low dosages prescribed in the herb formulas. All of the herbs chosen, however, do have an energetic effect on the body. Therefore, anyone considering taking Body Space Medicine herbs should first consult with their physician or other healthcare professionals.

This chapter on the key treatment aspects of Body Space Medicine is organized as follows:

- Key Herbs of Body Space Medicine
- Practical Considerations in Using Herbs
- Eight Basic Herb Formulas of Body Space Medicine
- Treatment Strategies and Applications
- Four Quantum Herb Formulas of Body Space Medicine
- Soul Herbs
- Practitioners of Body Space Medicine

KEY HERBS OF BODY SPACE MEDICINE

Body Space Medicine uses a very small selection of Chinese herbs to treat all illnesses and health conditions. Only fifteen herbs are routinely used in the *eight basic herb formulas* of Body Space Medicine, and the total number of herbs used in Body Space Medicine is fewer than fifty. This is remarkable considering that there are thousands of herbs in the Chinese herb compendium.

The small selection of herbs used in Body Space Medicine has been chosen by design. In developing this new healing science, one of my primary goals was to develop an easy-to-apply and effective healing system that would be accessible to as many people as possible, including those who have limited funds. I did not want Body Space Medicine to be inaccessible or impractical to apply for the poor.

Consequently, I researched and tested many Chinese herbs through the years to find the ones that best suited the Body Space Medicine system by satisfying the following criteria:

a) fewest herbs necessary

b) effective

c) low-cost

d) no toxicity or side effects

This sparing selection of herbs means that each herb has a special and unique function in Body Space Medicine. I am continuing to conduct research on herbs for Body Space Medicine to reduce the selection and dosage of herbs used. I have already further concentrated and simplified the eight basic herb formulas presented in this section to develop the *four quantum herb formulas* [patents pending] presented later in this chapter. I accomplished this further concentration of the essence of Body Space Medicine in early 2006. I envision a time when, eventually, physical herbs will no longer be necessary in the application of Body Space Medicine.

You may wish to leap to the most advanced, most distilled and most updated knowledge and practice of Body Space Medicine. If so, you may go directly to the chapter "Four Quantum Herb Formulas of Body Space Medicine" on page 115. This section contains the simplest and most accessible wisdom. You can do this and be an entirely successful student and practitioner of this revolutionary healing science. However, I recommend that you study the rest of this chapter so that you will have a greater understanding of tongue reading, body fluids, the functions and practical aspects of using physical herbs, the Gong Zhuan and applications of Body Space Medicine for serious conditions related to various major organs. You will gain all of this additional background and foundational information, along with a better perspective on the evolution of Body Space Medicine.

Table 6 lists the fifteen herbs that are used in the basic herb formulas of Body Space Medicine. The herbs are listed alphabetically by pinyin Romanization of the Chinese name. Included is a brief summary describing the main functions of each herb in Body Space Medicine and where it mainly acts (inside the cells, outside the cells, etc.). For easy cross-referencing, the Chinese, pinyin, scientific and common names are given for each herb. Photographs of the herbs are provided in Figure 3 below.

Although the basic formulas use a total of only fifteen herbs, Body Space Medicine makes use of additional herbs to modify the basic formulas based on the unique symptoms each patient presents. You will find occasional mention of these additional herbs throughout this book, particularly in the case studies in Chapter 5, Take the information provided, but do not allow it to distract you from the core and essence of this new healing system.

On the whole, the herbs used in Body Space Medicine are low in cost, effective in low doses and readily available anywhere around the world from herb shops supplying Chinese herbs as well as through the Internet.

Note that some of the herbs can come in different forms, which have different or even opposite properties and characteristics. Take care not to substitute a different form for the one specified. For example, the dried herb Mai Ya (sprouted barley) can be specified as Sheng Mai Ya, which is *raw* sprouted barley, or as Chao Mai Ya, which is *lightly roasted* sprouted barley. Herbs can also be roasted to different degrees. Chao means to lightly roast, while Jiao means to roast until dry and crispy.

The descriptor terms of Sheng, Chao and Jiao have been incorporated where appropriate into the herb lists in Table 6. Therefore, Sheng Mai Ya would be listed under "S" and Chao Mai Ya would be listed under "C." Be aware that mail-order catalogs and herb suppliers may list and categorize herbs differently. For example, they may forego the descriptor word, in which case sprouted barley would be found under "M" for Mai Ya. This is mentioned to aid readers who wish to look elsewhere for additional information on the herbs.

Regardless of the herb-referencing system, the herbs used in Body Space Medicine should be easy to find, identify and specify.

Fifteen Key Herbs of Body Space Medicine						
#	Chinese (simplified)	Pinyin	Scientific name	Common Name	Main Action	Body Space Medicine Function
1	炒麦芽	Chao Mai Ya	Fructus hordei germinatus	barley sprout (lightly roasted)	inside cells	• Component of Jiao San Xian and Jiao Si Xian
2	炒山楂	Chao Shan Zha	Fructus crataegi	hawthorne berry (lightly roasted)	inside cells	• Component of Jiao San Xian and Jiao Si Xian
3	炒神曲	Chao She Qu	Massa medicata fermentata	medicated leaven (lightly roasted)	inside cells	• Component of Jiao San Xian and Jiao Si Xian

Fifteen Key Herbs of Body Space Medicine						
#	**Chinese (simplified)**	**Pinyin**	**Scientific name**	**Common Name**	**Main Action**	**Body Space Medicine Function**
4	赤芍	Chi Shao	Radix paeoniae rubra	red peony root	inside cells	• Vitalizes blood, promotes blood circulation and clears blood stagnation • Causes matter to move in the cells
5	丹参	Dang Shen	Radix salviae miltiorrhizae	salvia, red sage root	inside cells	• Removes blood stagnation • Stimulates blood circulation, nourishing the heart, spleen and heart blood • Stops diarrhea
6	当归	Dang Gui	Radix agelicae sinensis	Chinese angelica root (aka "female ginseng")	inside cells	Vitalizes and nourishes blood; removes blood stagnation • Increases blood output volume of the left atrium and left ventricle • Promotes movement of matter and increases body's driving force • Increases moisture in the cells
7	独活 (大活)	Du Huo (Da Huo)	Radix agelicae pubescentis	pubescentis angelica root	outside cells	• Moves energy down from the head to the feet, which stimulates movement of matter and energy

Fifteen Key Herbs of Body Space Medicine						
#	Chinese (simplified)	Pinyin	Scientific name	Common Name	Main Action	Body Space Medicine Function
						in the Lower Jiao, thereby promoting Gong Zhuan circulation • Clears the Wai Jiao space
8	桂枝	Gui Zhi	Ramulus cinnamomi	cinnamon twig	cell membrane	• Opens cell membrane pathways • Balances and enables free exchange of matter (in cells) and energy (around cells) • Moves fire from the upper parts of the body to the Lower Jiao, thereby warming the Lower Jiao cells and space
9	藿香	Huo Xiang	Herba agastachis seu, Herba pogastemonis	agastache/patchouli/pogostemon herb	outside cells	• Clears fluid from the Middle Jiao • Use for loose stools or diarrhea; not to be used for constipation
10	焦三仙	Jiao San Xian	Chao Mai Ya + Chao Shan Zha + Chao Shen Qu	barley sprout, hawthorne berry, medicated leaven (roasted until crispy)	inside cells	• Jiao San Xian is comprised of 3 roasted herbs: Chao Mai Ya, Chao Shan Zha, Chao Shen Qu • The term Jiao means the herbs are dry-fried or

Fifteen Key Herbs of Body Space Medicine						
#	Chinese (simplified)	Pinyin	Scientific name	Common Name	Main Action	Body Space Medicine Function
						roasted until they are crispy. The process takes much longer and processes herbs beyond the Chao stage, which means to lightly dry-fry or roast. • Clears the matter and energy of all organs in the Middle Jiao • Restores the function of Middle Jiao organs • Increases appetite
11	桔梗	Jie Geng	Radix platycodi	root of platycodon, balloon flower	outside cells	• Clears the lungs • Moves energy up from the level of the ribs
12	连翘	Lian Qiao	Fructus forsythiae	forsythia fruit	outside cells	• Clears the heat and energy in the space of the Upper Jiao (space around the heart and the lungs) • Quickly clears energy and heat produced by the cells • Activates the spleen and stomach; lifts spleen *qi* • With Gui Zhi: clears the Upper

Fifteen Key Herbs of Body Space Medicine						
#	Chinese (simplified)	Pinyin	Scientific name	Common Name	Main Action	Body Space Medicine Function
						Jiao space and makes the *upper part deficient* • With Dang Gui and Gui Zhi, clears the San Jiao by moving *qi,* blood and water
13	佩兰	Pei Lan	Herba eupatorii	agueweed, boneset, eupatorium, hempweed	outside cells	• Removes dampness and turbid energy in the Middle and Lower Jiao • Clears fluid and moisture in the cells and in the space • Promotes the flow of water in the San Jiao pathway and balances water in the body • Can use for both constipation and loose stools
14	石菖蒲	Shi Chang Pu	Rhizome acori graminei	facorus root, grass-leaved sweetflag rhizome	outside cells	• Reduces the pressure in the space around the right atrium, right ventricle, Message Center • Lets energy flow freely between the head and the rest of the body • Releases

Fifteen Key Herbs of Body Space Medicine					
#	Chinese (simpli-fied)	Pinyin	Scientific name	Common Name	Main Action	Body Space Medicine Func-tion
						emotional and Message Center blockages; calms the mind
15	香附	Xiang Fu	Cyperus rhizome	rhizome of nut grass, nutsedge, coco sedge	outside cells	• Moves energy from the Middle Jiao (between the navel and the diaphragm) to the Gong Zhuan pathway, up through the diaphragm to the area of the Shan Zhong (midpoint between the nipples) and Mes-sage Center (be-hind the sternum)

Table 6. Fifteen Key Herbs of Body Space Medicine

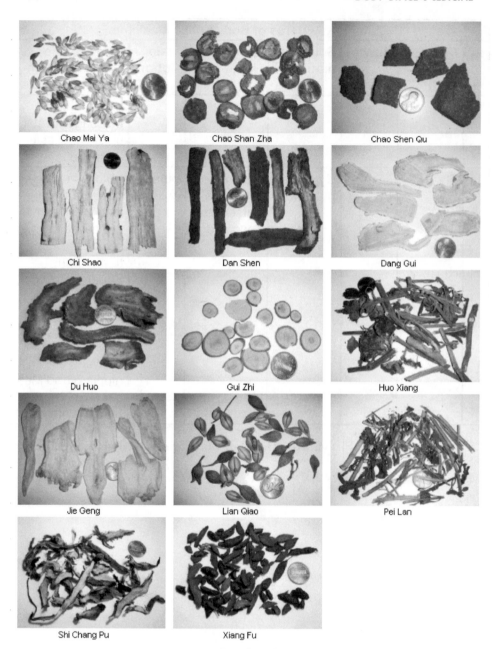

Figure 3. Key Herbs of Body Space Medicine

PRACTICAL CONSIDERATIONS IN USING HERBS

WHERE TO OBTAIN CHINESE HERBS

In most areas of the world, Chinese herbs are considered food products or dietary supplements and are not usually regulated as pharmaceutical products. They are usually dried materials of plant, animal or mineral origin. Therefore, they are readily available almost anywhere in the world, locally, through the Internet or by mail order.

Most of the Chinese herbs used in Body Space Medicine are readily available from any herb supply house that carries Chinese herbs. Cities with a large Chinese population will also have many Chinese herb stores where customers can walk in and have their prescriptions filled on the spot. The herb shops are usually located in the local Chinatown, or in marketplaces that sell Asian foods and services. Herb supply houses that cater to different ethnic groups and natural health stores may also carry Chinese herbs.

Chinese herbs are also readily available online through the Internet or by mail order. Simply perform an online search using one of the popular Internet search engines. Enter key words such as "Chinese herbs, supply, order" in the search field. Including additional terms such as location or herb name in the search field can narrow the search results. The search results are generated instantly and you will find many suppliers offering a variety of products and services.

Some suppliers only sell commercially produced herb extracts and prepackaged formulas; others may also fill prescriptions. In choosing a supplier, look for reputable companies that carry quality products, show clear pricing, have shipping procedures and a well-defined ordering process in place, and offer good customer support.

Herb pricing will vary with the quality and form of the herb, the quantity ordered and the processing involved. The manufacturer and whether or not preservatives were used are among the additional factors that can affect price. Herbs come in many different forms and sizes, so check your order to ensure that you are specifying the proper herb. For example, do you want the leaf, the stem or the flower of the herb? Do you want the entire root or just slices; the whole herb, the powder or the capsules? Be very specific as different parts of the same herb plant will have different properties, as will the raw form vs. the prepared form, and so on.

Whether ordering herbs in bulk for dispensing or in smaller quantities for personal use, practitioners should consider preservative-free or non-sulfured herbs. Naturally processed herbs will not appear as white as herbs that have been bleached or contain chemical preservatives. However, they contain fewer contaminants and other chemicals. Because they are purer, their taste and properties are less affected.

Look for fresh, good quality herbs from a reputable manufacturer. Be wary of buying from a shop with less than ideal herb handling practices or from a place where product is not stored properly. When possible, always inspect the herb before purchasing it. Smell it. Fresh herbs are more potent so they will smell stronger than herbs that have been stored for a while. Look at the packaging; is it intact? Inspect herbs for insect infestation, color, mold, dirt and breakage to ascertain their quality.

To avoid confusion when ordering herbs, especially for non-Chinese speaking practitioners, it is best to write down the Chinese name, the pinyin Romanization, and the scientific name of the herb with the dosage or amount required. Bring this information into the herb store. The more information you provide for the shop to cross-reference, the less confusion and fewer mistakes will result, especially if the shop staff is not fluent in English or the local language.

STORING HERBS

When obtaining herbs, buy only as much as will be consumed in a reasonable length of time. Depending on circumstances, this may range

from one week to a few months. For example, buy at most the full dura-
tion of an herb formula, which may be one or two weeks as specified by
the issuing practitioner.

Generally, it is not necessary to stock up on a particular herb formula. The soul, mind and body respond to the herbs, so it is natural
that one's formula will change over time, which is what usually happens
when the patient returns to the practitioner for follow-up consultations.
The less herb stock on hand, the less of an issue storage becomes.

Another factor to consider is that herbs age and lose their potency
upon exposure to air and light. How much stock to keep will depend
on usage and demand. Are herbs being purchased for self-use or for a
clinical practice? How much is being used? How often does the supply
turn over?

Proper storage and identification of herbs are important considerations for those who plan on stocking herbs onsite. Herbs should
be kept in a cool, dry place. Too much humidity can encourage mold
growth which damages the herbs. Moldy herbs should be discarded
and never used.

Keeping herbs in sealed containers will help retain freshness and
minimize pest infestation. If transferring herbs to another container,
always label the containers so as not to mix up the herbs. A systematic
herb storage and management system is important if herbs are stored
onsite for clinical dispensing.

Those intending to work with bulk herbs will find an accurate gram
scale with a minimum resolution of 0.1 gram very useful for filling prescriptions onsite. Alternatively, some practitioners may prefer the traditional way of weighing Chinese herbs using a simple handheld pan
balance.

FORMULA BASICS

In Body Space Medicine, herb formulas are prescribed as treatment after an analysis of the tongue and assessment of the patient's stool, urine and other relevant symptoms. The prescription is valid for the pathological conditions at the time of evaluation. Prescriptions will change as the body changes, so an herb formula issued one month ago may not be valid today, depending on the patient's current health condition.

The herb formulas given in this chapter constitute a daily dose of herbs. The practice of writing herbs as daily dosages is standard when working with Chinese herbs. The herbs are to be taken on a daily basis for the length of time specified by the practitioner. The practitioner will recommend that the patient return for a follow-up consultation to monitor progress and modify the prescription as necessary.

All herb dosages in this book are given in grams, as signified by the abbreviation "g." To put the gram into perspective, one thousand grams is equivalent to one kilogram (1,000 g = 1 kg), which is approximately 2.2 pounds. There are about twenty-eight grams (more precisely, 28.35 grams) in one ounce. The format used for the herb formulas lists the name of each constituent herb followed by its dosage (e.g., Pei Lan 17 g).

For the treatment of general health issues or for preventive health, herb formulas are usually prescribed for a period of two to three weeks or even longer. At the end of this initial treatment period, patients are urged to return for follow-up consultations to determine if their conditions have been satisfactorily resolved and, if not, to have their herb formulas updated.

For those with more serious health conditions, the Body Space Medicine practitioner will suggest more frequent follow-up consultations as body conditions can change in a matter of a few days. In such cases, the practitioner may prescribe herbs for a period of one week or less and request that the patient return for a follow-up assessment. Some situations require closer monitoring than others. Appropriate adjustments of the herb formula will need to be made as the body changes.

Preparing an Herb Formula

When herb prescriptions are filled in a Chinese herb dispensary or herb store, the herbs are usually packaged as single-day dosages. This is based on the concept that the prescription given is a daily prescription, which is standard practice with Chinese herb formulas. There will be one package made up for each day the formula is prescribed for. For example, a seven-day prescription will be measured and packaged as seven packages.

Instructions for preparing single and multiple packages of herbs and guidelines for taking the herbs follow.

Preparing One Daily Herb Package

1. Place one package of herbs (one day's dosage) in a clay, ceramic, glass or stainless steel pot. Do not use aluminum, copper or cast-iron pots.

2. Add two to three cups of cold water or enough to cover the herbs. Let the herbs sit and soak in the water for at least 15 minutes before boiling.

3. Bring the herbs to a boil. Then, reduce the heat and cook at a low boil for 15-20 minutes, or until approximately one cup of liquid remains.

4. Drain off and save the liquid (approximately one cup).

5. Add about two cups of cold water to the herbs in the pot.

6. After bringing the herbs to a boil again, reduce the heat and cook at a low boil for 10-15 minutes, or until approximately one cup of liquid remains.

7. Drain off and save the liquid (approximately one cup).

8. Combine and mix the two cups of saved liquid; this is the herb tonic or "soup."

9. Drink one cup (warm) of the saved liquid 30 minutes before or after breakfast.

10. Cover and refrigerate the remaining cup of saved liquid.

11. Warm and drink the remaining cup of saved liquid in the evening 30 minutes before or after dinner.

Continue to prepare and drink the herbs daily for the prescribed number of days. If indicated, see your practitioner again to determine if the herb formula needs to be changed as your condition changes.

Note: While preparing the herbs, do not let the pot boil dry or the herbs will burn. If this happens, do not add more water and reboil the burnt herbs! Discard the burnt herbs and start over by boiling a new package.

Preparing Several Days' Dosages of Herbs

To save time and effort, several days of herbs can be prepared at the same time by boiling them all together in the same pot. In general, do not prepare more than three or four days' supply of herbs at the same time.

Follow the same instructions given for preparing one package of herbs, except apply them to preparing multiple packages together. The main differences are to boil the herbs with more water and to store the unused herb tonic properly.

1. After boiling the herbs twice, make sure to end up with two cups of herb tonic per package (one day's dosage) of herbs. For example, you should have about six cups of herb tonic after preparing three days' supply of herbs.

2. Pour the liquid into a clean glass jar. When the liquid is cool, cover and refrigerate.

3. Before using, first stir and blend the herb tonic, then pour one cup of the liquid into a cup or bowl. Warm the herb tonic before drinking it.

4. Drink one cup of herb tonic in the morning 30 minutes before or after breakfast.

5. Drink one cup of herb tonic in the evening 30 minutes before or after dinner.

6. Cover and refrigerate any unused herb tonic.

Guidelines to Observe While Taking Herbs

1. Always drink herb tonics warm.

2. Avoid eating cooling foods. Examples of cooling foods include raw vegetables, cucumber, lettuce, sprouts, seaweed, fruit juices, watermelon and citrus fruits.

3. Avoid eating oily and spicy foods that are hot in character. Examples of hot foods include coffee, alcohol, ginger, cayenne, onions, garlic and prawns.

EIGHT BASIC HERB FORMULAS OF BODY SPACE MEDICINE

Body Space Medicine herb formulas are determined after the practitioner has performed a tongue reading and taken into consideration the conditions of the stool and urine and any other relevant symptoms. The tongue reading, however, is the primary factor for determining the herb formula.

Body Space Medicine recognizes eight main types of tongue bodies for tongue reading. Each tongue body type is treated with a different herb formula. Consequently, there are eight basic herb treatment formulas involving a total of fifteen key herbs which can treat all manner of illnesses and disorders of the entire body.

Table 7 below summarizes the eight basic tongue body types of Body Space Medicine and the herb formulas used for each. The herbs comprising each formula and their dosages are shown. For example, the Chi Shao/Gui Zhi Tang herb formula is used for a tongue body that features blisters or raised areas on the tip of the tongue. These basic Body Space Medicine herb formulas are very simple. Each of the eight basic formulas uses three to five herbs in very low dosages.

Note that the name of each formula ends with "Gui Zhi Tang," which essentially means cinnamon tea. *Gui Zhi* is the Chinese name for cinnamon bark. *Tang* means "soup" in Chinese. The herb formula is boiled, making an herbal cinnamon tea that the patient drinks (i.e., the "soup"). Each Gui Zhi Tang formula contains the same three herbs: Gui Zhi 7 g, Lian Qiao 17 g and Du Huo 7 g. Therefore, each formula is identical to the others except for one or two additional herbs. The names of these unique herbs precede "Gui Zhi Tang" to form the full name of the formula.

For example, the Chi Shao/Gui Zhi Tang formula is distinct from the others in that it contains Chi Shao; the Dang Gui/Gui Zhi Tang formula contains Dang Gui, and so on. The herbs that are unique to each formula are also identified by being bolded in Table 7. Each tongue body condition and its corresponding basic herb formula are discussed thoroughly in the sections that follow.

Prior to applying Body Space Medicine herb formulas, practitioners are urged to learn the eight basic formulas, the tongue body characteristics they apply to, and the fifteen basic herbs. Familiarity with this knowledge will help practitioners apply Body Space Medicine healing efficiently.

Eight Basic Herb Formulas of Body Space Medicine		
#	Formula Name	Tongue Body for Which the Formula Applies	Herbs and Dosage (unique herbs bolded)
1	Chi Shao/ Gui Zhi Tang	Raised or Blistered Tip • The tip of the tongue is raised or has blisters	• **Chi Shao 17 g** • Gui Zhi 7 g • Lian Qiao 17 g • Du Huo 7 g
2	Dang Gui/Gui Zhi Tang	Raised Edges • The edges of the whole tongue are raised Whole Tongue Surface is Raised (dry stool) • The surface of the whole tongue is raised or shows an abnormal elevation	• **Dang Gui 17 g** • Gui Zhi 7 g • Lian Qiao 17 g • Du Huo 7 g
3	Dan Shen/ Gui Zhi Tang	Whole Tongue Surface is Raised (loose stool) • The surface of the whole tongue is raised or shows an abnormal elevation	• **Dan Shen 17 g** • Gui Zhi 7 g • Lian Qiao 17 g • Du Huo 7 g
4	Xiang Fu/Gui Zhi Tang	Raised Area Behind the Tip • The region behind the tip of the tongue is raised	• **Xiang Fu 17 g** • Gui Zhi 7 g • Lian Qiao 17 g • Du Huo 7 g
5	Shi Chang Pu/Gui Zhi Tang	Raised Shan Zhong (Message Center) Area • The tongue has a raised area or bump in the Shan Zhong or Message Center area (see Figure 2)	• **Shi Chang Pu 17 g** • Gui Zhi 7 g • Lian Qiao 17 g • Du Huo 7 g
6	Jiao San Xian/Gui Zhi Tang	Raised Areas at Both Sides of the Middle Jiao Line • The left and right sides of the Middle Jiao line are raised or have bumps	• **Jiao San Xian 17 g for each of its three component herbs** • Gui Zhi 7 g • Lian Qiao 17 g • Du Huo 7 g

Eight Basic Herb Formulas of Body Space Medicine			
#	Formula Name	Tongue Body for Which the Formula Applies	Herbs and Dosage (unique herbs bolded)
7	Jie Geng/ Gui Zhi Tang	Raised Areas on Both Sides with Trench Along the Midline • The tongue is raised on both sides of the vertical midline, from the root (back) to the front of the tongue • There is a trench along the tongue midline	• **Jie Geng 7 g** • Gui Zhi 7 g • Lian Qiao 17 g • Du Huo 7 g
8	Pei Lan/Huo Xiang/ Gui Zhi Tang	Many Raised Areas Plus Watery Coating • The tongue has different raised areas • The coating is wet and watery	• **Pei Lan 17 g** • **Huo Xiang 12 g** • Gui Zhi 7 g • Lian Qiao 17 g • Du Huo 7 g

Table 7. Eight Basic Herb Formulas of Body Space Medicine

Raised or Blistered Tip

The tip of the tongue is raised or has blisters. This is the most common type of tongue condition. Raised areas indicate blood stagnation. A raised tip of the tongue therefore indicates heart blood stagnation.

In Body Space Medicine tongue reading, raised areas on any part of the tongue indicate blood stagnation in the corresponding part of the body. Remember this as it is very important. When the tip of the tongue is raised or has blisters, the flow of *qi* and blood is affected in the entire San Jiao. The basic herb formula to use for this condition is the Chi Shao/Gui Zhi Tang.

Chinese herbalists follow the maxim, "Upper part deficient and lower part excessive." In Body Space Medicine, *upper part deficient* means that the space in the Upper Jiao (the body space above the diaphragm) must be deficient or light. *Lower part excessive* means that the space in the Lower Jiao (below the navel) must be in excess; in other words, matter and energy must be adequate in the space below the navel to provide a strong foundation for the body. *Upper part deficient and lower part excessive* is necessary for a healthy body. If the condition of the upper part and the lower part is not in this balance, many health issues will develop. This is the case when the tip of the tongue is raised or has blisters.

The basic Body Space Medicine formula to use for a tongue tip with raised areas or blisters is the Chi Shao/Gui Zhi Tang, as summarized in Table 8. Modifications to the basic formula are given in Table 9.

FORMULA	CHI SHAO/GUI ZHI TANG	
Herb	**Grams**	**Function of the Herb**
Chi Shao	17	• Stimulates matter movement inside cells • Vitalizes blood and clears blood stagnation
Gui Zhi	7	• Opens the cell membrane pathways to enable free exchange between matter inside cells and energy outside cells
Lian Qiao	17	• Instantly clears the energy and heat radiated from inside cells • Used together with Gui Zhi, reaches up to clear the Upper Jiao space and makes the *upper part deficient* • Used together with Gui Zhi (and Dang Gui), clears the San Jiao and moves *qi*, blood and water in the San Jiao
Du Huo	7	• Clears the Wai Jiao

Table 8. Chi Shao/Gui Zhi Tang Formula

MODIFICATIONS TO CHI SHAO/GUI ZHI TANG		
Herb	**Grams**	**Modification Use Guidelines and Function of the Herb**
Dang Gui	17	For constipation, **add** Dang Gui **or** Rou Cong Rong • Vitalizes, stimulates and nourishes blood • Removes blood stagnation
Rou Cong Rong	17	For constipation, **add** Dang Gui **or** Rou Cong Rong • Stimulates cellular vibration in the intestines
Chao Zao Ren	7	For loose or frequent stool, **add** Chao Zao Ren **or Chao Bai Zhu**
Chao Bai Zhu	7	For loose or frequent stool, **add** Chao Zao Ren **or** Chao Bai Zhu
Wu Wei Zi	7	For night urination more than 3 times per night, **add** Wu Wei Zi

Table 9. Modifications to the Chi Shao/Gui Zhi Tang Formula

Raised Edges

The edges of the whole tongue are raised. This tongue body characteristic is due to blockage in the San Jiao body space; liver *qi* is not smooth. The basic formula to use is the Dang Gui/Gui Zhi Tang, as summarized in Table 10 below.

Whole Tongue Surface is Raised

The entire surface of the tongue is raised. This tongue body characteristic is due to energy blockage in the Wai Jiao. The treatment strategy is to clear the Wai Jiao and promote energy flow in the Gong Zhuan (vertical energy circle). Once the Gong Zhuan flows freely, the Zi Zhuan (horizontal energy circles) will also flow freely.

Two different herb formulas are used depending on the stool conditions:

1. If the stool is dry or the patient has constipation, use the Dang Gui/Gui Zhi Tang, as summarized in Table 10.

2. If the stool is frequent, loose or is morning stool (before 8:00 a.m. or before breakfast), replace Dang Gui with Dan Shen. The resultant formula is the Dan Shen/Gui Zhi Tang, as summarized in Table 11.

FORMULA	DANG GUI/GUI ZHI TANG	
Herb	Grams	Function of the Herb
Dang Gui	17	• Vitalizes, stimulates and nourishes blood • Removes blood stagnation
Gui Zhi	7	• Opens the cell membrane pathways to enable free exchange between matter inside cells and energy outside cells
Lian Qiao	17	• Instantly clears the energy and heat radiated from inside cells • Used together with Gui Zhi, reaches up to clear the Upper Jiao space and makes the *upper part deficient* • Used together with Gui Zhi (and Dang Gui), clears the San Jiao and moves *qi,* blood and water in the San Jiao
Du Huo	7	• Clears the Wai Jiao

Table 10. Dan Gui/Gui Zhi Tang Formula

FORMULA	DAN SHEN/GUI ZHI TANG	
Herb Name	Grams	Function of the Herb
Dan Shen	17	• Vitalizes blood and removes blood stagnation • Stimulates blood circulation; the resulting energy nourishes the heart, spleen and heart blood • Stops diarrhea
Gui Zhi	7	• Opens the cell membrane pathways to enable free exchange between matter inside cells and energy outside cells
Lian Qiao	17	• Instantly clears the energy and heat radiated from inside cells • Used together with Gui Zhi, clears the Upper Jiao space and makes the *upper part deficient* • Used together with **Dan Shen** and Gui Zhi, clears the San Jiao and moves *qi,* blood and water in the San Jiao
Du Huo	7	• Clears the Wai Jiao

Table 11. Dan Shen/Gui Zhi Tang Formula

Raised Area Behind the Tip of the Tongue

The region behind the tip of the tongue is raised. For example, the Upper Jiao area behind the tip of the tongue is raised. This tongue body characteristic is due to inadequate energy or driving force for the Upper Jiao or Middle Jiao. Consequently, energy does not flow freely or properly in the Gong Zhuan (vertical energy circle). The basic formula to use is the Xiang Fu/Gui Zhi Tang, as summarized in Table 12.

FORMULA	XIANG FU/GUI ZHI TANG	
Herb	**Grams**	**Function of the Herb**
Xiang Fu	17	• Promotes energy from the Middle Jiao area below the diaphragm to move along the Gong Zhuan pathway • Moves energy up through the diaphragm and up to the Shan Zhong point (midpoint between the nipples) or through the Message Center behind the sternum
Gui Zhi	7	• Opens the cell membrane pathways to enable free exchange between matter inside cells and energy outside cells
Lian Qiao	17	• Instantly clears the energy and heat radiated from inside cells • With Gui Zhi, clears the Upper Jiao space and makes the *upper part deficient* • With Gui Zhi and Dang Gui), clears the San Jiao and moves *qi,* blood and water in the San Jiao
Du Huo	7	• Clears the Wai Jiao

Table 12. Xiang Fu/Gui Zhi Tang Formula

Raised Shan Zhong Area (Message Center)

The tongue body that shows a raised area or mound in the Shan Zhong or Message Center area (see Figure 2) is a special case. The raised area is due to blocked energy in the Message Center that cannot dissipate.

Message Center blockage affects the movement of energy in the head and the San Jiao body space. Because the Message Center is the emotional center, the love center, the forgiveness center and the karma center, blockage there also affects the emotions and the soul. Various disorders in the head, mental illnesses and emotional problems are connected with the Message Center. The basic formula to use to treat these issues of the brain, soul and emotions is the Shi Chang Pu/Gui Zhi Tang, as summarized in Table 13.

FORMULA	SHI CHANG PU/GUI ZHI TANG	
Herb	Grams	Function of the Herb
Shi Chang Pu	17	• Lowers the density and pressure in the outer space (the space around) of the right atrium and the right ventricle • Strengthens the flow of venous blood from the extremities back to the heart • Lowers the density and pressure of the energy in the Message Center, allowing energy in the head to flow downward
Gui Zhi	7	• Opens the cell membrane pathways to enable free exchange between matter inside cells and energy outside cells
Lian Qiao	17	• Instantly clears the energy and heat radiated from inside cells • With Gui Zhi, clears the Upper Jiao space and makes the *upper part deficient* • With Gui Zhi and Dang Gui), clears the San Jiao and moves *qi,* blood and water in the San Jiao
Du Huo	7	• Clears the Wai Jiao

Table 13. Shi Chang Pu/Gui Zhi Tang Formula

Raised Areas at Both sides of the Middle Jiao Line

The left and right sides of the Middle Jiao line on the tongue (see Figure 2) *have raised areas.* This tongue body characteristic is due to stagnant energy in the Middle Jiao; the energy of the digestive system is blocked. The basic formula to use to treat this tongue condition is the Jiao San Xian/Gui Zhi Tang, as summarized in Table 14.

FORMULA	JIAO SAN XIAN/GUI ZHI TANG	
Herb	Grams	Function of the Herb
Jiao San Xian	17 each	• Jiao San Xian is comprised of Chao Mai Ya, Chao Shan Zha, Chao Shen Qu • Clears the matter and energy of all the organs in the Middle Jiao
Gui Zhi	7	• Opens the cell membrane pathways to enable free exchange between matter inside cells and energy outside cells

FORMULA	JIAO SAN XIAN/GUI ZHI TANG, cont.	
Herb	Grams	Function of the Herb
Lian Qiao	17	• Instantly clears the energy and heat radiated from inside cells • With Gui Zhi, clears the Upper Jiao space and makes the *upper part deficient* • With Gui Zhi and Dang Gui), clears the San Jiao and moves *qi,* blood and water in the San Jiao
Du Huo	7	• Clears the Wai Jiao

Table 14. Jiao San Xian/Gui Zhi Tang Formula

Raised Areas on Both Sides with Trench Along the Midline

There are raised areas on both sides of the tongue's vertical midline, and consequently a trench or valley down the midline. The raised areas extend from the root (back) of the tongue to the front of the tongue. This type of tongue body is due to blockage in the San Jiao body space. The basic formula to use is the Jie Geng/Gui Zhi Tang, as summarized in Table 15.

FORMULA	JIE GENG/GUI ZHI TANG	
Herb	Grams	Function of the Herb
Jie Geng	17	• Clears the lungs, makes the energy from the ribs move up
Gui Zhi	7	• Opens the cell membrane pathways to enable free exchange between matter inside cells and energy outside cells
Lian Qiao	17	• Instantly clears the energy and heat radiated from inside cells • With Gui Zhi, clears the Upper Jiao space and makes the *upper part deficient* • With Gui Zhi and Dang Gui), clears the San Jiao and moves *qi,* blood and water in the San Jiao
Du Huo	7	• Clears the Wai Jiao

Table 15. Jie Geng/Gui Zhi Tang Formula

Many Raised Areas Plus Watery Coating

The tongue body has multiple raised areas on its surface, and the tongue coating is wet and watery. The basic formula to use for this type of tongue is the Pei Lan/Huo Xiang/Gui Zhi Tang, as summarized in Table 16. Modifications to the basic formula are summarized in Table 17.

FORMULA	PEI LAN/HUO XIANG/GUI ZHI TANG	
Herb	Grams	Function of the Herb
Pei Lan	17	• Clears fluid and moisture inside and outside of all cells in the body • Can be used for constipation or loose stools
Huo Xiang	12	• Clears the fluid in the Middle Jiao • Use for loose stools or diarrhea; not to be used for constipation
Gui Zhi	7	• Opens the cell membrane pathways to enable free exchange between matter inside cells and energy outside cells
Lian Qiao	17	• Instantly clears the energy and heat radiated from inside cells • With Gui Zhi, clears the Upper Jiao space and makes the *upper part deficient* • With Gui Zhi and Dang Gui), clears the San Jiao and moves *qi,* blood and water in the San Jiao
Du Huo	7	• Clears the Wai Jiao

Table 16. Pei Lan/Huo Xiang/Gui Zhi Tang Formula

MODIFICATION TO PEI LAN/HUO XIANG/GUI ZHI TANG		
Herb	Grams	Modification Use Guidelines and Function of the Herb
Zhi Mu	4	Add Zhi Mu if there is fever • Clears internal heat and clears the Wai Jiao

Table 17. Modification to the Pei Lan/Huo Xiang/Gui Zhi Tang Formula

TREATMENT STRATEGIES AND APPLICATIONS

Body Space Medicine is a new science that is simple in its methods, powerful in its herb applications, and quick in its diagnosis and treatment. The large majority of herb formulas in Body Space Medicine consist of only four or five herbs, yet Body Space Medicine can treat all illnesses, including chronic and serious conditions. In particular, Body Space Medicine's clinical results for lung cancer, liver cancer, pancreatic cancer, esophageal cancer and other cancers are astounding.

The application of Body Space Medicine follows various treatment protocols which are critical to its successful implementation and application. This section presents the background, methodologies and treatment strategies to deal with complex cases such as cancer. Thorough study and understanding of the methods discussed will empower practitioners to effectively treat patients with cancer or other serious illnesses.

Treatment in Body Space Medicine focuses on the characteristics displayed by the tongue and the symptoms displayed by the body. Its treatment strategy is based on an understanding of the functions of the cells and organs, the activity and energy of cells, the collision of energies, and the density in the space within the body.

In the sections that follow, I discuss symptoms with respect to the Five Elements theory, feng shui and the movement of energy in the body space. The final treatment strategy involves finding an exit for blocked energy, after assessing all relevant symptoms, considering the name of the disease, illness or condition, and finding the root cause of the disorder.

In Body Space Medicine the whole organism is treated — soul, mind, heart and body. In addition to adjusting the matter and energy of the body, the body's messages are also adjusted so as to enable total transformation of the illness. Messages are used to change the energy of the body so that energy collides with matter and restores the body's functions. Messages are also used to change the messages carried by the matter and energy of the body to better enable healing.

BASIC GONG ZHUAN CONCEPTS

To understand symptoms from the perspective of Body Space Medicine and to determine the appropriate treatment approach, the following concepts need to be understood:

1.   The Gong Zhuan is the Key Energy Circle of the Body

Normal functioning of the body's organs and cells is closely connected with the Gong Zhuan, or vertical energy circle. In the treatment of illness, the Gong Zhuan must function normally; that is, energy must circulate freely through it. The Gong Zhuan is the main thoroughfare for the movement of energy in the body space, and so it is also the main thoroughfare for adjusting this movement. The Gong Zhuan can be used to adjust the transformation of matter and energy in the organs, the cells and the body space. Body Space Medicine considers the Wai Jiao to be the body's energy market, the central repository for the exchange (deposit and withdrawal) of energy.

2.   The Gong Zhuan Flows Up the Front and Down the Back

The Gong Zhuan starts from the Hui Yin acupuncture point in the perineum, between the genitals and the anus. It moves up past the Lower Dan Tian energy center in the lower abdomen, the navel, and the acupuncture points Zhong Wan, Shan Zhong (midpoint between the nipples) and Tian Tu (at the base of the throat) to the Bai Hui point (top of the head), then downward in front of the Da Zhui (below C7 of the cervical vertebrae), Zhong Shu and Ming Men points (on the lower back below L2 of the lumbar vertebrae), and back to the Hui Yin. Energy flows continuously in the Gong Zhuan, which is the conduit for the space energy and saturated vapor of the body. The Gong Zhuan energy circle is shown in Figure 4.

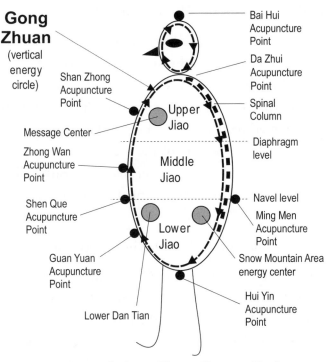

Figure 4. Gong Zhuan Energy Circle

3.   Gong Zhuan Is Not the Ren-Du Meridians

The Gong Zhuan energy circle of Body Space Medicine is not the same as the Ren and Du meridians of traditional Chinese medicine. The Ren (Conception Vessel) meridian runs up the front midline of the body, while the Du (Governing Vessel) meridian travels up the back inside the spinal column to the head. In traditional Chinese medicine, the meridians are pathways through which vital energy or *qi* circulates. The Ren and Du meridians are different from the Gong Zhuan. The Gong Zhuan is wider by two *cun* (pronounced "chuen," this unit of measurement used in traditional Chinese medicine is equivalent to the width of the thumb at its widest part) on each side of these two meridians. The Du meridian travels *up* the back *inside* the spinal column, whereas the Gong Zhuan runs *down* the back and in *front* of the spinal column, in the Wai Jiao space. I discovered and named this largest of all body spaces, which extends down the entire back of the body in front of the spinal column, and up through the back of the head.

4.   Gong Zhuan Is Not the Microcosmic Orbit

The Gong Zhuan energy pathway is not the same as the Micro-cosmic Orbit (Small Heaven) pathway familiar to Taoist practitioners. Although many of the key points are the same, the Microcosmic Orbit route goes *up* the back along the Du meridian and *down* the front mid-line along the Ren meridian. This direction of flow is *opposite* that of the Gong Zhuan. Also, the back part of the Gong Zhuan circle does not go through the upward-flowing Du meridian, but rather flows down through the body space in front of the spinal column, through the Wai Jiao.

5.   Each Gong Zhuan Part Is a Driving Force and an Exit

Every part of the body along the Gong Zhuan pathway serves as the driving force for the area downstream and also provides an exit for the area upstream on the route. Note the direction of flow in the Gong Zhuan — energy flows continuously up the front and down the back. Take for example the chest area. The chest is the exit for abdominal energy, because the chest is downstream from the abdomen along the Gong Zhuan. At the same time, the chest is also the driving force of en-ergy for the back, which is downstream from the chest along the Gong Zhuan. In turn, the back is the exit for chest energy and also the dri-ving force for the tailbone. This principle holds true for every part of the body along the Gong Zhuan.

6.   Consider Several Exits to Ensure Smooth Gong Zhuan Flow

To treat illness, the practitioner should consider the driving force and exit of the affected area, as well as the second and third exits down-stream from the affected area, to ensure that the Gong Zhuan flows smoothly. Therefore, for a person with abdominal problems, resolve any chest issues (the first exit for the abdomen) and also look at the conditions in the back space of the body (the second exit for the abdo-men). If energy is blocked at the back, the chest energy cannot dissi-pate and so the abdominal problem cannot be resolved.

In determining a treatment strategy, the practitioner needs to consider the entire body to be able to heal effectively. **In the practice and application of Body Space Medicine, the goal is to have smooth and unimpeded flow in the Gong Zhuan.** All treatment methods and diagnoses are tied to the Gong Zhuan. Therefore, proper adjustment of the Gong Zhuan is central to the effective application of Body Space Medicine.

In the sections that follow, the application and treatment approach of Body Space Medicine are discussed for several key organs of the body — the lungs, esophagus, pancreas, intestines, liver and kidneys.

A brief introduction is given for each organ, including its main functions and the implications of impaired organ function for health. Treatment strategy for common organ symptoms, illnesses and disorders is explained. Herb formulas and appropriate modifications of the basic formulas are given, along with explanations of the role and function of each herb. Of special interest is the understanding and approach Body Space Medicine uses for the effective treatment of cancer, diabetes and other diseases that are difficult to treat with standard medical methods.

LUNGS

The lungs are located above the diaphragm in the thoracic cavity. Traditional Chinese medicine considers the lungs in the Upper Jiao as Heaven in the body. If Heaven is clear, people feel open and comfortable. If Heaven has clouds or rain, people feel heaviness, pressure and blocked. Therefore, in assessing any illness, one must also consider whether lung function is normal. If lung energy does not transform properly, this malfunction affects the heart, spleen, kidney, liver, etc. So, consider the source and the exit of lung energy as it is the key for treatment.

The term *lung* not only refers to the lobes of the right and left lungs and their functions, but includes the area and space around the lungs which is the central depot for receiving and distributing energy to the other areas of the body. (In traditional Chinese medicine, the lungs are in charge not only of respiratory *qi*, but also of whole body *qi*.) There are two sources of energy for the lungs: (a) the spleen and (b) nature.

The lungs receive food essence from the spleen, the source of the body's post-natal energy, and then distribute the energy to the entire body. The "Yellow Emperor's Classic of Internal Medicine" states, "The spleen disperses essence to the Shan Zhong[2]," which is to say the source of the lung energy is directly connected to the energy radiated by the spleen in the Middle Jiao. The energy produced by the spleen cells radiates upwards to the Shan Zhong, where it bumps and collides with lung energy, forming one of the driving forces for lung cell vibration.

The lungs also receive energy from nature, which is the energy in the body space. This energy provides the internal driving force for the body's clearing function of *light energy ascends, turbid energy descends.* Through the process of respiration, the lungs exchange, integrate and transform their energy with the energy of nature. Inhalation and exhalation is also the process by which the energy of the body mixes and transforms with the energy of nature.

Treatment

The cell activity of the lungs and lung area can affect the heart. Traditional Chinese medicine has long recognized the relationship between the lungs and the heart. Body Space Medicine understands that if lung energy is too strong, this excessiveness can lead to muscle contraction on the right side of the heart, and eventually to myocarditis.

Myocarditis, or inflammation of the muscular tissue of the heart, is a serious condition that is sometimes fatal. To treat myocarditis, one must first clear the lungs and reduce the pressure of the energy in the lung space. When pressure in the lungs is reduced, the heart will recover much faster.

The herbs used to address myocarditis in Body Space Medicine are Ye Jiao Tang, Ban Lan Gen, Ge Geng and Lian Qiao as summarized in Table 18.

HERBS FOR TREATING MYOCARDITIS		
Herb	Dose	Function of the Herb
Ye Jiao Tang	7 g	• Increases the return flow of venous blood to the right atrium of the heart
Ban Lan Gen	17 g	• Eliminates inflammation, clears heat, increases body fluids and has the quenching action of *water over fire*
Ge Geng	7 g	• Opens up the capillary system in the muscles, eliminates heat and enables water to reach the extremities
Lian Qiao	17 g	• Clears heat from the space in the lungs and reduces heat in the space around the heart • The herb of choice for clearing heat from around the heart

Table 18. Herbs for Treating Myocarditis

Normally, lung energy goes up and moves across the back to exit through the two shoulder blades. The Wai Jiao serves as the conduit for the exit of lung energy. When lung energy has an exit, the environment of the lungs can be clear and the lungs can be healthy. The Body Space Medicine herbs to move lung energy up and open the exit at the back are listed in Table 19.

HERBS TO MOVE LUNG ENERGY AND OPEN THE BACK	
Herb	Function of the Herb
• Ge Geng • Ma Huang	• Open the muscle cells of the back
• Zhi Mu • Pu Gong Ying	• Open the Gong Zhuan in the space of the back, clear heat and reduce inflammation

HERBS TO MOVE LUNG ENERGY AND OPEN THE BACK, cont.	
Herb	Function of the Herb
• Yi Mi Ren • Bai Tou Weng	• Clear the Gong Zhuan in the Lower Jiao space

Table 19. Herbs to Move Lung Energy and Open the Back

Body Space Medicine can also be applied to treat other common symptoms of lung disorder as listed in Table 20:

HERBS FOR COMMON LUNG SYMPTOMS		
Case	Common Lung Symptoms	Herbs to Use
1	• Dullness in the chest • Heaviness or sinking feeling in the back • Pain in the shoulder blade(s)	• Ren Dong Teng • Zhe Bei • Ge Geng
2	• Expanded feeling in the head • Dullness in the chest • Heaviness or sinking feeling in the back	• Shi Chang Pu • Ren Dong Teng • Zhe Bei • Ge Geng
3	• Cough	• Chao Pi Pa Ye (roasted)
4	• Phlegm	• Fu Shi • Chen Pi • Ban Xia

Table 20. Herbs for Common Lung Symptoms

ESOPHAGUS

The esophagus is a soft muscular tube in the center of the chest that delivers food from the mouth and throat to the stomach. The driving force for the esophagus and its function comes from the abdomen below the diaphragm. The direct exit for esophageal energy is the space in the back; the second exit would be the space in the tailbone area. At the same time, the esophagus is connected to the energy in the chest area. High energy pressure in the space of the chest therefore affects the function of the esophagus. The exits for chest energy are also in the spaces of the back and tailbone.

Esophageal cancer occurs when malignant tumors form anywhere along the length of the esophagus. From the perspective of Body Space Medicine, esophageal cancer develops when energy becomes highly congested and cannot dissipate from the esophagus area. In essence, cancer is a form of energy blockage. To enable recovery from esophageal cancer, one needs to make energy circulate normally and freely in the Gong Zhuan.

Treatment

With esophageal cancer, the tongue coating is often thick and greasy. In particular, there will often be a thick, yellow and greasy coating on the middle and back of the tongue. A thick and greasy tongue coating indicates that the Wai Jiao is blocked; energy cannot dissipate from the Wai Jiao space. Body Space Medicine uses the following herb formulas to treat esophageal cancer:

- Basic Formula

  Use Bai Tou Weng 30 g, Gui Zhi 7 g, Lian Qiao 17 g, Du Huo 7 g. This formula disperses the energy and clears the damp turbidity in the middle and the lower parts of the Wai Jiao.

- If the Stool is Dry

  Use Dang Gui 17-30 g, Gui Zhi 7g, Lian Qiao 17 g, Du Huo 7 g. This formula activates the cells of the San Jiao (the Upper, Middle and Lower Jiao) and activates the driving force of the whole body.

- If Constipated or Morning Stool

  If the patient is constipated, add roasted Bing Lang (Chao Bing Lang 7g). If the patient has morning stool (i.e., bowel movement before breakfast), replace Chao Bing Lang with Chao Zao Ren 7 g.

- If the Coating is Watery and the Tongue is Full

  Use Pei Lan 17 g, Gui Zhi 7 g, Lian Qiao 17 g, Du Huo 7 g. This formula adjusts the distribution of water and *qi* in the body.

The key points to remember when treating esophageal cancer are to vitalize blood appropriately and bring the turbid *qi* down appropriately. Only when light energy ascends can turbid energy descend.

Guidelines for Treating Illness

In the application of Body Space Medicine, observe the following guidelines when treating any illness:

1. Prevent colds and flu from developing. Ensure that the spaces in the Upper Jiao and the Wai Jiao are clear.

2. Prevent fatigue. Maintain the driving forces of the Middle and Lower Jiao.

3. Follow a light and bland diet so as to keep the digestive system clean and functioning well.

4. When treating esophageal cancer, it is very important to observe whether the tongue coating on the vertical midline is clean. Only when the tongue midline is clean will the San Jiao and Wai Jiao spaces be clear for good treatment results.

5. When the tongue coating is raised along the midline, herbs that aid digestion (e.g., Jiao San Xian) must be used to clear the San Jiao.

6. If the patient is constipated, add Chao Bing Lang 7 g to the herb formula. If the patient has morning stool (i.e., bowel movement on waking and before breakfast), replace Chao Bing Lang with Chao Zao Ren 7 g.

PANCREAS

The pancreas is located behind the stomach across the back of the abdomen. The pancreas' digestive and hormonal functions help break down food and regulate blood sugar levels. Disorders of the pancreas include diabetes, cystic fibrosis, pancreatitis, tumors and cancer.

Pancreatic cancer is the growth of a malignant tumor in the pancreas. Modern medicine considers pancreatic cancer very difficult to treat. It is one of the most lethal forms of cancer. Body Space Medicine, however, has a different perspective on pancreatic cancer. The pancreas lies on the Gong Zhuan. Consequently, any problem of the pancreas spreads quickly and affects the upper and lower exits of the entire body. On the positive side, it is easy to determine the source of the driving energy for the pancreas, as well as its energy exit. If one understands the concept of providing an exit for the energy radiating from the cells around the pancreas, then the root cause of problems with the pancreas can be solved quickly.

Pancreatic cancer and all disorders of the pancreas are caused by dampness and blocked energy pathways. To address these issues, the Upper Jiao and Wai Jiao spaces should be clear and empty. Only when these spaces are empty can the energy around the pancreas radiate externally and dissipate. The energy given off by the pancreas must go upward through the diaphragm, as that is the direction of dispersion in the Gong Zhuan. The energy can dissipate when it moves up through the diaphragm and passes through the Upper Jiao and Wai Jiao. Pancreatic cancer, like all other cancers and all illnesses, must be solved through the Gong Zhuan.

A common observation with patients who have pancreatic cancer is that the tip or front part of the tongue is often raised. In Body Space Medicine, a raised tongue tip or raised area at the front of the tongue indicates that lung energy cannot move upward. In other words, the Upper Jiao energy and the Wai Jiao energy are not able to connect and exchange.

Common symptoms associated with pancreatic cancer, pancreatitis and other disorders of the pancreas include a sinking or heavy feeling in the back, tightness in the back and hiccups. These symptoms occur because lung energy cannot move first up and then down the Gong Zhuan to collide with, stimulate and nourish the kidneys. Consequently, cell movement in the kidney area is diminished, kidney cell energy weakens and kidney function suffers. This situation is known as *deficient kidney* in traditional Chinese medicine.

Traditionally, the kidneys are the main source of energy for the fetus. After birth, the lungs are the main energy source for the body. Thus, kidney energy begets all things before birth and lung energy begets all things after birth. In other words, the kidneys are responsible for the body's storehouse of pre-natal or congenital energy, known as *yuan qi* or original *qi;* the lungs are responsible for the body's post-natal energy, known as *ying qi* or acquired *qi.*

The energy of the pancreas is dissipated via the Wai Jiao space (in front of the spinal column) through the lungs. In the Wai Jiao space around the lungs, pancreas energy collides with that of the kidney cells. Gong Zhuan flow dictates that the generated energy can only move down to collide with Lower Dan Tian energy and produce *ying qi.* The post-natal driving energy of the body is thus derived from lung *qi* moving down and supplementing the body's store of congenital essence or *yuan qi.* Consequently, in treating any illness, one must focus on clearing the Upper Jiao so as to maintain the lungs' function of replenishing the body's energy.

There are some notable differences between Body Space Medicine and traditional Chinese medicine. Traditional Chinese medicine considers the Lower Jiao to be the provider of the main driving energy or force for the body. Body Space Medicine, however, focuses on the Upper Jiao and, specifically, the lungs as the *source* of the body's driving energy. According to the theory of traditional Chinese medicine, the body's driving force is created when *light energy ascends* and *turbid energy descends*.

The Body Space Medicine perspective is to first let the light energy (lung energy) descend. After this occurs, the body's driving energy can be produced. Only when the light energy in the Wai Jiao space descends can the body's driving energy be produced. Then, when light energy ascends along the Gong Zhuan, turbid energy will descend.

The first step in treating any condition is to clear the Wai Jiao.

This rule applies no matter what kind of illness, tumor, inflammation or cancer one is dealing with. As borne out by thousands of clinical cases and tongue observations, the energy exchange in the Middle Jiao and Upper Jiao is key in the treatment of illness. One must provide an exit for blocked energy.

Pancreatic cancer is often accompanied by a raised area on the tip or the front part of the tongue. However, many patients with similar tongue conditions do not have pancreatic cancer. The specific illness is not relevant. For all such tongue bodies, one must dissipate the energy in the Middle Jiao and Upper Jiao to address the root of the illness, whatever the illness may be.

With pancreatic cancer, the common symptoms of tightness in the back or a sinking or heavy feeling in the back can be due to the liver area's cell energy radiating and directly affecting the function of the pancreas. Anatomically, the liver is to the right, in front of and above the pancreas. The liver, stomach and pancreas are all located below the diaphragm in the Middle Jiao. The energy condition immediately below the diaphragm therefore directly affects the function of the pancreas; the dampness of the San Jiao also directly affects the function of the pancreas; and the energy movement of the San Jiao directly affects the action of the pancreas.

Treatment

During treatment of pancreatic disorders, ensure that the Gong Zhuan flows freely. The Gong Zhuan serves as the reference for all treatment. Identify any blockages in the Gong Zhuan. Ensure that the Upper Jiao and Wai Jiao are clear. If not, emphasize treatment for the part of the body that presents a blockage by promoting the action of *light energy descends* in the San Jiao so as to subsequently lead the San Jiao light energy to ascend and the turbid energy to descend. The focus of the herb formulas that follow is on clearing dampness from the space:

- Basic Formula

  Use Pei Lan 17 g, Gui Zhi 7 g, Lian Qiao 17 g, Du Huo 17–30 g.

- If the Tongue is Dry and the Stool is Dry

  Use Dang Gui 17 g, Gui Zhi 7 g, Lian Qiao 17 g, Du Huo 17–30 g.

- If the Tongue is Purple and Wet

  Use Yi Mu Cao 30 g, Gui Zhi 7 g, Lian Qiao 17 g, Du Huo 17 g.

- Wet and Purple Tongue, Abdominal Fullness, Stool Not Dry

  Use Dan Shen 17 g, Gui Zhi 7 g, Lian Qiao 17 g, Du Huo 7–17 g. This formula is used if the tongue is slightly purple and wet, the abdomen is full and the stool is not dry.

- If Morning Stool (Bowel Movement Upon Waking)

  Use Chao Zao Ren 7 g, Gui Zhi 7 g, Lian Qiao 17 g, Du Huo 17 g. Note that Chao Zao Ren cannot be used too much as it will block the Upper Jiao pathway.

- If the Stool is Loose and Wet

  Use Huo Xiang 12 g, Pei Lan 17 g, Gui Zhi 7 g, Lian Qiao 17 g, Du Huo 17 g.

- If the Edge of the Tongue is Thick, Hard and Purple

  Use Chi Shao 17 g, Gui Zhi 7 g, Lian Qiao 17 g, Du Huo 17 g.

- If the Middle Part of the Tongue Front Tip is Raised

  Use Shi Chang Pu 17-30 g. Shi Chang Pu resolves the area 2 cun above the Shan Zhong (midpoint between the two nipples). This area is the key for treating the Upper Jiao pathway blockage associated with pancreatic cancer.

INTESTINES

The intestines include the small intestine and the large intestine, both of which are located in the Lower Jiao (the area of the body below the navel). The primary function of the small intestine is digestion and the primary function of the large intestine is disposal.

The digestive function of the small intestine requires energy from the Middle Jiao as its driving force. The disposal function of the large intestine requires the pressure of the space to be reduced. The actions of the intestines require both the driving energy from the space as well as the clearance of the space in an around the intestine itself in order to function. This is why traditional Chinese medicine advises one to *clear the intestines* often as the key for trouble-free intestinal absorption and digestion.

Fluid in Body Space Medicine

The exits for the intestines are the main exit routes for solid matter and fluid in the body. The exit route of matter has disposal as its outcome. This function belongs to the large intestine. The exit route of fluids arises from the functional movement of the small intestine. Western medicine, in contrast, associates the fluid exit with the kidneys. However, Body Space Medicine considers *all* cell activity, not only that of the kidneys, to be related to fluid. The processes of digestion and absorption involve fluid formation in both the space around the cells and also around the matter inside the cells, for every cell in the body.

The body space defined by Body Space Medicine is where water, other fluids and moisture are released. This space around the organs contains the essence of the organs. Thus, the flow of fluid in the body arises from the normal process of digestion and absorption in the cells. However, digestion and absorption is not a discrete process that is complete after one or two cycles, but rather an ongoing process that continuously forms fluid, cycle after cycle.

The body's functions can be summarized in one word: *saturation.* All cells of the body absorb and dispose at the same time, forming fluid in the process. This fluid is released into the body space, moistening and saturating it, and is transported along the Gong Zhuan.

The process can be likened to the function of blood vessels in the body where the arteries, which conduct oxygen-rich blood from the heart to the body, and the veins, which return oxygen-depleted blood back to the heart, are both functioning at the same time. When there are arteries, there are also veins. Where there is fluid outflow, there is also fluid inflow or return flow.

Consequently, fluid absorption and fluid elimination are not limited to the kidneys as is thought to be the case in Western medicine. Rather, the continuous process of digestion and absorption involves every cell of the body. It is a normal part of the action of the body space. This phenomenon forms the foundation for the matter and energy functions of the entire body.

Traditional Chinese medicine has a saying that nutritious *qi* or energy from food essence comes from the Middle Jiao (from the action of the lungs and the spleen) and defensive *qi* (*wei qi*) comes from the Lower Jiao. However, both types of *qi* are actually different forms of matter. Nutrition is provided by the turbid part of matter, and defense by the light part of matter. Basically, nutrition is matter inside the cells and defense is matter outside the cells.

LIVER

The liver is located directly under the diaphragm on the right side of the upper abdomen. To the left is the stomach and above, the heart and the right lung. The liver's functions include metabolism, digestion of food, breakdown of toxic substances, storage of glycogen, synthesis of plasma protein and production of bile. In traditional Chinese medicine, the liver is an organ for storing blood, purging stagnation in the spleen and stomach, nourishing the tendons, nails and hair, and opening on the eyes (clean and nutrient-rich blood from a healthy liver can flow easily and nourish the eye tissues well). Disorders of the liver include jaundice, hepatitis, cirrhosis and cancer, as recognized by Western medicine. Additionally, traditional Chinese medicine cites digestive problems, eye problems, emotional issues, irregular menstruation, numbness in the extremities, aching joints and pain or distension in the sides of the chest as liver disorders.

In Western medicine, liver transplants are the main course of treatment for those with liver failure. In traditional Chinese medicine, herbs are used to effect change in the liver for those with liver illness. Body Space Medicine differs significantly from both modalities in that its treatment involves the integration of Xiu Lian practice and restoration of free flow in the Gong Zhuan.

Body Space Medicine's approach to treating disorders of the liver is to adjust the body by using Gong Zhuan theory. Knowing the main direction of the Gong Zhuan flow, all treatment focuses on leading, pushing and changing small sections along the Gong Zhuan pathway to enable free flow in the entire Gong Zhuan. Traditional Chinese medicine looks for the causes of disease in the *six excesses* and the *seven emotions*. (The six excesses are the exogenous factors of wind, cold, heat, dampness, dryness and fire. The seven emotions are the endogenous factors of overjoy, anger, melancholy, anxiety, grief, fear and fright.) **Body Space Medicine is different in that it looks to the accumulation of fluid and the imbalance in fluid distribution as the causes of illness.**

In traditional Chinese medicine, the Five Elements theory gives the concept of Wood (liver) generating Fire (heart), where the energy of the mother organ (liver) nourishes the son organ (heart). Body Space Medicine understands the concept of Wood generating Fire from the perspective of energy flow. In this case, the energy radiating from the activity of the liver cells moves to the left (below the diaphragm) and then collides with the lower part of the heart (above the diaphragm), which increases the activity and movement of the heart cells, thereby strengthening the heart.

Body Space Medicine further understands that the clarity of the space below the diaphragm is directly related to the energy radiated by the liver cells. The normal pathway is for the radiation of energy from the liver to move left below the diaphragm. However, if the radiated liver energy moves horizontally excessively, it will unfavorably affect the stomach and its digestive functions.

Treatment

In the treatment of liver diseases, the first step is to clear the pressure and density of the body space of the liver and its surroundings. The basic formula and two modifications thereof follow:

- Basic Formula

  Gui Zhi, Lian Qiao, Xiang Fu, Bo He

- If the Tongue Coating Is Thick, Greasy and Wet

  Add Pei Lan.

- If the Coating Is Dry

Add Dang Gui and drop Pei Lan. The formula then contains Dang Gui, Gui Zhi, Lian Qiao, Xiang Fu and Bo He. Its purpose is to increase the cell water content, blood content and overall blood circulation, and to improve the flow of the Gong Zhuan.

Clear damp heat and make the pathway free; then, dampness will be eliminated by itself. This is a key principle to grasp in the determination of treatment. The clearance of energy allows new energy to enter and also nourishes energy. The clearance of energy provides nourishment to the area as it is a method of renewing energy. In Body Space Medicine, clearance is the main approach used for renewing energy. In other words, nourish the energy of the area by using elimination as the treatment approach. Therefore, the main approach for treating diseases of the liver is to clear the Upper, Middle and Lower Jiao. The following herbs are used for clearing the space and freeing the pathway:

• Gui Zhi and Lian Qiao —key herbs for stretching and clearing the cells. In the process of clearing, these herbs also clear away the heat of cell radiation.

• Xiang Fu — clears the energy in the Middle Jiao space and moves Middle Jiao energy up through the diaphragm to the Shan Zhong (acupuncture point midway between the nipples). This clears the Middle Jiao energy and opens the Middle Jiao space.

• Bo He — clears the matter inside the liver cells by transforming matter into energy, which radiates out of the cells. It allows liver cell energy to radiate outwards into the space below the diaphragm and disperse in the Middle Jiao and Lower Jiao.

• Sheng Mai Ya — clears the energy below the diaphragm by causing energy on the right side of the diaphragm to move to the left. It is used to move liver energy horizontally to the left to stimulate vibration of the heart cells, thus nourishing and strengthening the heart.

- Yin Chen — clears matter blockage and moves liver energy to the left. This clears the space between the liver and the stomach, allowing liver energy to dissipate.

- Bing Lang and Jin Yin Hua — clear the stomach and intestines. In treating liver disease, it is important to clear any stagnation or blockages of the stomach and intestines. Use 15 g each of these key herbs and take them on an empty stomach.

Guidelines for Treating Diseases of the Liver

Use the following guidelines for treating diseases of the liver:

- Clear damp heat and make the pathway free.

- Clear the matter by clearing the space in the stomach and intestines.

- Pay attention to water retention in the abdomen (blocked matter) and the level of cell activity in the Lower Dan Tian.

- Increase Lower Dan Tian energy to avoid or to treat water retention in the abdomen.

- Be alert to the portal vein[3] and the inferior vena cava; do not excessively use herbs that affect blood flow. Do not increase the return flow of blood to the heart by increasing venous blood flow. Allow the liver cells to function naturally.

Dispersing the energy radiated by the cells, clearing the pathway and finding an exit are all important methods for treating illness. Normal liver function and pressure in the space of the chest above the diaphragm are related to normal pressure in the spaces of the spleen and stomach below the diaphragm. The circulation of energy in the surrounding space requires the driving force of the Gong Zhuan to attain a relative balance. Consequently, in treating the liver, one must also clear the lungs, reduce the pressure and density of the space in the chest, and reduce the pressure and density of the Wai Jiao. Only by accomplishing all these requirements can the liver energy be cleared.

Dispersion creates wind and accumulation creates form. So says the *Huang Di Nei Jing* (the "Yellow Emperor's Classic of Internal Medicine"). This provides the insight that stagnation of liver energy easily leads to the formation of liver cysts and tumors.

In traditional Chinese medicine, the liver houses the soul. Therefore, in addition to changing the energy and matter in the space and changing the matter inside the cells, the treatment of liver disease must also include message healing (soul healing).

In the case of liver cancer, dissipation is required but the prenatal *jing qi* or kidney essence must also be strong. In the process of dissipation, one has to follow the route indicated by the Five Elements and act according to its theory. Specifically, Water (kidneys) generates Wood (liver). This will solve liver stagnation without spreading it to other organs. Follow the regular energy route and direction of the Gong Zhuan. Then treatment will be successful and all subsequent problems avoided.

To summarize, first consider the exit when treating any disease. Next, consider the Wai Jiao, which needs clearance as well as driving force and energy. This can be generated by having the Wai Jiao energy flow downwards to strike the Ming Men (the kidney area). The resulting collision of energies nourishes the kidneys to strengthen the body's foundation energy. Then, apply the Gong Zhuan method to solve liver cancer and other liver diseases.

KIDNEYS

The kidneys are a pair of bean-shaped, fist-sized organs located in the abdomen near the lower back, one on each side of the spine. The right kidney lies just below the liver and the left kidney below the spleen. In Western medicine, the kidneys are part of the urinary system, filtering wastes from the body and excreting them as urine. In traditional Chinese medicine, the kidneys store the body's prenatal essence or *jing;* they are the source of Ming Men fire, the root of the San Jiao. They also control water metabolism, nourish the marrow and the brain, and open on the ears and the two genital orifices. Kidney disorders include urinary problems, water imbalance, organ failure, kidney stones, infection, tumor, cancer and other kidney diseases.

Kidney cancer is the disorder that creates the biggest blockage in the body's primary energy pathway, the Gong Zhuan. To treat kidney problems, first consider the clarity of the lungs; then consider the energy flow in the upper part of the Wai Jiao. Kidney sickness is caused mainly by lack of clarity in the lungs, spleen, stomach and intestines. Blockage in the Wai Jiao space weakens lung energy with the result that the lungs in the Upper Jiao are not cleared. Middle Jiao blockage leads to energy blockage in the Lower Jiao, which blocks the energy pathway of the kidneys.

In the process of adjusting the Gong Zhuan to promote recovery from illness, first locate the source of the problem, then look downstream of the problem area to see whether it is open or not. Thus, when asking a patient about his symptoms, ask also about the areas above and below the problem area and analyze the information accordingly. When the source of the problem is not cleared, it leads to downstream issues in the Gong Zhuan. Downstream blockages, in turn, create blockages at the source, leading to sickness.

For example, the three symptoms of tightness in the chest, a sinking or heavy sensation in the back, and an uncomfortable stomach are all considered upstream blockages.

The source cause is a back problem leading to chest issues. So for any sickness, one must always determine the real source of the problem. Kidney sickness, kidney cancer, a sinking sensation in the back, sore backs, tightness in the chest and upper respiratory tract problems can all be traced to issues with the kidneys.

Downstream symptoms of kidney illness include fullness of the ab-domen and of the Middle Jiao, which can lead to vomiting and other symptoms. These symptoms are kidney issues caused by blockage of the lower pathway of the Gong Zhuan.

Treatment

In the treatment of diseases, always use Gong Zhuan theory as the guiding key. The Gong Zhuan must flow freely for health to prevail. Any strategy used should increase the circulatory power and strength of the Gong Zhuan. Traditional Chinese medicine focuses particularly on the phenomenon of *light energy ascending and turbid energy descending.* This natural law increases the potential for change in the energy in the body space, increases cell absorption, and strengthens its drive. The action of *light energy ascending and turbid energy descending* can be used to adjust the energy movement of the Lower, Middle and Upper Jiao and enhance Gong Zhuan circulation.

The key herbs to use for the treatment of kidney disease are as follows:

- To Treat Kidney Cancer

  Use Qiang Huo 4 g, Gui Zhi 7 g, Lian Qiao 17 g, Du Huo 17 g. This formula promotes Gong Zhuan circulation and enables cell action. During treatment, one must strengthen the function of the intestines in the Lower Jiao, otherwise constipation can result. Constipation is caused by functional imbalance of the intestines, which blocks the energy movement of the kidneys.

- To Clear Kidney Energy Blockage

  Use Rou Cong Rong 17 g, Gui Zhi 7 g, Xiang Fu 7 g, Du Huo 17 g to enhance intestinal movement.

- If the Stool is Loose and Frequent

Use Pei Lan 17 g, Huo Xiang 7 g, Gui Zhi 7 g, Xiang Fu 17 g, Du Huo 17 g to dissipate dampness and to open the kidney pathway. Loose and frequent stools are an indication that the dampness in the intestines cannot dissipate.

- Interrupted Menstruation and Internal Fever

Use Dang Gui 17 g, Gui Zhi 7 g, Lian Qiao 17 g, Du Huo 17 g to nourish the blood, unblock *qi* and clear the pathway. Use this formula if a woman's menses have stopped for a few months and there is internal fever. Traditional Chinese medicine considers internal heat to be due to yin deficiency, which also causes kidney disease.

- For Frequent Flu

Use Pu Gong Ying 30 g, Gui Zhi 7 g, Du Huo 17 g to clear the back and to clear the energy in the Wai Jiao space. For patients who catch flu frequently, the lung energy must first be dispersed.

ALL DISORDERS BELOW THE NAVEL

All cancers below the navel can follow the same treatment method used for kidney disease. Refer to the symptom analysis given. For example, urinary bladder issues, prostate gland issues and gynecological issues should all adhere to the following treatment principles:

- Maintain the condition of *upper part is light, lower part is solid*.

- Promote the action of light *energy ascends, turbid energy descends*.

- Enhance Gong Zhuan circulation.

When analyzing the symptoms presented by the patient, look at the symptoms of the upper part of the body; then look at the symptoms of the lower part with respect to the upper part. In treating various illnesses, use herbs to drive up the energy from the lower parts.

For example, Huang Qi makes the Hui Yin area's cells active, such that the force generated by their movement goes upward and reaches the lungs. (The Hui Yin area is located just above the perineum.) In traditional Chinese medicine, Huang Qi nourishes the lungs. Huang Qi has a much more important role in Body Space Medicine, where it is used to activate Hui Yin area energy. This is very important as Hui Yin area energy provides the driving force for the entire body. The Hui Yin is also the starting point of the Gong Zhuan so a strong Hui Yin is vital for healthy Gong Zhuan flow.

In traditional Chinese medicine, herbs are used to affect the meridians, whereas in Body Space Medicine, herbs are used to address the root source of the problem or the illness. *Root source* refers to the area that the herb can act on to increase the driving force of the sickness area. For example, the *root source* for herbs to act on for all disorders below the navel is the back, so applying herbs to work on the back will enable the driving force of the Lower Jiao.

The following herbs are used to treat all abdominal disorders:

• To Treat All Abdominal Disorders

Use Du Huo, Qiang Huo, Qi Zi, Du Zhong, Mao Gou.

4

The Four Quantum Herb Formulas of Body Space Medicine

You have learned the *eight basic herb formulas of Body Space Medicine.* You have learned which specific tongue conditions call for which formula. Combined, these eight basic herb formulas use a total of only fifteen herbs. You have learned some specific, more advanced applications for conditions of the lungs, esophagus, pancreas, intestines, liver and kidneys, including cancer and other serious, chronic and life-threatening illnesses.

You have seen that the basic herb formulas are very simple and practical — amazingly simple. You do not have to spend years studying the hundreds, even thousands of herbs used in traditional Chinese medicine. Body Space Medicine uses a core formulary of fewer than twenty herbs and, in fact, fewer than ten herbs are used to address almost all unhealthy conditions. Moreover, a typical herb formula in Body Space Medicine consists of four or five herbs at most, whereas a typical herb "soup" in traditional Chinese medicine includes ten or more different herbs. Some herb formulas in Body Space Medicine consist of three and even only two herbs.

Now, I am honored to give you, wholeheartedly and without reservations, the results of my latest research, insights and inspirations on this revolutionary healing science and system. The basic theories and herb formulas are already a dramatic breakthrough from traditional

Chinese medicine and other healing modalities that use tongue diagnosis or herbs. Using only fifteen key herbs may already be too difficult
for some to believe. I can only say: Try it. Experience it. Benefit from
it. Then you will know for yourself the efficacy of the tongue reading
methods and the basic herb formulas. I did not create them out of the
air. They are based on decades of practice, research, refinement and
breakthrough inspirations. They have been proven to work for hundreds of thousands of beneficiaries.

Now, I would like to simplify even further. I offer my most recent,
most updated, most advanced, most simple and most powerful concepts
and formulas. I offer you the *four quantum herb formulas of Body Space
Medicine* [patents pending]. If what you have learned already were not
simple enough, the dosages used in these four quantum formulas for
individual herbs are exceptionally small — seven grams or even four
grams of each herb. This is why I call my herb formulas "the small prescriptions of Body Space Medicine" in Chinese. For this book, I will use
the English term "quantum herb formulas" of Body Space Medicine. I
call this newest and most refined herb system of Body Space Medicine "quantum formulas" because these formulas, which I have finally
developed after more than fifty years of research, theoretical development, clinical practice and spiritual communication and observation,
are indeed a quantum leap beyond traditional Chinese medicine or any
other healing modality that applies herbs as healing through matter.

With my latest research, clinical testing and spiritual messages and
inspiration, I offer these *four quantum herb formulas,* which can be used
to address all kinds of sickness. They represent the essence of the essence of Body Space Medicine. They are the essence of the essence of
my life's work. This is my gift to you, to all humanity and to the universe. Use quantum herbs to prevent, heal, bless, rejuvenate, prolong
life and transform soul, mind and body. Use quantum herbs to serve
humanity and all souls well.

The four quantum herb formulas of Body Space Medicine are:

FOUR QUANTUM HERB FORMULAS OF BODY SPACE MADICINE		
#	Herbs and Dosage (unique herbs bolded)	Indicated for	Function of Herbs
1	• Gong Ying 4 g • Du Huo 7 g • **Dang Gui** 4 g (patent pending)	Constipation • All kinds of sickness with constipation	• Gong Ying promotes free flow in the entire front part of the Gong Zhuan • Du Huo promotes free flow in the entire back part of the Gong Zhuan • Dang Gui is for constipation, nourishes the blood and promotes blood flow
2	• Gong Ying 4 g • Du Huo 7 g • **Pei Lan** 4 g (patent pending)	Loose Bowels or Morning Stool (before 8 am) • All kinds of sickness with loose bowels or stool before 8 am	• Gong Ying promotes free flow in the entire front part of the Gong Zhuan • Du Huo promotes free flow in the entire back part of the Gong Zhuan • Pei Lan is for loose bowels or early morning stool
3	• Gong Ying 4 g • Du Huo 7 g • **Dang Gui** 4 g • **Pei Lan** 4 g (patent pending)	All Kinds of Sickness • All kinds of sickness regardless of stool condition, including alternating constipation and diarrhea	• As above. Dang Gui and Pei Lan can be used together when there is alternating constipation and diarrhea, or with normal stool conditions (no constipation or diarrhea)
4	• Gong Ying 4 g • Du Huo 7 g • Dang Gui 4 g • Pei Lan 4 g • **Huo Xiang** 4 g (patent pending)	Communicable Diseases and All Kinds of Sickness • A secret for AIDS and other communicable diseases	• As above. • Huo Xiang is the secret herb for all communicable diseases, including AIDS.

Table 21. Four Quantum Herb Formulas of Body Space Medicine

The two herbs that all four of these quantum herb formulas have in common are **Gong Ying** (also called Pu Gong Ying) and Du Huo. Gong Ying, which is dandelion, moves energy from the genital area all the way up to the top of the head. It promotes fluid and energy flow in the entire front side of the Gong Zhuan. **Du Huo** moves energy from the top of the head to the genital area through the Wai Jiao. It promotes fluid and energy flow in the entire back side of the Gong Zhuan.

Together, Gong Ying and Du Huo create and promote flow in the entire Gong Zhuan, front and back. *If Gong Zhuan flows, one is healthy. If Gong Zhuan is blocked, one is sick.* This is the core theory and philosophy of Body Space Medicine. Gong Ying and Du Huo are the essence of herbs for Body Space Medicine. Because they work precisely for the Gong Zhuan, these two herbs can and should be applied for any illness, regardless of the cause of the illness. Gong Ying and Du Huo can and should be applied for chronic pain, other chronic conditions and life-threatening conditions such as cancer.

Dang Gui is for constipation. It is also the key herb to nourish and enhance the blood and promote blood flow.

Pei Lan is used for diarrhea or loose bowels or early morning stool (bowel movement before breakfast), which could be considered as a mild form of loose bowels.

❋ ❋ ❋ ❋

These four quantum herb formulas are even simpler than the eight basic herb formulas I presented earlier. The quantum formulas use three, four or five herbs. Every herb in each formula is used in a very low dosage, either 4 grams or 7 grams. And yet, the quantum formulas yield very quick results. The formulas are very economical, with no side effects. However, they act so quickly that some people could re-act with diarrhea several times a day. Do not worry about this kind of reaction. It is actually a beneficial cleansing and balancing effect. It is not an adverse side effect. If this cleansing reaction occurs, continue to drink your herbs. The diarrhea will stop naturally by itself. This kind of reaction is due to the rapid changes within the body after drinking the quantum herbs.

The quantum formulas can yield quick healing results because they are totally focused on adjusting the functions of the body. If the body's functions are restored to their normal conditions, you are healed. The quantum formulas center around two herbs, Gong Ying and Du Huo. These two herbs focus on creating and promoting free flow in the Gong Zhuan. We do not need to consider the name of the sickness at all. We do not need to consider the diagnosis by Western medicine. The names of the sickness and, to a large extent, even the symptoms are just used as references. Instead of paying attention to the symptoms, we pay attention only to the tongue reading and the stool condition. According to the tongue's condition, we apply the appropriate herb formula. As the tongue changes, we adjust the herbs. We pay attention to which parts of the tongue are raised. You can say that we are actually adjusting the tongue. Because the tongue reflects every part of the body, when we adjust the tongue, we will adjust the functions within the body. That is how Body Space Medicine works. Every sickness has its foundation in matter and in message. To heal is to adjust matter and to adjust message.

These four quantum formulas are the total essence of Body Space Medicine. I have done research, clinical practice and confirmation of results for more than fifty years. My efforts have proven the efficacy of these four formulas. I have consulted and treated hundreds of thousands of people physically in my life, addressing all kinds of chronic and life-threatening conditions. I contribute these formulas to humanity and to all healing professionals in all healing modalities. I thank all the people who have given me the opportunity to serve them. I thank Heaven for spiritual inspiration and guidance.

According to my whole life's experience, these four formulas have no side effects at all. They are completely safe. Anybody can use them by following the explanations I have given. I wish these formulas can serve millions of people worldwide.

Use the quantum herb formulas of Body Space Medicine. Benefit from them. Restore your health as soon as possible.

QUANTUM HERB FORMULAS AND THE GONG ZHUAN

A human being can be thought of as a mechanical system of energy. This system must always have a driving force to push and move energy within the body. Without this driving force, there would not be life. This driving force, and the resulting flow of energy, must follow certain rules and regulations. The principle rule is that movement should follow the Gong Zhuan pathway.

The Gong Zhuan is the main hub of the body's energy. It is the main switch for the collision of energies. For example, liver cells and stomach cells vibrate and radiate energy. These energies collide and meld together in the space to produce new energy. The pathway of the Gong Zhuan must flow without blockage, freely and fluently. Any blockage or lack of flow in the Gong Zhuan pathway will directly affect the radiation, movement, collision and melding of energies and, consequently, the body's functions.

In 1998 I announced my discovery of the Wai Jiao and its significance. The force of energy must move through the Wai Jiao. Western anatomy confirms the existence of the four largest spaces in the body, the Lower Jiao, Middle Jiao, Upper Jiao and Wai Jiao. Western medicine also confirms the existence of the body fluids in the space, but it does not recognize that the space is where energy moves.

The quantum formulas adjust fluid and energy flow in the four major body spaces (Lower Jiao, Middle Jiao, Upper Jiao, Wai Jiao). The formulas also adjust the distribution and flow of fluid in the body space, and promote the relative balance of fluid in the body. The focus is on the four big spaces of the body. The focus is on the free flow of the Gong Zhuan pathway. It is an integrative, holistic view. Focus on the body as a whole, as ONE concept. Do not limit your thinking to one group of cells or one organ or even one system. Break through the limitations of the name of the sickness. Throw out the diagnosis or the name of the sickness. Adjust the body's functions directly to restore health.

As the major circuit of fluid and energy, the Gong Zhuan leads the flow of fluid and energy in the whole body. To put it another way, the Gong Zhuan is the big movement of feng shui in a human being.

Feng means wind. *Shui* means water. So feng shui is literally the study of wind and water. Water is yin. Wind is yang. Energy, which is tiny matter, moves within the body. So energy movement is feng shui movement. When you go to a home or an office or a place in nature, you can feel the movement. If energy does not flow, it is blocked, creating an uncomfortable feeling. The body works in exactly the same way. If the Gong Zhuan flows freely, you can clean and purify the four big body spaces.

If the Gong Zhuan flows normally, the transformation between matter inside the cells and energy outside the cells will be balanced. If this transformation is balanced, cell functions will be normal and one will be healthy. The Gong Zhuan is absolutely *the* key for healing. The Gong Zhuan is *the* secret for healing, prevention of illness, rejuvenation and long life.

When the Gong Zhuan flows, it both nourishes matter and reduces the density of matter. For example, the herb Zhe Bei can reduce the density in the Upper Jiao. If the Upper Jiao has high pressure or density of energy, use Zhe Bei and it will reduce the density at the starting point. It will open the space in the starting area (the Upper Jiao), improve and restore the function of the cells, and improve the driving force.

Zhe Bei can dissipate energy in the Upper Jiao, causing this energy to flow to the Wai Jiao. When the density in the Upper Jiao is reduced, the density in the Middle Jiao will be relatively high. Because high density flows to low density naturally, Middle Jiao energy will then flow up to the Upper Jiao. When the density in the Middle Jiao is reduced, Lower Jiao energy will flow up to the Middle Jiao. Thus, when you use an herb or herbs to reduce the density of energy in one area of the body, energy from the area upstream along the Gong Zhuan will flow to it. When we use herbs in Body Space Medicine, we must pay attention to the starting point, to the pathway and to the ending point.

In the example of Zhe Bei, which acts in the Upper Jiao, when Upper Jiao energy flows to the Wai Jiao, energy in the Wai Jiao will flow down the whole back. We can say that Zhe Bei starts at the Upper Jiao and ends at the kidneys. In this way, the action of Zhe Bei has three stages. First, Zhe Bei reduces energy in and around the lungs (starting point is the Upper Jiao). Second, it promotes energy flow around and down the entire spinal column (pathway continues downstream through the Wai Jiao). Third, it stimulates and nourishes the kidneys (ending point).

With this concept, we are breaking through the constraints of ancient Chinese herb wisdom. Another example involves the herb Xiang Fu. In traditional Chinese medicine, Xiang Fu promotes *qi* flow. In Body Space Medicine, Xiang Fu reduces, reinforces and promotes flow. It promotes flow in the Middle Jiao, since Xiang Fu can promote energy movement from the Middle Jiao to the Upper Jiao. This movement of energy nourishes the Upper Jiao. At the same time, it reduces the density and pressure in the Lower Jiao. In this way, we pay attention to the starting point, to the pathway and to the ending point.

Traditional Chinese medicine has the concept of *qing sheng zhuo jiang,* which means lighter energy ascends, heavier energy descends (within the San Jiao). This is the normal condition within the body. The herb formulas of Body Space Medicine adjust abnormal conditions to restore normalcy. If lighter energy cannot flow up and heavier energy cannot flow down, abnormal and pathological conditions result. The essence and the secret of the quantum herb formulas is that they promote free flow in the Gong Zhuan.

The importance of the Gong Zhuan cannot be overstated.

1.   Gong Zhuan is key for healing.

2.   Gong Zhuan is key for prevention of illness.

3.   Gong Zhuan is key for rejuvenation.

4.   Gong Zhuan is key for long life.

5.   Gong Zhuan is key for Xiu Lian. To purify your soul, mind and body, you have to move your Gong Zhuan.

Fluid

In the entire body, remember just one issue: fluid. How does fluid flow? An excess of fluid or a deficiency of fluid are problems. All blockages in the body are due to fluid. We understand and honor traditional Chinese medicine, which posits six excesses (wind, cold, heat, damp, dry, fire) and seven emotions (overjoy, anger, melancholy, anxiety, grief, fear, fright) that cause illness. However, Body Space Medicine simplifies the theory of the causes of illness in traditional Chinese medicine. We simplify to one word: The cause of all illness is **fluid.**

Fluid is the cause of illness in human beings. Fluid in the body, like fog, clouds and rain in nature, can ascend, descend and float. Changes in fluid in the body space also parallel changes of nature. Whatever the changes in nature, all are related with fluid. Whatever the changes in the human body, all are related with fluid. Fluid is everywhere in nature. Even in the driest desert, there is fluid. Fluid is everywhere in the human body. There is no place in the body without fluid.

Fluid comprises 70% of the adult human body, and more in infants. Fluid is the most important factor for life. Fluid in the body has many forms: intestinal fluid, saliva, sweat, urine. Blood is another form of fluid. Different kinds of fluid conditions cause different illnesses. In fact, *qi* itself is another form of fluid, only in vapor form, like steam. Western medicine talks about only the lungs having *qi,* and no other organ. For decades, medical experts in China have tried to integrate Western medicine and traditional Chinese medicine, but they could not overcome the obstacle that Western medicine does not recognize *qi* except in the lungs. However, Western medicine also does not recognize that the essence of matter radiates out from cellular vibration. When cells contract, they radiate energy outside the cells. Energy is simply tiny matter, the tiny essence of matter. This tiny matter exists and flows in the body space. Tiny matters collide with each other to stimulate the cells. This tiny matter is called *qi* in traditional Chinese medicine.

Body Space Medicine agrees with the concept of *qi,* but explains that *fluid* is the cause of illness. Energy and matter are all different forms of fluid. Energy outside the cells and matter inside the cells are different forms of fluid; they just have different essences. The understanding of fluid in Body Space Medicine resolves the conflict and contradiction between Western medicine and traditional Chinese medicine. The tiny matter must flow freely in the space. This is the key for health. In nature, in the heavens, we can have a clear blue sky, but there is still moisture in the space. When this moisture accumulates, fog and clouds are produced. When the accumulation continues, the clouds become heavier. When the space cannot hold any more fluid, rain will start to fall. In nature, there are different types of water conditions. Inside the body, it is exactly the same. If fluid or moisture is distributed in balance, we are healthy. If fluid accumulates, illness occurs. Because the fluid blockages can occur in different parts of the body, different illnesses can result.

As moisture accumulates more and more, those with open Third Eyes will be able to see spiritual images which "seem there, seem not there." This is Lao Zi's theory. The "seems there, seems not there" images are the accumulation of fluid (matter), which will block the normal flow, distribution and balance of fluid. Illness will occur. It doesn't matter what kind of blockage or what kind of illness one has — all are caused by fluid.

Illness does not happen suddenly. It always comes on gradually. At first, as the fluid density begins to increase gradually, no symptoms or signs may be manifest. As the fluid density continues to increase, eventually, illness will be apparent. As the quantity changes, the quality will also change, causing the moisture to becomes a major sickness. Do not treat the major sickness right away. Treat the small blockages first.

In traditional Chinese medicine, when sickness comes, it is just like a mountain falling down — very heavy and very fast. When sickness leaves, it is just like silk being spun — very slow.

When you observe nature outside, this is the macro level. When you look within the body, this is the micro level. The quantum herb formulas work at the micro level within the body, within the capillaries and even at the cellular level. Little by little, the quantum formulas address and solve the problem, but then suddenly the mountain can be restored. Thus, Body Space Medicine reverses the view of traditional Chinese medicine. Sickness comes slowly and gradually, but health can be restored quickly, even suddenly.

In Western medicine, illness is thought to be caused by bacteria, viruses, mental factors, emotional factors and so on. When you are really sick, Western medicine often gives you an IV, administering nutrients through the circulatory system. A 10% or high density glucose solution promotes movement of fluid *into* the cells from the skin and tissues. A 5% or low density glucose solution promotes movement of fluid *out of* the cells into the tissues and skin. Both IV therapies adjust the fluid balance in the body, which is exactly what the quantum herb formulas of Body Space Medicine do. In effect, the quantum formulas are doing IV treatment to balance fluid within the body, removing fluid (matter) blockages to promote free flow in the Gong Zhuan. This is the essence and the secret of the quantum herb formulas: they promote free flow in the Gong Zhuan.

If stool is dry, that indicates a lack of fluid. If you have diarrhea, that means there is too much fluid in the body. Both are fluid problems. From the stomach and intestines, the essences of food and other matter, including the fluids inside, will radiate out. They are different forms of fluid and have different essences. Illness is due to an imbalance of fluid distribution in the body. Wherever the blockage is, the illness occurs. This is why we do not pay attention to the diagnosis or the name of the sickness. We only need to recognize where the fluid blockage is and, secondarily, how significant the blockage is. This is why Body Space Medicine can treat all kinds of cancer with great simplicity and effectiveness. Only know where the blockage is and how severe the blockage is. This is revolutionary thinking.

Accumulation of fluid inside the cells produces tumors. Accumulation of fluid outside the cells is called *pi*, which means that it feels like a lump or growth, but there is no actual solid growth. In the *Shang Han Lun,* one of the authoritative herb texts of traditional Chinese medicine, the herb Wu Pi is designated for this condition.

Pi has different forms, which become different illnesses. When *pi* forms (accumulation of fluid outside the cells), water inside the cells cannot transform out of the cells. This is why cancer can result.

Accumulation of fluid inside blood vessels produces blood clots. Depending on where the clot forms, different illnesses result. A clot in the heart results in a heart attack. A clot in the lungs is called a lung clot. A clot inside an artery is called an arterial blood clot. A clot inside the veins is called a venous blood clot. Dampness in the joints causes joint illnesses such as arthritis. Rheumatoid arthritis is fluid in the space, because the cells can no longer absorb any more of that fluid.

This kind of illness is difficult to treat. Fluid around the cells cannot easily be absorbed into the cells.

Fluid imbalance is also the cause of death. The name or kind of illness involved doesn't matter. Commonly, death is by heart attack (failure) or by lung inflammation (failure). Both heart attacks and lung inflammations are very dangerous. For example, phlegm can remain within the bronchial tubes, leading to a lung infection. The lung infection can in turn affect the heart, causing a heart attack. These are all different forms of fluid.

Inflammation of the kidneys or the liver is due to fluid. Liver cancer is due to fluid. Skin problems are due to fluid. Diabetes is due to fluid. *Medicine is no longer difficult. All illness is due to fluid imbalance.* The location of the fluid blockage is the location of illness. Remove the fluid blockage and one will get well. If there is fluid blockage in the shoulder, it doesn't matter what or how many conditions of the shoulder there are. Move the fluid, clear the blockage. This is the breakthrough theory.

I deeply appreciate the practitioners of traditional Chinese medicine who have developed profound wisdom, knowledge and practice over thousands of years. I also appreciate all Western doctors and practitioners for their great contributions to humanity. It was their contributions that inspired me to strive toward and reach the quantum formulas of Body Space Medicine. I thank all my predecessors and peers for their great efforts, methods and results. Without their yesterdays, we would not have this today.

History is always moving. Science is always moving. Change is the only constant. I believe that the quantum formulas can be spread all over the world. But perhaps someone more intelligent and with greater insight than I will then be able to simplify the Body Space Medicine system even further.

KINGS OF HERBS

Gong Ying is the number one "king" of herbs. It dissipates density, so it can be used for all kinds of inflammation. At the same time, if there is not enough energy, it can nourish energy. So, Gong Ying works in both directions. If there is too much energy, it can dissipate the excess energy. If there is not enough energy, it can increase the insufficient energy.

Du Huo can be used to reduce high blood pressure and to treat back pain, because it moves energy down the back, causing energies to collide there. It can also be used to treat joint problems.

Gong Ying and Du Huo are very special because they have the capacity not only to promote energy flow but also to nourish energy at the same time. That is the secret of these herbs. That is why they are so important and so powerful. That is why they are *universal quantum herbs*. Some herbs that nourish energy can create blockages. Gong Ying and Du Huo do not create blockages.

For example, Huang Qi is a very well known herb for nourishing *qi*. However, if one uses too much Huang Qi, it can *over*nourish, thereby actually *creating* blockages. Similarly, I used to use Gou Ji Zi to nourish the kidneys, but I no longer use herbs strictly for nourishment.

This is why the quantum herbs of Body Space Medicine do not have side effects. Because the herbs nourish energy and promote flow at the same time, balance is always maintained, For example, when used to treat bronchitis, which is a blockage in the Upper Jiao, Gong Ying and Du Huo dissipate the blockage and promote the free flow of unstuck energy down the back, through the Wai Jiao, to nourish the kidneys and Snow Mountain Area. Just like Robin Hood (and there was a Robin Hood in China too), we rob from the rich to give to the poor. We take from the blocked accumulated energy to give to the deficient energy.

GONG YING

Gong Ying is dandelion. It moves energy upward from the genital area to the top of the head, or from Earth to Heaven. Du Huo moves energy from the head to the genital area, or from Heaven to Earth. Together, Gong Ying and Du Huo move the entire Gong Zhuan.

I used to use 20 to 40 grams of Gong Ying. Now, I use only 4 grams because the soul of Gong Ying told me directly that 4 to 7 grams are enough.

To treat any illness, the Gong Zhuan must flow freely. If there is too much moisture in the space, free flow of the Gong Zhuan will remove the excess moisture. If there is not enough moisture in the space, free flow of the Gong Zhuan will increase the moisture. Free flow of the Gong Zhuan will automatically balance fluid, energy and matter. Free flow of the Gong Zhuan is the key for health, prevention, rejuvenation and long life.

If there is too much moisture in the space, as indicated by the tongue reading and/or the stool condition, use Pei Lan.

If there is not enough moisture in the space, use Dang Gui.

Du Huo

Du Huo clears the entire Wai Jiao. Usually, we use 7 grams of Du Huo. In traditional Chinese medicine, Du Huo is the most effective herb for treating rheumatic conditions. Why can Du Huo treat rheumatic illnesses? Because it can remove fluid blockage.

Du Huo can dissipate fluid and energy blockages around the cells. It is very effective in treating arthritis, as was already known in the *Sheng Neng Ben Cao,* an ancient authoritative herb treatise. However, the ancient herb experts did not explain why Du Huo works. Now we know that Du Huo can not only remove fluid around the joints, it can also remove fluid and energy blockages in all the body spaces. Think of density in the space as clouds in the sky. Du Huo is like the sun that dissipates the clouds. It can dissipate all excess fluid and energy in the space. Consequently, Du Huo, together with Gong Ying, is a key to addressing all kinds of illness. Furthermore, I have realized that Du Huo can push energy in the space into the cells, by promoting the transformation of energy outside the cells to matter inside the cells. In essence, Du Huo has the power to turn energy into matter. This is why Du Huo works for arthritis. This is also an example of how Body Space Medicine expands the understanding of the power of certain herbs.

Together, Gong Ying and Du Huo can dissipate the invisible shape blockages (which are visible if your Third Eye is open). Lao Zi made the famous statement: *In blurred images, there is matter inside.* On other words, even spiritual images have a foundation of matter. With an open Third Eye, you can see tiny matter (*shang*) blockages and rough matter (*wu*) blockages. *Shang* (tiny matter) flows up the front side of the Gong Zhuan. *Wu* (rough matter) flows down in the Wai Jiao.

Du Huo follows the principle of *qing shang zhuo jiang* — light energy ascends, heavy energy descends. For example, if energy is blocked in the Upper Jiao, Du Huo dissipates this energy so that light energy can go up. At the same time, Du Huo promotes flow from the head flow down to the kidneys to nourish and increase the energy density of the kidneys. Reduce first (light energy goes up), and then heavy energy sinks. Upper parts empty and lower parts solid, then humans will be healthy.

Dosages

The dosage for each herb in the quantum formulas is either 4 grams or 7 grams. These dosages came from my spiritual or soul communication, literally a conversation with the souls of the herbs. I used to use 20 or 30 grams of Gong Ying typically, but the soul of Gong Ying was not happy, and told me that 4 grams are enough. When I spoke with the soul of Zhe Bei, which is not part of the quantum formulas, Zhe Bei told me, "If Gong Ying can work at a dosage of 4 grams, so can I." The quantum dosage for Xiang Fu is also 4 grams.

If children under ten years old drink 1 gram of Zhe Bei each day, they will be very healthy. (This could be in the form of powder in water. Children between the ages of one and five should drink 0.5 grams of Zhe Bei each day. Babies can drink only a tiny teaspoon of herb solution.) Children's illnesses are generally due to lung heat and dampness staying in the stomach area. Zhe Bei works for the lungs and reduces the density within and around the lungs. The excess energy flows to and through the Wai Jiao, ultimately nourishing the kidneys.

This is radical new thinking compared to the traditional understanding and use of herbs. With these few herbs in extremely low dosages, some of my patients with cancer have healed very quickly.

❈ ❈ ❈ ❈

The historical task of the Yellow Emperor has ended. Five thousand years of herb practice in traditional Chinese medicine has ended. The ancient, traditional understanding of herbs had weaknesses and gaps. A new era has begun, with Body Space Medicine as the standard. Body Space Medicine addresses the old weaknesses. The old King of Medicine has ended his historical task. Now the new Kings of Medicine are on duty, in the form of six kings of herbs:

1. Gong Ying

2. Duo Huo

3. Xiang Fu

4. Gui Zhi

5. Pei Lan

6. Dang Gui

These are the six new kings of herbs. Heaven has given an order that these herbs will now work. We are empowered to develop the potential power of herbs. This is our new contribution.

The Quantum Dimension

You have learned how to offer Body Space Medicine herbs in a physical formula, with specific herbs in specific amounts. You have learned that the entire herb system of Body Space Medicine is very simple, and that the quantum herb formulas are amazingly simple.

I call the ultimate herb system of Body Space Medicine "quantum formulas" because these formulas, which I have finally developed after more than fifty years of research, theoretical development, clinical practice and spiritual communication and observation, are indeed a quantum leap beyond traditional Chinese medicine or any other healing modality that applies herbs as a means of healing through matter. However, the term "quantum herb formulas" has a much broader and deeper significance.

As described previously, Body Space Medicine is quantum medicine. It is not limited by the physical dimensions of time and space. A major part of the great simplicity, power and, indeed, *beauty* of Body Space Medicine is its use of Soul Power. Body Space Medicine teaches how to chant herbs, how to use the soul of the herbs to heal.

Herbs have a soul. Everything has a soul or message. Matter and energy, or *qi,* have messages. According to the Message Energy Matter Theory, they are also carriers of message. What is message? Message is soul. Message is spirit. Soul or message can transform matter and energy, because it can transform the message that matter and energy carry. Soul can heal. Soul can transform any aspect of existence.

In the Say Hello Healing of my worldwide representative Zhi Gang Sha's soul healing system called Soul Mind Body Medicine, one directly asks souls to heal: *Dear soul of my back, dear soul of my liver, I love you. Can you heal me, please? Thank you.* In the same way, in Body Space Medicine you can use the herbs simply by calling the souls of the herbs. The souls of the herbs can directly influence the transformation between matter in the cells and energy outside the cells. The souls of the herbs can directly clear fluid and energy blockages.

If you do not have the physical herbs, or even if you do have physical herbs, you can just use the soul of the herbs. Chant the names of the herbs to invoke their souls and you will be fine. Chant your herbs before you have actually filled your prescription and received physical herbs.

Developing the message of herbs is another major contribution of Body Space Medicine. The purpose of developing the message of herbs is to awaken every soul in the universe to join hearts and souls to move further together.

When you chant the herbs, honor the power of the herbs. Honor the souls of the herbs. Relax your body. Trust that these low dosages can treat your physical body as well as emotional issues. Trust.

QUANTUM BODY SPACE MEDICINE: A SUMMARY

The quantum aspects of Body Space Medicine are its essence. Because this essence is concentrated, yet simple, I feel the following summary, which also adds some essential new wisdom, will be useful.

Gong Ying moves energy up from the Lower Jiao to the top of the head. On the map of the tongue (Figure 2, page 42), Gong Ying promotes movement from the root of the tongue to the tip of the tongue. Gong Ying is the king of the herbs. Then Du Huo moves energy down through the Wai Jiao, which corresponds to movement from the tip of the tongue back to the root of the tongue. Gong Ying moves up the front side of the Gong Zhuan; Du Huo moves down the back side of the Gong Zhuan. These two herbs alone promote free flow through the entire Gong Zhuan, which is basically enough for all healing.

For tongue and stool reading, focus on the following:

1. Is the tip of the tongue raised or indented?

    Du Huo solves the issues related to a raised area at the tip of the
    tongue. Because the tip of the tongue represents the heart and
    the Upper Jiao, Du Huo precisely makes blocked energy in the
    Upper Jiao flow down.

2. Pay attention only to the raised areas on the tongue.

    Which part of the tongue is raised? The tip? The sides? Make
    sure that the person presents the entire tongue so that you can
    see all the raised areas. The locations of the raised areas in-
    dicate the locations of the blockages in the body. In general,
    even though there may be many raised areas on the tongue,
    we can just use the same basic formula. Don't become "stuck"
    on tongue reading. (Some exceptional cases are discussed in
    #5 below.) For example, if the tongue is raised at the left front
    of the tongue, that would indicate heart problems. Use Du
    Huo again! Du Huo will address all conditions in and around
    the heart.

    Some tongues have raised areas on the sides or in the middle.
    You can use the herb Xiang Fu for these conditions. Xiang Fu
    moves energy UP from the Middle Jiao to the Upper Jiao. Use
    Xiang Fu to make blocked energy in the Middle Jiao go up to
    initiate and promote free flow in the Gong Zhuan circle. The
    typical quantum dosage for Xiang Fu is also 4 grams.

    If the middle of the tongue is raised *and* the person has constipa-
    tion, you may use the roasted herb Chao Bing Liang[1]. Alterna-
    tively, if you do not use Chao Bing Liang, you can of course use
    Dang Gui.

Diarrhea and Constipation

Plain rice congee is the best food when one has diarrhea.

Oven-roasted garlic is another excellent food for diarrhea.

For stubborn cases of diarrhea, use Sheng Bai Zhu, 4 to 7 grams.

Jiao Si Xian can also be used to treat diarrhea.

For stubborn cases of constipation that persist even after using the basic quantum formula of Gong Ying, Du Huo and Dang Gui, use Chao Bing Liang (4 to 7 grams) to remove the stool blockage.

One should also use Sound Power, the number sounds 3-9 in Chinese, *san jiu* (pronounced "sahn joe").

3. Pay attention to the key stool conditions.

    Ask the person, "Are you constipated?"

    If so, add the herb Dang Gui, so the quantum formula for this condition is:

    Gong Ying 4 g
    Du Huo 7 g
    Dang Gui 4 g

    If the person has diarrhea or loose bowels, use the herb Pei Lan. Morning stool, generally before 8:00 a.m., is considered to be loose bowels, so use Pei Lan. In this case, the quantum formula is:

    Gong Ying 4 g
    Du Huo 7 g
    Pei Lan 4 g

If the stool condition alternates between constipation and diarrhea, then use both Pei Lan and Dang Gui. Even if you don't know whether the person is constipated or has diarrhea, you can use this quantum formula:

Gong Ying 4 g
Du Huo 7 g
Dang Gui 4 g
Pei Lan 4 g

4. Is the tongue coating dry or wet?

   Use Dang Gui for a dry tongue and Pei Lan for a wet tongue.

5. Is the tongue body wide or narrow?

   When the tongue is long, stiff and hard, energy and matter are blocked. Use the herb Jiao San Xian, which actually is a combination of three roasted herbs: Chao Mai Ya, Chao Shan Zha, Chao Shen Qu. You may also use Jiao San Xian when there are raised areas in the Middle Jiao area of the tongue. The raised areas may be on the sides or in the center. This tongue condition indicates a blockage in the digestive system. The usual dosage for Jiao San Xian is 10 to 15 grams for each of its three component herbs. The *quantum* dosage is 4 grams each.

6. Note other significant tongue conditions.

   Dark, purple, red or white blisters on the tongue indicate blood stagnation. Use 4 grams of Chi Shao to dissipate blood stagnation.

   Caution: Do *not* use Chi Shao if the person has cancer or blood disorders because it can cause more bleeding.

   If there is too much bleeding, use the herb Ou Jie.

   If the tongue is raised in the Shan Zhong or Message Center area, that indicates a blockage in the Message Center. Use the herb Shi Chang Pu to dissipate this blockage.

If the tongue points out at an angle to one side, that indicates a blockage in the capillaries in the brain, possibly a hardening of the blood vessels, with a potential for a stroke.

I have given you the standard quantum formulas, but even with them we can be flexible. Using only one herb can work as well! For example, for knee pain, you can try to use only Xiang Fu (4 grams). Xiang Fu moves energy up from the Middle Jiao. It clears the energy there, so that energy below the Middle Jiao (in particular, from the knees) can move up. One herb can also make the Gong Zhuan circle flow. One herb may be a little slower, but it still works. As long as you make the circle flow, the solution is there.

More on the Gong Zhuan

The main functions of the herbs are to reduce (dissipate), promote (move) and reinforce (nourish).

In applying Body Space Medicine, we must pay greatest attention to the blockages in the Gong Zhuan pathway. If one doesn't feel well, there must still be a blockage in that circle. It is simplest and most accurate if you can see the root of the blockage with medical intuitive capabilities. As long as you move the area of blockage, everything will improve.

Only promoting the Gong Zhuan will allow you to balance all of the matter and energy through all twelve of the yin yang meridians (liver, gallbladder, heart, small intestine, spleen, stomach, lung, large intestine, kidney, urinary bladder, pericardium, San Jiao) plus the Ren and Du meridians. Flow in all of the yin yang meridians depends on flow in the Gong Zhuan. When the Gong Zhuan flows fluently, all the energy and all the matter will be in balance.

Whatever sickness you are treating, do not pay attention to the name of the sickness. Do not be concerned with which organs are affected. Focus first and foremost on moving the Gong Zhuan circle.

Wherever the blockage is, always open the area one step ahead (or downstream) of it in the Gong Zhuan circle. For example, if a patient has an upset stomach, heaviness in the chest and throat pain, do not bother with the lower parts. Concentrate on the upper parts. In this case, the top part is the throat. The next step downstream along the Gong Zhuan is the Wai Jiao. This is the fundamental principle underlying the development and application of the quantum herb formulas of Body Space Medicine.

Follow the circle. The Middle Jiao is the driving force for the Upper Jiao. At the same time, the Middle Jiao is also the dissipating area for the Lower Jiao. In general, the area downstream on the Gong Zhuan from a given area is usually the dissipating area for the given area. Every area along the Gong Zhuan is the ending point for the previous step and the starting point for the next step. For the San Jiao as a whole, the Lower Jiao is usually the driving force and the Upper Jiao is usually the dissipating area.

For Du Huo, the starting point is the head and the ending point is the tailbone (Wei Lu). That is why Du Huo can dissipate energy in the head. The ending point of Du Huo is the starting point of the Ren meridian, which is in accordance with traditional Chinese medicine theory. Find the gate. Open the gate for the sickness. In this way we ensure that the circle will flow.

Xiang Fu starts in the Middle Jiao. Du Huo starts at C7. Gong Ying starts at the Hui Yin point. Pei Lan and Dang Gui can start anywhere in the body; their usage depends on whether the stool condition is constipation or diarrhea.

Consider the prostate gland, which is a potential trouble spot for males. The prostate is in the Lower Jiao. If the sickness is in the Lower Jiao, the kidneys are in charge. In the Five Elements, kidneys belong to Water. We could use Gong Ying because it acts on the starting point. For every sickness we must pay attention to the starting point.

What about the ending or exit point? It is the Middle Jiao, so we use Xiang Fu.

Examine the Five Elements theory more deeply and we can ask what produces the starting point? In this case, Metal (the lungs) produces and nourishes Water. The Metal herb is Zhe Bei. Gong Ying is OK, but using the Five Elements theory to find the one herb that produces the starting point, we would use Zhe Bei.

So our formula would consist of Xiang Fu and Zhe Bei. What we have done is to "dig a hole" downstream on the Gong Zhuan. We use Xiang Fu to reduce density in the ending point, which is the Middle Jiao. This is the "hole." We use Zhe Bei to push on the back side, to drive energy down from the lungs to the kidneys. Then from the Lower Jiao, including the prostate, energy will flow up and the entire Gong Zhuan will flow.

For middle back pain, Shi Chang Pu (7 grams) is the key herb. Shi Chang Pu opens the Message Center and dissipates its energy. Then lower abdomen energy can flow up, which will drive middle back energy to flow down.

Find the exit point. Do not think that the excess energy actually exits the body. We are promoting the flow of the excess energy through the exit point to continue flowing through the Gong Zhuan. The energy does not flow out of the body. We are helping it move within the body, along the Gong Zhuan. Stimulate the exit area. Make the exit area extremely empty *(zhi xu)*. Dissipate that energy from the exit point.

Key exit points for the body and some major organs are:

• The main exit for the Upper Jiao is the tailbone or Wei Lu.

• The main exit for the head is the Shan Zhong (acupuncture point located in the middle of the chest on the heart chakra or Message Center).

- The upper back is the exit for the liver. (The liver is in the Middle Jiao. The lungs are in the Upper Jiao, one step ahead or downstream. To treat the liver, dissipate the energy in the lungs. The next step for lungs is the Wai Jiao. So the second dissipation point for the liver is the upper part of the Wai Jiao, or the upper back. Empty the upper back and liver energy will flow up.)

- The kidneys are the exit for the lungs. (Treat the kidneys by stimulating the lungs.)

- The abdomen is the exit for the spinal column. (Treat illnesses of the spinal column by treating the abdomen. Find and treat the exit for the illness.)

- The abdomen is also the exit for the back.

Make sure that these four areas flow freely:

- Da Zhui (C7)

- Wei Lu (tailbone)

- Middle Jiao

- Shan Zhong

These are key areas for energy to be free flowing. Also, for any sickness, to promote matter flow and to ensure that intestinal and stomach energy flows, stool must flow freely. If the person has constipation, the first task is to resolve the constipation. Promoting the stool and adjusting the stool conditions are vital for treating all kinds of sickness. Because the stool is directly related to energy flow in the Middle Jiao, normal stool condition is very important. Think of the whole body as having one entrance (the mouth) and one exit (the anus). If either of those has a problem, the whole body will have a big problem. That's why we must address the stool condition first.

If the intestinal cells vibrate, the Middle Jiao and Lower Jiao will flow. To clear the Middle Jiao and Lower Jiao, you can also chant 1–10 (yi shi) to stimulate the head and the anus. Also, coffee enemas excite the intestinal cells and can be very beneficial for emptying the colon.

Together, these are the keys for promoting the Going Zhuan and the whole body.

In general, the best place is to dissipate is one step ahead or downstream of the blockage along the Gong Zhuan. The dosage for the driving force area is usually uses 4 grams, while for the dissipating area it is usually 7 grams.

Traditional Chinese medicine talks about yin yang balance. Body Space Medicine teaches yin yang absolute imbalance. The temporary imbalance will move energy, allowing it to balance itself later. Some parts must be extremely empty, while others must be extremely solid. Use the principle of imbalance by finding the major exit.

OTHER HERBS IN BODY SPACE MEDICINE

We know that Gong Ying moves energy up and that Duo Huo can move energy from the head to the feet. Qiang Huo can move energy from the feet to the head.

In traditional Chinese medicine, each herb is associated with specific meridians. The idea is that the herb will end in that meridian. **Body Space Medicine specifies the starting point, the ending point and the whole pathway that the herb acts on.**

Huang Qi is very good for wounds. It extracts pus and alleviates edema. In traditional Chinese medicine, Huang Qi belongs to the spleen meridian and the lung meridian. In Body Space Medicine, the starting point for Huang Qi is the Hui Yin point in the perineum. It can strengthen the energy radiation from the bottom of the Sea Wheel in the genital area, making it an excellent herb to treat prolapsed organs. The end point for Huang Qi is the spleen and lungs.

Digging a Hole

Always put the sickness between the two herbs for the starting point and the ending point. It will actually help to write the formula in the indicated order, following the Gong Zhuan pathway. If the sickness is on the back side, write Gong Ying first at the starting point, then follow with Du Huo to go to the ending point. If the sickness is on the front side, then write Du Huo first and follow with Gong Ying. Gong Ying and Du Huo together will promote flow in the entire Gong Zhuan.

The ending point herb "digs the hole." That is, it dissipates, reduces and empties downstream of the sickness area. The starting point herb *pushes* energy along the Gong Zhuan, beginning upstream of the sickness area.

For example, if the tip of tongue is raised, we know an Upper Jiao blockage is indicated. (See area B in Figure 5.) In this case, we use Du Huo to dig the hole.

If there are blockages in the middle of the tongue, Xiang Fu will make things flow. For all Middle Jiao disorders, use Xiang Fu. If Xiang Fu is not enough to move the Gong Zhuan, for Gong Ying to add an upward "push." Then all blockages will be removed.

If both sides of the tongue are raised (see areas C and D in Figure 5), Du Huo will reduce the density there. For example, if there are breast problems, use Du Huo to dig the hole.

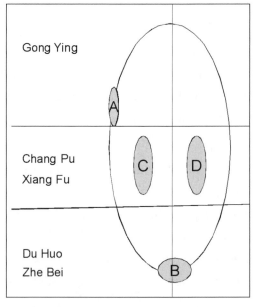

Figure 5. Quantum Herbs
and the Gong Zhuan

Chang Pu and Xiang Fu are two herbs that can be used interchangeably for the middle part of the body.

For women's diseases (menstrual problems, ovarian cysts, etc.), use Xiang Fu to dig the hole.

For asthma, dig the hole in the tailbone. Use Gong Ying, Chang Pu and Du Huo.

So we have the fifth quantum herb formula of Body Space Medicine, which can be used for all illnesses:

(patent pending)
Du Huo or Zhe Bei (these can be used interchangeably) 7 g
Gong Ying 4 g
Xiang Fu 4 g

❋ ❋ ❋ ❋

The quantum herb formulas of Body Space Medicine are universal. They do not distinguish by gender or age. Male or female, young or old — as long as you are a human being, the quantum herb formulas will work. In fact, they will work for animals because animals also have a Gong Zhuan with the same properties as a human being's Gong Zhuan. Similarly, the quantum herb formulas will serve every department in a hospital. Even within internal medicine, for example, there are several different departments. Body Space Medicine, however, has only one department.

The quantum herb formulas of Body Space Medicine bring us back to the ancient original healing methods for humanity. They offer a very economical and unified approach for healing all kinds of illnesses and imbalances.

The principles of Body Space Medicine and the Gong Zhuan are also linked with the universal law of universal service.

Energy that is produced in an area cannot be used for that area. For example, with a cough, the energy in the throat or the upper respiratory system cannot be used for those areas. For back pain, the energy in the painful area cannot be used for that area. The blocked energy must move to other parts of the body for healing to occur.

In essence, illness is due to selfishness. For example, the vibration of the cells of the liver causes energy to radiate out. If this energy stays around the liver and does not flow to other parts of the body, this selfishness of the liver will make the liver sick. Similarly, if the energy radiating from the vibration of the cells of the lungs does not flow, any illness of the lungs may result, including lung cancer.

In this way, all illness is due to selfishness. Illnesses of the liver are due to the selfishness of the liver. Illnesses of the lungs are due to the selfishness of the lungs. Illnesses of the stomach are due to the selfishness of the lungs. Illnesses of the stomach are due to the selfishness of the stomach. Mental confusion, unclear thinking and mental illnesses are due to the selfishness of the heart (since the heart houses the mind).

This is a universal law. Is your organ self-oriented or other-oriented (service-oriented)? Are you self-oriented or service-oriented? In the universe, one cannot serve oneself. One must serve others to serve oneself. The apple tree produces apples, but the apple tree does not eat apples. Human beings eat apples. Human beings produce stool. Human beings do not eat stool, but will give stool to the apple tree for nourishment.

One always uses another's energy and another's matter to nourish oneself. Each major organ must contribute its own energy to others. Only then will that organ be healthy. The theory of the Five Elements in traditional Chinese Medicine is an example. Wood produces and nourishes Fire. Fire produces and nourishes Earth. Earth produces and nourishes Metal. Metal produces and nourishes Water. Water produces and nourishes Wood. One serves another, and then the organ will be healthy.

We must remove selfishness. You, I, every human being must contribute our energy and our service to others. Only then can we advance. Only with generosity can we be healthy. Only with generosity can we receive intelligence and wisdom. These are the keys to health and intelligence: generosity and service. Serve, serve, serve.

5

Case Studies

In this chapter, I present a collection of 32 Body Space Medicine case studies. Each case study documents the consultation and treatment of a patient at my healing center in China. For convenience, the studies are arranged alphabetically by symptom or name of illness, even though you have learned that this information is not particularly important in the quantum application of Body Space Medicine.

For some case studies, there is only one main symptom. For other case studies, there is more than one major symptom or illness involved. For example, a case study may involve prostatitis, gastritis and varicose veins. Another case study may involve a particular tongue characteristic or symptoms such as poor appetite, noisy breathing and bleeding gums.

To aid the reader in quickly finding a case study of interest involving a particular symptom or issue, all major symptoms and illnesses of the case studies are summarized in Table 22.

> Note: These case studies predate my development of the quantum herb formulas of Body Space Medicine. As such, they do not represent the "state of the art." However, they still offer valuable wisdom and insights that will benefit any reader who studies them.

Each case study includes a description of the consultation, photographs of the tongue, tongue analysis, the herb formula prescribed, a discussion of the pathology and an explanation of the herbs used. A discussion of the treatment may or may not be included. Each of these key components is further described as follows:

CONSULTATION

- A brief description of the main symptoms is provided. If known, the name of the illness is also included.

- The date format used in all case studies is yyyy.mm.dd.

- A photograph of the tongue before treatment is shown. Some case studies may also show a photograph of the tongue after treatment.

- Tongue photographs are labeled by case study ID and by consultation number; the date of the consultation may or may not be included. For example, a photograph with the caption "Tongue 07-#5 (2005.12.04)" is a tongue photograph for the patient of Case Study 07 taken during Consultation #5 on December 4, 2005.

- An herb formula is prescribed based on the tongue conditions and symptoms presented at the time of consultation. The prescription is a daily dosage with all dosages listed in grams. The formula is usually taken daily until the patient's next consultation.

PATHOLOGY

- The condition of the patient's tongue is described and discussed from the perspective of Body Space Medicine.

- Photographs illustrate the tongue analysis. Close-ups of different parts of the tongue may be included. These photographs are also labeled with the same date and tongue identification format described above.

- The root cause of the dysfunction or symptoms, the mechanism of illness and the resulting consequences are explained from the perspective of Body Space Medicine.

- The treatment approach used is outlined and the rationale given.

EXPLANATION OF THE FORMULA

- The key herbs used in the herb formula are explained from the perspective of Body Space Medicine.

DISCUSSION OF TREATMENT

- Discussions are included for some case studies that feature a series of follow-up consultations and treatment.

ID	Title	Sex	Age	Main Symptoms
01	Abdominal Pain and Fullness	F		inflammation in lower abdomen, stomach fullness, frequent dreams
02	Abdo-minal Tumor	F	19	abdominal tumor, constipation, difficulty walking, sweats with effort
03	Atrophic Gas-tritis	M		shrinking-style stomachitis, stomach distension, poor appetite, heavy back
04	Chest Problems	M	37	heavy chest, backache, poor sleep
05	Diabetes, Hyperten-sion	F	75	diabetes, vision, night sweats, heart issues, R-hip and leg feel cold, obstruction when swallowing
06	Esophageal Cancer	M	70	esophageal cancer
07	Gallbladder Cancer	M	73	GB cancer, GB stone & inflammation, abdominal inflammation
08	Gallbladder Disease	M	35	gallbladder problems
09	Gastritis, Prostatitis	M	27	prostatitis, gastritis, stomach issues, pain at head of penis
10	Heart Problems	F	50	heart problems, constipation
11	Heat Stagnation	F	4	adjustments
12	Hepatitis B	M	49	Hepatitis B, abdominal pain
13	Hypertension	F		hypetension (arterial HT, high blood pressure), fatigue, leg pain, cold navel, anxiety

Stool/ day	Urine	Tongue Characteristics	Tongue Coating	Root Problem
1X am		big, thick, full, stagnant	wet	excess water in cells
none in 3 d	pain	thick, high front	yellow greasy MJ+LJ	UJ blockage
2X loose		thick. median cracks, blisters	root greasy	UJ stagnation
1X am		tongue on tongue, red indented tip	sticky yellow	UJ+MJ blockage
1-2X loose	frequent, yellow, foamy, odor	indented tip, raised middle	yellow greasy MJ+LJ	MJ blockage
1X 3-4 days, dry		curled edge	thick, sticky at LJ	UJ blockage
2-9X	yellow	bump on tip. cracks, R-side thicker		UJ stagnation
2X loose		thick. median cracks, blisters	root greasy	UJ stagnation
1X am		tongue on tongue, red indented tip	sticky yellow	UJ+MJ blockage
1-2X loose	frequent, yellow, foamy, odor	indented tip, raised middle	yellow greasy MJ+LJ	MJ blockage
1X		stick tongue, raised Shan Zhong, narrow tip	damp	UJ stagnation
1X noon		raised edges + Shan Zhong, L-skew, indented tip	light yellow	UJ stagnation
1X am		stick tongue, R-skew, tip blisters, narrow front	none	sticky yellow root

ID	Title	Sex	Age	Main Symptoms
14	Intestinal Inflammation	M	33	intestinal inflammation, itchy body, swollen lymphs in R-lower jaw
15	Kidney Cancer, Liver Tumor, Diabetes	M	44	kidney cancer, liver tumor, diabetes, chest feels stuffy
16	Kidney Infection	M	42	kidney infection, back pain, leg sore & swollen, bloated stomach
17	Knee Joint Degeneration, Stomach Fullness	F		tight shoulders, fullness R-side of head, knee joint problems, stomach fullness
18	Liver Cancer	M	52	liver cancer, cough with phlegm, abdominal pain, R-rib pain
19	Liver Pain, Edema, Numb-ness	F	48	liver pain, edema L-calf, numbness right side, back pain
20	Lung Cancer (Right Lung)	M	65	cancer R-lung, cough with phlegm, heart issues, salty taste
21	Lung Cancer, Facial Numbness	M	57	lung cancer, cough with phlegm, transient pain L-ribs, numbness
22	Pancreatic Cancer	M	47	pancreatic cancer, metastasis to liver & GB, abdominal pain, cannot eat fatty food
23	Prostatitis, Joint Pain	M	39	prostatitis, liver pain, back pain, skin problems
24	Psoriasis	M	23	psoriasis, itchiness
25	Rheumatoid Arthritis, Amenorrhea	F	28	rheumatoid arthritis, cervix pain, amenorrhea
26	Rickets (Osteomalacia)	M	16	rickets, discomfort in L-hip, spine and sides, pain, eye issues

Stool/ day	Urine	Tongue Characteristics	Tongue Coating	Root Problem
1X am		high Shan Zhong, thick, fat, indented tip	thick white at root	Shan Zhong blockage
1-2X am		full, purple, cracks in MJ+LJ	none	weak Ming Men
1X am		thick. purple, raised middle	wet	UJ blockage
2X		hard, curled tip/ edges	none	UJ stagnation
2-3X loose	yellow	hard tip, raised edges (R-side higher)	root greasy, yellow	Lung/Heart stagnation
1X am loose		indented tip, high middle, L-side larger	watery	MJblockage
1X am	normal	raised front, cracks in MJ, dry	greasy yellow MJ+LJ	UJ stagnation
1X / 2 days	normal	bump on narrow tip, red edges, blisters & stagnation spots	root	UJ stagnation
1X / 2-3 d, dry	yellow	moist, thick, purple	yellow sticky root	excess water in cells
1X am	incomplete	fat, thick, weak, red, indented tip, blisters	watery, thick, sticky at LJ	excess water in cells
1-2X		big, thick, full; indented tip	none	excess water in cells
1X		fat, thick, soft, raised tip, 3 high areas, 3 dents	MJ greasy white	UJ stagnation
1-2X		red tip, raised middle, turbid root	MJ+LJ greasy white	excess water in cells

ID	Title	Sex	Age	Main Symptoms
27	Stomach Cancer, Ulcer	M	63	stomach cancer, ulcer, distended stomach
28	Stomach Ulcer, Breast Lump	F	60	stomach ulcer, hot chest, lump L-breast, hiccup, heavy back
29	tongue: Upper Jiao Blockage	F	43	chest tight, hiccups, weak lower limbs, dizziness
30	Uterine Fibroid Tumor	F	40	uterine tumor, distension in lower abdomen, frequent urination
31	Uterine Tumor, Fatigue	F	39	uterine tumor, no energy
32	Uterine Tumor, Hypo-menorrhea	F	43	uterine tumor, hypomenorrhea, headaches & dizziness, fatigue
20	Lung Cancer (Right Lung)	M	65	cancer R-lung, cough with phlegm, heart issues, salty taste
21	Lung Cancer, Facial Numbness	M	57	lung cancer, cough with phlegm, transient pain L-ribs, numbness
22	Pancreatic Cancer	M	47	pancreatic cancer, metastasis to liver & GB, abdominal pain, cannot eat fatty food
23	Prostatitis, Joint Pain	M	39	prostatitis, liver pain, back pain, skin problems
24	Psoriasis	M	23	psoriasis, itchiness
25	Rheumatoid Arthri-tis, Amenorrhea	F	28	rheumatoid arthritis, cervix pain, amenorrhea
26	Rickets (Osteomalacia)	M	16	rickets, discomfort in L-hip, spine and sides, pain, eye is-sues

Table 22. Case Studies

Stool/ day	Urine	Tongue Characteristics	Tongue Coating	Root Problem
1-2X, loose		thick, red, cracks	none	excess Lung *qi*
1X / 2 days		tip raised, indented, median crack	thick, sticky at LJ	UJ blockage
		high front, dip in middle	none	UJ blockage
1X low vol, no form	frequent	pale, soft, weak, stagnant	none	heart lacks drive
		raised tip, low front, high middle, stagnation blisters		MJ stagnation + dry heat
1X / 2 days, dry		thick, big, dip at front & root	none	MJ blockage
1X am	normal	raised front, cracks in MJ, dry	greasy yellow MJ+LJ	UJ stagnation
1X / 2 days	normal	bump on narrow tip, red edges, blisters & stagnation spots	root	UJ stagnation
1X / 2-3 d, dry	yellow	moist, thick, purple	yellow sticky root	excess water in cells
1X am	incomplete	fat, thick, weak, red, indented tip, blisters	watery, thick, sticky at LJ	excess water in cells
1-2X		big, thick, full; indented tip	none	excess water in cells
1X		fat, thick, soft, raised tip, 3 high areas, 3 dents	MJ greasy white	UJ stagnation
1-2X		red tip, raised middle, turbid root	MJ+LJ greasy white	excess water in cells

The case studies are examples of the real-life application of Body Space Medicine. They document the assessment and treatment of actual patients with a wide variety of health conditions. Study each one well, look at the tongue analysis provided and understand the pathology, the rationale for the treatment chosen and the herbs prescribed.

Armed with this library of valuable references, practitioners can confidently apply the same principles in their own practice. With time and practice, they will become experienced Body Space Medicine practitioners with great healing skills and abilities to share with others. The day will come when they are one with Body Space Medicine.

When that moment occurs, I will know in my heart of hearts and in my soul of souls, and I will proudly say to them: *Congratulations and welcome to Body Space Medicine!*

CASE 1: ABDOMINAL PAIN AND FULLNESS

Consultation #1: 2006.01.09

ID: 01   **Sex:** Female

Symptoms: Stomach fullness,
pain in lower abdomen when palpated
(some inflammation), frequent dreams

Stool/Urine: Stool once in the morning

Formula: Chi Shao 17 g, Shi Chang Pu 30 g,
Jie Geng 4 g, Jin Yin Hua 7 g, Du Huo 30 g

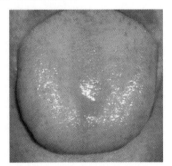

**Photo 1. Tongue 01-#1
(2006.01.09)**

PATHOLOGY

Details of the tongue diagnosis are shown in Photo 2. The whole tongue is big, thick and full with stagnation inside the cells, which indicates lack of energy. The tongue coating is watery. Both sides and the front of the tongue are raised. There are also many small white

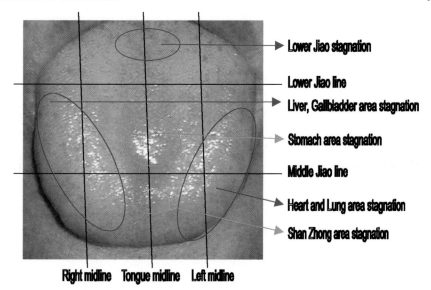

Lower Jiao stagnation

Lower Jiao line

Liver, Gallbladder area stagnation

Stomach area stagnation

Middle Jiao line

Heart and Lung area stagnation

Shan Zhong area stagnation

Right midline   Tongue midline   Left midline

Photo 2. Analysis of Tongue 01-#1 (2006.01.09)

blisters on top of the tongue as seen in the close-ups of Photo 3. The flat area in the middle of the tongue corresponding to the stomach and spleen shows a bump, on top of which are many small white blisters. The whole area from the Lower Jiao line back to the root of the tongue shows blood stagnation.

These conditions indicate excess water in the cells. Water is not able to properly dissipate from the cells, which causes excess energy to build up and stagnate in the areas of the lungs and chest. This leads to congested energy in the areas of the Middle Jiao, stomach and spleen. The subsequent blockage of the pathways for moving energy and matter in the Middle Jiao, in turn, causes Lower Jiao blockage. Consequently, the San Jiao (Upper, Middle and Lower Jiao) energy does not move. The Gong Zhuan does not flow freely.

To solve these problems, the treatment strategy must first dissipate the excess water in the cells so as to reduce the pressure in the lungs and promote the transformation between matter and energy. This will open a pathway to allow the Middle Jiao and the Lower Jiao to flow. Once the San Jiao flows smoothly, normal Gong Zhuan function will return and the body will recover its health.

EXPLANATION OF THE FORMULA

- *Chi Shao* promotes matter movement in the cells, promotes blood circulation, removes stagnation and reduces pain. This herb helps dissipate energy.

- *Shi Chang Pu* dissipates energy from the head area by promoting energy flow down to the chest area, removes damp heat energy in the space of the heart area, and reduces the density and pressure in the space around the right atrium and right ventricle.

- *Jie Geng* opens the lung cells, lifts lung *qi*, reduces lung pressure, promotes the transformation between matter and energy, and also dissipates water.

- *Jin Yin Hua* transforms damp heat into energy and matter.

- *Du Huo* promotes the downward flow of energy from the head to the toes. It moves energy down to give the Lower Jiao a push, activates the movement of matter and energy in the Lower Jiao, and promotes the normal circulation of the Gong Zhuan.

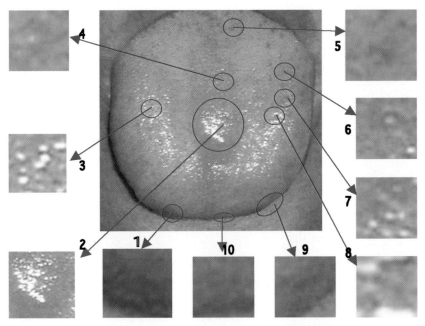

Photo 3. Close-ups of Tongue 01-#1 (2006.01.09)

CASE 2: ABDOMINAL TUMOR (SERIOUS)

Consultation #1: 2006.02.11

ID: 02   **Sex:** Female   **Age:** 19

Symptoms: Abdominal tumor pressing on nerves affecting the legs, especially the right leg, leading to walking difficulties. Over time, the left leg developed numbness. The patient's face is dull and yellow, the body thin. Patient cannot walk without two assistants and any motion generates profuse perspiration.

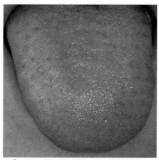

Photo 4. Tongue 02-#1 (2006.02.11)

Stool/Urine: Pain with bowel movements and urination. No bowel movement in three days, not even with enema.

Formula: Jin Yin Hua 30 g, Chao Bing Lang 20 g, Jie Geng 7 g, Du Huo 30 g. Urgent: 3 doses every 2 days, taken 3 times a day. Less urgent: 1 dose a day, taken twice a day (normal intake).

PATHOLOGY

This is a very serious case. The upward and downward paths of the San Jiao are blocked. If stool can exit, the patient has a chance of survival as it would be a sign that *qi* is moving. If stool does not exit, there is no path for the lightness to rise and turbidity to sink, in which case death would ensue in a matter of time.

In addressing the situation, a critical constraint is to not disturb the tumor. Treatment must avoid breaking or disrupting the boundaries of the tumor; otherwise, new issues can result. The best strategy and only course of action for this case is to open the top of the body to clear the bottom, much like lifting a lid off of a pot to relieve pressure.

The density on the inside of the left hipbone is very high so nothing can move up. There has been no bowel movement in three days and urination has also been difficult, so making things move up is the only option.

With the bottom blocked, a way must be found to open up the top to relieve the pressure in the body. Treatment must have the effect of stimulating and bringing the energy up to exit from the upper parts of the body. In this case, stimulation may not be possible as the tumor is too large.

Details of the tongue diagnosis are shown in Photo 5. The tongue is large, thick and fills the mouth. The front third of the tongue is raised, indicating Upper Jiao blockage. The coating at the center of the Middle Jiao and Lower Jiao is yellow and greasy. The tip of the tongue is slightly red and has a slight indentation or notch. There are stagnation spots which can be seen more clearly in Photo 6, along with the color variations and density for select areas of the tongue. All these tongue characteristics are indications of accumulated matter in the cells; the matter energy is blocked, the San Jiao is blocked and the Gong Zhuan cannot circulate normally.

To solve the root problem of the Upper Jiao blockage, treatment must first stimulate the matter inside the cells and increase the driving force of matter and energy. The objective is to increase and generate more powerful collisions between cells to open a pathway for the movement of matter.

Providing an exit for the pathway will allow energy and matter to quickly dissipate from the Upper Jiao, with the result that the raised area at the front of the tongue will be leveled. When pressure is reduced in the upper parts of the body, it will lead the matter at the back upward, which will stimulate the stagnated matter in the lower parts. As a result, the San Jiao can start to flow smoothly, which will allow the Gong Zhuan to circulate normally. Only then will the patient have a chance to survive.

EXPLANATION OF THE FORMULA

- *Jin Yin Hua* eliminates excess energy in the lung space, clears impurities without affecting *jing qi*[1] (one's inherited life essence),

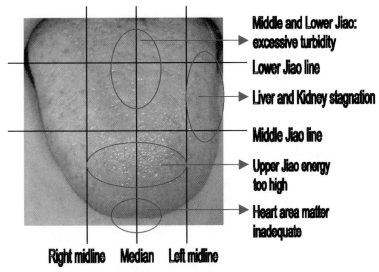

Middle and Lower Jiao:
excessive turbidity

Lower Jiao line

Liver and Kidney stagnation

Middle Jiao line

Upper Jiao energy
too high

Heart area matter
inadequate

Right midline   Median   Left midline

Photo 5. Analysis of Tongue 02-#1 (2006.02.11)

dissipates energy, reduces the pressure in the space, and fosters the transformation of matter to energy. It is used to treat problems with matter movement and matter imbalance due to high density in the space. The Upper Jiao can be thought of as the sky of the body. Jin Yin Hua has the effect of clearing the sky of clouds, allowing the sun to shine through.

- *Chao Bing Lang* drives the matter in the cells and makes energy move downward. It leads the energy in the spleen and lungs down to the toes, clearing heat from the Middle Jiao, Lower Jiao and the intestines. Like a street cleaner, Chao Bing Lang clears the water pathway, opening the pathway and allowing turbidity to sink.

- *Jie Geng* is like the pen that dots the dragon's eye; it leads the lung energy up, reduces the lung pressure, lifts lung *qi* and opens the lung door or exit. The action of lifting first will induce sinking. This approach is akin to lifting the lid on a boiling pot; lifting relieves the tongue's stuffiness from the top part of the body (lungs, Upper Jiao), thereby allowing turbidity to sink.

• *Du Huo* induces the energy of the upper back to charge downwards through the Wai Jiao space to the Lower Jiao, in effect run-
ning energy down from the head to the feet. This one herb alone
is enough to stimulate the Gong Zhuan to automatically move,
there-by leveling the raised parts of the tongue (the heart and
lungs). Du Huo combined with Jie Geng guides the lung energy
down to nourish the kidney area, an example of using Five Elements theory in healing (Metal produces and nourishes Water).

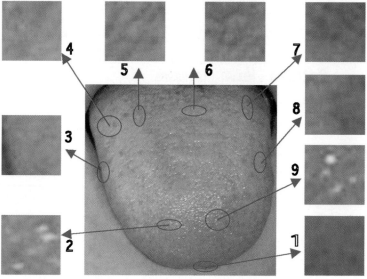

Photo 6. Close-ups of Tongue 02-#1 (2006.02.11)

CASE 3: ATROPHIC GASTRITIS

Consultation #1:

ID: 03   **Sex:** Male

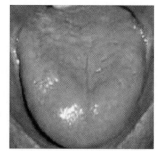

Symptoms: Atrophic stomach inflammation
(atrophic gastritis), a process of chronic inflammation of the stomach which leads to a
loss of stomach cells and replacement by intestinal and fibrous tissues. Distension of the
stomach, poor appetite, heaviness of the back.

Photo 7. Tongue 03-#1

Stool/Urine: Loose, unformed stool twice a day.

Formula: Pei Lan 17 g, Gui Zhi 7 g, Lian Qiao 17 g, Jiao San Xian 15 g each, Du Huo 30 g.

PATHOLOGY

Photo 8 shows details of the tongue diagnosis. This tongue shows no coating above the navel area; instead, the tongue coating is greasy and localized in the Lower Jiao area. There is a vertical crack along the midline of the tongue. The front of the tongue is raised, thick and full. Although the raised area is larger on the right than on the left, both sides have clusters of white blisters. The center middle of the tongue has a slight depression and is darker in color. Photo 9 shows the variations in tongue color, density and blisters more clearly.

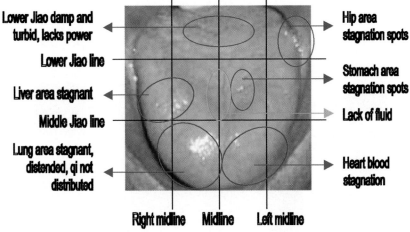

Lower Jiao damp and turbid, lacks power

Lower Jiao line

Liver area stagnant

Middle Jiao line

Lung area stagnant, distended, qi not distributed

Hip area stagnation spots

Stomach area stagnation spots

Lack of fluid

Heart blood stagnation

Right midline   Midline   Left midline

Photo 8. Analysis of Tongue 03-#1

The thickness at the front of the tongue indicates stagnation in the Upper Jiao; energy cannot move, which causes the heart and lung function to become unbalanced. As a result, the patient feels irritated and frustrated. The chest and back feel heavy and tight with pressure. The patient catches cold easily.

With the Upper Jiao not moving, matter in the Middle and the Lower Jiao also cannot move normally. The blockage in the Middle

Jiao causes liver energy stagnation, distension of the spleen and stomach, and abnormal function of the stomach and intestines.

To resolve the problems indicated by this tongue, treatment must first address the thickness and fullness at the front of tongue so that matter can flow freely in the Upper Jiao. The energy stagnation of the heart and lung will then be able to dissipate. The San Jiao will clear, the Gong Zhuan will move freely and the body will then be healthy and well.

EXPLANATION OF THE FORMULA

- *Pei Lan* removes dampness and turbidity in the Middle Jiao. It promotes the free flow of water within and around the cells.

- *Gui Zhi* balances the transformation between matter (inside) and energy (outside) the cells.

- *Lian Qiao* removes heat and energy from the Upper Jiao space, dissipating it through the pores of the skin. It clears the field

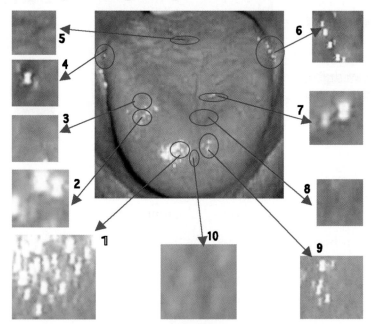

Photo 9. Close-ups of Tongue 03-#1

around the heart and the energy of the lung space. It activates greater cellular vibration of the spleen and stomach, lifts spleen *qi* and clears heat from the inside and the outside of the cells.

- *Jiao San Xian* clears stagnation in the San Jiao by inducing energy to flow up and down. It activates cellular vibration of the Middle Jiao, promotes movement of matter and promotes digestion, thereby increasing appetite.

- *Du Huo* promotes energy flow to charge downward from the head, giving the Lower Jiao a big push, increasing the energy of the Lower Jiao and increasing the transformation of matter, which in turn nourishes the kidneys and brain and restores the body's health.

CASE 4: CHEST PROBLEMS

Consultation #1:

ID: 04   **Sex:** Male   **Age:** 37

Symptoms: Backache, chest problems, poor sleep. The tongue is shown in Photo 10.

Urine/Stool: Morning stool; bowel movement upon waking

Formula: Chao Zao Ren 7 g, Pei Lan 17 g, Gui Zhi 7 g, Lian Qiao 17 g, Du Huo 17 g, Chi Shao 17 g.

PATHOLOGY

Photo 10 shows the details of the tongue analysis. This tongue has a second, smaller tongue in the middle to front part of the main tongue. This small tongue is very hard and raised quite high. This tongue characteristic is referred to as having a *tongue on top of the tongue*.

The tip of the tongue is red and indented; there is a blister on the left side of the tip. The back of the tongue shows dampness and heat.

In general, this tongue shows high turbidity and has a sticky yellow coating.

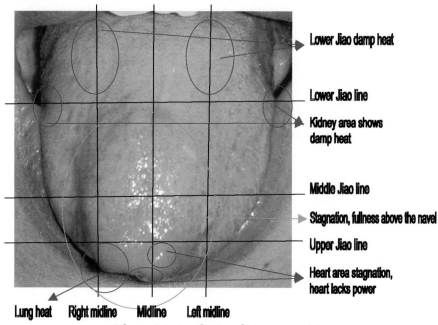

Photo 10. Analysis of Tongue 04-#1

The small tongue on top of the tongue indicates that the Middle Jiao and Upper Jiao are blocked. Energy cannot flow through the space and matter inside the cells cannot move or transform properly. This prevents the energy in the Lower Jiao from going upward (as per the Gong Zhuan flow), thereby creating excessive dampness and turbidity. As a result, the Lower Jiao and Meng Men areas have no driving power, causing the symptoms in the back and chest, as well as the sleeping disorders.

The treatment strategy must first focus on removing the small tongue on top of the tongue. Dispel the blockage in the body's upper parts so that the Lower Jiao can drive the Gong Zhuan flow to heal the body.

EXPLANATION OF THE FORMULA

- *Chao Zao Ren* increases the pressure of the space (outside the cells) around the left atrium of the heart. It nourishes the cells by increasing matter inside the cells.

- *Gui Zhi* adjusts the balance and transformation between matter inside cells and energy outside cells.

- *Chao Zao Ren,* used with Gui Zhi, nourishes and moistens the skin and balances the energy inside and outside of the cells.

- *Chi Shao* promotes blood circulation and removes blood stagnation in the blood vessels.

- *Pei Lan* removes dampness and turbid energy in the Middle Jiao and promotes the function of the stomach.

- *Lian Qiao* removes the excess heat generated by the action of Gui Zhi.

- *Du Huo* quickly drives Upper Jiao energy down to the Lower Jiao. At the same time, it nourishes the kidneys and increases the driving force for the Meng Men area.

CASE 5: DIABETES, HYPERTENSION

Consultation #1: 2005.11.18

ID: 05   **Sex:** Female   **Age:** 75

Symptoms: Diabetes, heart issues, poor sleep, fuzzy vision in both eyes, obstruction felt upon swallowing, right hip and leg feel cool. The tongue is shown in Photo 11.

Stool/Urine: Stool once a day.

Formula: Yi Mi Ren 17 g, Jie Geng 6 g, Gui Zhi 7 g, Lian Qiao 30 g, Yin Chen 17 g.

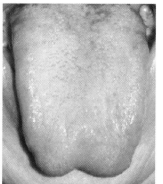

Photo 11. Tongue 05-#1 (2005.11.18)

PATHOLOGY

Photo 12 shows the details of the tongue analysis. The tip of the tongue has a deep indentation. The left side of the tip is slightly red which explains the insufficient drive, stagnation and heat in the heart. The middle of the front part of the tongue is raised, which explains the feeling of fullness in the chest area above the diaphragm; the matter inside the cells is not moving smoothly.

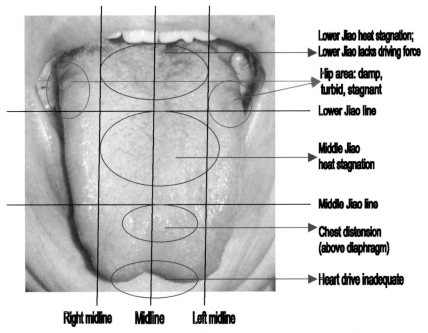

Right midline   Midline   Left midline

Photo 12. Analysis of Tongue 05-#1 (2005.11.25)

The Middle Jiao and Lower Jiao areas of the tongue show a greasy yellow coating, indicative of excessive damp heat, which is why the hip and leg feel cool.

The middle area of the front part of the tongue is raised, which indicates that the cells are inactive internally. This blocks matter in the Middle Jiao from moving up, so that Middle Jiao energy cannot dissipate normally and becomes stagnated. Stagnation in the Middle Jiao means that Lower Jiao energy cannot radiate and move upward. All of these issues combined lead to the symptoms experienced by the patient. The treatment strategy is to dissipate the blockage of the Middle Jiao.

EXPLANATION OF THE FORMULA

- *Yi Mi Ren* absorbs the water of the energy and matter in the space of the middle and lower part of the Wai Jiao. Yi Mi Ren absorbs water into the cells of the Middle and Lower Jiao, enhances *jing qi*, clears the water pathway, clears internal damp heat, and relieves back and leg pain.

- *Jie Geng* opens the lung door and lifts lung *qi*. It leads the lung energy up and activates the matter above the diaphragm. It opens a pathway for the lung matter.

- *Gui Zhi* opens the cell walls, adjusts and balances the transformation between matter inside the cells and energy outside the cells.

- *Yin Chen* causes energy to move to the left side of the liver region, which reduces the pressure in the space between the liver and the stomach. This increases the driving force for energy to dissipate from the liver cells, thereby restoring the functions of the liver and gallbladder.

Consultation #2: 2005.11.25

Symptoms: Diabetes, poor vision in the left eye, high blood pressure, insomnia, apprehension, headache, toothache, back feels tight and taut, weakness and lack of strength, night sweats. The tongue condition is shown in Photo 13.

Stool/Urine: Stool 1 or 2 times per day, loose. Urine is frequent, yellow and foamy with odor.

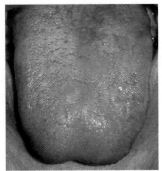

Photo 13 Tongue 05-#2 (2005.11.25)

Formula: Gui Zhi 7 g, Ge Gen 17 g, Lian Qiao 17 g.

EXPLANATION OF THE FORMULA

- *Ge Gen* is used to level the raised area in the middle of the front part of the tongue. Once this part of the tongue is leveled, the Middle Jiao energy can move up. Once the San Jiao pathway is open, the Gong Zhuan energy pathway can then flow normally about the body and the patient recover from diabetes and other symptoms.

CASE 6: ESOPHAGEAL CANCER

Consultation #1: 2005.11.01

ID: 06   **Sex:** Male   **Age:** 70

Symptoms: Cancer in the lower part of the esophagus. The tongue is shown in Photo 14.

Stool/Urine: Stool once every 3 to 4 days and very dry.

Formula: Ma Huang 6 g, Gui Zhi 7 g, Zhe Bei 7 g.

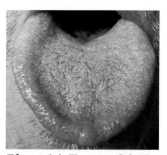

Photo 14. Tongue 06-#1 (2005.11.01)

PATHOLOGY

Photo 15 shows the details of the tongue analysis. The overall appearance of the tongue is big, hard, red and thin. The coating is thick and sticky in the Lower Jiao area, indicating high turbidity, lack of *yuan qi*[2] and lack of driving power in the Lower Jiao. All this explains why the stool is very dry.

From the tip of the tongue to the Ming Men area, there are cracks in the middle of the tongue. The edge of the tongue is curled and raised

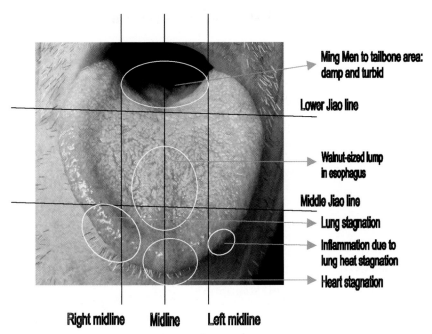

Ming Men to tailbone area: damp and turbid

Lower Jiao line

Walnut-sized lump in esophagus

Middle Jiao line

Lung stagnation

Inflammation due to lung heat stagnation

Heart stagnation

Right midline   Midline   Left midline

Photo 15. Analysis of Tongue 06-#1 (2005.11.01)

while the middle is flat. The tongue body is red, indicating lack of matter in the Upper and Middle Jiao. The body lacks fluid and the cells have heat stagnation. The liver and spleen are also stagnant.

The tongue is hard in the area of the esophagus indicating inflammation.

The blister at the tip of the tongue indicates heart blood stagnation and lung heat. The Upper Jiao is blocked so the Middle Jiao cannot move, which in turn blocks matter and energy in the Lower Jiao from moving. Because the energy of the lungs cannot descend to nourish the lower parts, the Lower Jiao has inadequate energy to drive the Gong Zhuan to clear the congestion in the body.

To resolve the problems described, treatment must first focus on removing the bump at the tip of the tongue and the raised areas along the front edges. The key is to open the Upper Jiao by dissipating the blockages in the lungs and the heart. Then the matter and energy of the Middle Jiao, Lower Jiao and San Jiao can all flow, which will allow the Gong Zhuan to flow. When this happens, the body will recover and health will prevail.

EXPLANATION OF THE FORMULA

- *Ma Huang* opens all cells in the body. It dissipates matter from inside the cells. It simultaneously promotes energy movement, removes heat and stagnation, and adjusts the heart.

- *Gui Zhi* balances matter and energy inside and outside of the cells. When used together with Ma Huang, it causes energy to radiate from the inside to the outside of the body. The combined effect of these two herbs extracts matter from inside the cells to the outside and dissipates heat and stagnation.

- *Zhe Bei* dissipates the stagnation in the lungs and bronchial tubes; it clears the lumps formed by accumulated energy. When used with Ma Huang, it clears the space in the chest and opens the skin pores, thereby dissipating accumulated energy out of the body through the skin.

- This formula is used to dissipate stagnation and blockages in the heart, lung and bronchial tubes. It promotes the movement of matter and reduces the pressure in the space of the Upper Jiao, making the energy matter of the Lower Jiao flow much better and restoring the body's health.

Consultation #2: 2005.11.11

Symptoms: Cancer of the esophagus. The tongue condition is shown in Photo 16.

Stool/Urine: Stool once a day in the evening

Formula: Bai Tou Weng 40 g, Dang Gui 12 g, Gui Zhi 7 g, Lian Qiao 30 g, Zhe Bei 30 g.

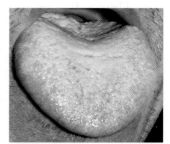

Photo 16. Tongue 06-#2 (2005.11.11)

DISCUSSION OF TREATMENT

Photo 16 shows the condition of the tongue after ten days of Body Space Medicine herb treatment. The tongue is fat, thick and very stagnant. However, the bump at the tip and the raised edges have been removed and the tongue is lighter in color. A thick and greasy coating covers the entire tongue and is particularly thick at the root indicating heavy stagnation of damp heat in the Lower Jiao and Ming Men area.

In Consultation #2, the herb prescription is changed based on the changes in tongue condition and corresponding symptoms. To reduce the high degree of heat and stagnation, heavier dosages of some herbs are used.

- *Bai Tou Weng* reduces density and dampness in the Lower Jiao by increasing the capillary action of the colon.

- *Dang Gui* removes blood stagnation and increases the output volume of blood of the left atrium and left ventricle to the rest of the body. It increases the body's driving force, promotes movement of matter (bowel movement) and increases moisture in the cells.

- *Lian Qiao* clears lung heat and heart energy in the space of the Upper Jiao, activates the spleen and stomach, and lifts spleen *qi*. With Gui Zhi, it clears the Upper Jiao space and makes the upper part deficient (lighter). With Dang Gui and Gui Zhi, it clears the San Jiao pathway by moving *qi*, blood and water.

- *Zhe Bei* dissipates energy, heat, stagnation and pressure in the Upper Jiao space in the lungs, bronchial tubes and chest, which nourishes the kidneys.

CASE 7: GALLBLADDER CANCER

Consultation #1: 2005.11.06

ID: 07   **Sex:** Male   **Age:** 73

Symptoms: Tumor in the lower end of the gallbladder duct, gallstones in the gallbladder and gallbladder duct (cholelithiasis), chronic inflammation of the gallbladder (cholecystitis), swollen lymph node in the abdomen. The tongue is shown in Photo 17.

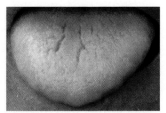

Photo 17. Tongue 07-#1 (2005.11.06)

Stool/Urine: Stool 2 to 3 times per day, urine yellow

Formula: Ma Huang 4 g, Gui Zhi 7 g, Zhe Bei 17 g, Yin Chen 30 g.

PATHOLOGY

The analysis of the tongue is shown in Photo 18. The tongue is hard and purple, indicating blood stagnation. The tip of the tongue has a bump, which indicates stagnation in the heart area. Matter is stuck and energy does not flow. On the left front side of tongue there is a stagnation spot, which indicates problems in the area of the heart.

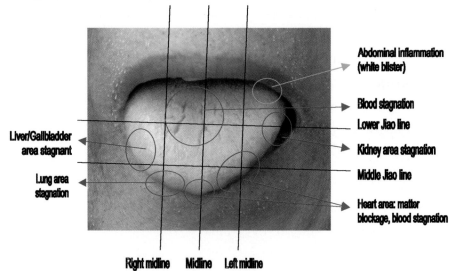

Photo 18. Analysis of Tongue 07-#1 (2005.11.06)

The right front side of the tongue has a stagnation spot in the Upper Jiao area, which indicates heat stagnation in the lung area. The right middle side of the tongue is thicker than the left side, which indicates stagnation in the area of the liver and gallbladder. Matter is stuck in and energy does not flow around the cells.

The rear left Middle Jiao area of the tongue has dark stagnation spots in the area of the kidney, which indicates problems with the kidneys. The rear left Lower Jiao area of the tongue has a white blister, which indicates inflammation in the abdomen.

The cracks in the center of the tongue in the Middle Jiao and Lower Jiao areas point to blood stagnation. The bump on the tip of the tongue shows that matter is stuck in the Upper Jiao so energy cannot flow. This also prevents the Middle Jiao matter from flowing up, therefore causing matter to accumulate in the area of the liver and gallbladder. All these blockages slow down the smooth movement of matter in the Lower Jiao as there is now insufficient power and drive to move the matter.

The issues described are responsible for all the symptoms experienced by the patient.

EXPLANATION OF THE FORMULA

- *Ma Huang* opens all the cells in the body. It dissipates matter and energy from inside the cells and facilitates the smooth flow of energy in the space.

- *Gui Zhi* balances the areas inside and outside of the cells. Ma Huang used with Gui Zhi promotes the transformation of matter to energy, which can then dissipate from the body.

- *Zhe Bei* dissipates energy in the chest and bronchial tubes. It clears local knots of stagnation and accelerates the reduction of excess lung energy by transforming matter to energy. When used with

Ma Huang, Zhe Bei speeds up the clearing of the lung space; it disperses excess energy through the skin by opening up the skin pores.

- *Yin Chen* helps dissipate the energy on the left side of the liver. This promotes the transformation of matter to energy and restores cell vitality and organ function.

Consultation #2: 2005.11.13

Symptoms: Metastasis of the cancer in the gallbladder duct to the pancreas and to the lymph nodes in the abdomen. The whole body is jaundiced and itchy. (Photo of the tongue is not available.)

Stool/Urine: Stool 2 to 3 times per day, urine yellow.

Formula: Gui Zhi 7 g, Jin Yin Hua 17 g, Lian Qiao 17 g, Du Huo 6 g.

Consultation #3: 2005.11.19

Symptoms: Cancer of the gallbladder duct, cough. The tongue is shown in Photo 19.

Stool/Urine: Bowel movement right after meals three times a day.

Formula: Huo Xiang 12 g, Pei Lan 17 g, Gui Zhi 7 g, Jiao San Xian 15 g each.

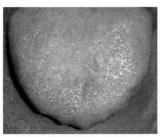

Photo 19. Tongue 07-#3 (2005.11.19)

Consultation #4: 2005.11.27

Symptoms: Pancreatic cancer. Cannot tolerate greasy food. The whole body shows jaundice. The tongue is shown in Photo 20.

Stool/Urine: Stool 8 to 9 times a day, sometimes green in color.

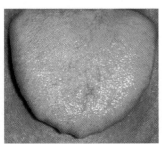

Photo 20. Tongue 07-#4 (2005.11.27)

Formula: Huo Xiang 12 g, Gui Zhi 7 g, Jiao San Xian 20 g each, Chi Shao 4 g.

Consultation #5: 2005.12.04

Symptoms: Jaundice, tumor in the lower end of the gallbladder duct, gallstones in the gall bladder and gallbladder duct, cannot tolerate greasy food, indigestion. The tongue is shown in Photo 21.

Stool/Urine: Stool 8 to 9 times a day; yellow and black in color.

Photo 21. Tongue 07-#5 (2005.12.04)

Formula: Jiao San Xian 30 g each, Pei Lan 17 g, Gui Zhi 7 g, Du Huo 7 g.

Consultation #6: 2005.12.11

Symptoms: Cancer of the gallbladder duct, bronchitis, dislike of greasy food, poor appetite. The tongue is shown in Photo 22.

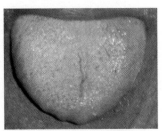

Stool/Urine: Stool 2 to 3 times a day, not loose.

Photo 22. Tongue 07-#6 (2005.12.11)

Formula: Pei Lan 17 g, Chi Shao 17 g, Gui Zhi 7 g, Lian Qiao 17 g, Du Huo 7 g, Jiao San Xian 15 g each.

CASE 8: GALLBLADDER DISEASE

Consultation #1: 2005.11.05

ID: 08   **Sex:** Male   **Age:** 35

Symptoms: Gallbladder disease. The tongue is shown in Photo 23.

Formula: Dang Gui 17 g, Gui Zhi 7 g, Lian Qiao 17 g.

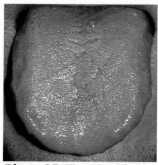

Photo 23. Tongue 08-#1
(2005.11.05)

PATHOLOGY

Photo 24 shows the details of the tongue analysis. The tongue is big, full and red. It has no coating and there are many cracks on the surface. This tongue lacks energy and vitality. Both sides of the tongue are raised and thick in the front and the middle is depressed.

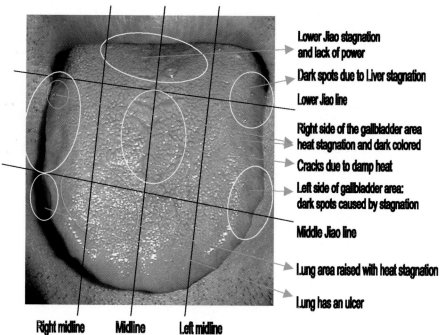

Lower Jiao stagnation and lack of power

Dark spots due to Liver stagnation

Lower Jiao line

Right side of the gallbladder area heat stagnation and dark colored

Cracks due to damp heat

Left side of gallbladder area: dark spots caused by stagnation

Middle Jiao line

Lung area raised with heat stagnation

Lung has an ulcer

Right midline   Midline   Left midline

Photo 24. Analysis of Tongue 08-#1 (2005.11.05)

At the front of the tongue, there is no wall to keep the energy in and protect against pathogenic Wind[3]. This causes problems with the lungs, as indicated by the conditions of the tongue. The resulting *qi* and blood stagnation cause irritability.

The stagnation in the Upper Jiao leads to blockages in the Middle Jiao, such that energy and matter cannot move or dissipate appropriately. As a result, heat is produced in the organs, distension develops in the organs and the patient experiences symptoms such as gallbladder dysfunction. With the Middle Jiao blocked, the space does not clear and its increased density prevents Lower Jiao energy from flowing up. This inhibits matter from entering the Lower Jiao cells with the consequence that the Lower Jiao lacks power and the whole body will feel tired and have no vitality. If untreated over time, this condition can lead to more serious illnesses.

EXPLANATION OF THE FORMULA

- *Dang Gui* works on the space outside of the cells. It increases the density, pressure and energy of the space.

- *Gui Zhi* balances the cells inside out, and assists Dang Gui with the transformation of energy around the cells into matter inside the cells. This nourishes the body, increases power and promotes blood circulation.

- *Lian Qiao* removes the heat generated by the action of Gui Zhi. It removes heat in the space of the Upper Jiao and clears the field of the heart area, dissipating this energy in the space of the lung area. It promotes the function of the spleen and stomach, lifts spleen *qi* and dissipates accumulated matter quickly, returning the body to normal health.

Consultation #2: 2005.11.14

Symptoms: Gallbladder disease. The tongue is shown in Photo 25.

Stool/Urine: Normal.

Formula: Bai Zhu 17 g, Gui Zhi 7 g, Mao Gou 30 g.

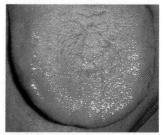

Photo 25. Tongue 08-#2 (2005.11.14)

CASE 9: GASTRITIS, PROSTATITIS

Consultation #1: 2005.12.19

ID: 09   **Sex:** Male   **Age:** 27

Symptoms: Prostatitis, varicose vein on the scrotum, stomach issues, cough without phlegm, insomnia, fatigue, scrotum damp, pain at the head of penis. The tongue is shown in Photo 26.

Stool/Urine: Stool 1 to 2 times per day.

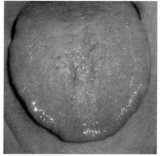

Photo 26. Tongue 09-#1 (2005.12.19)

Formula: Chao Zao Ren 7 g, Jiao San Xian 15 g each, Chi Shao 17 g, Gui Zhi 17 g, Lian Qiao 17 g, Xiang Fu 17 g, Du Huo 7 g, Pei Lan 17 g.

Consultation #2: 2005.12.24

Symptoms: Varicose vein on the spermatic cord, stomach issue, poor sleep patterns. The tongue is shown in Photo 27.

Stool/Urine: Stool twice in the morning.

Formula: Chi Shao 17 g, Gui Zhi 7 g, Lian Qiao 17 g, Pei Lan 17 g, Qiang Huo 5 g, Du Huo 17 g,

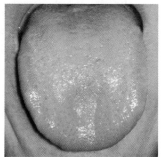

Photo 27. Tongue 09-#2 (2005.12.24)

Consultation #3: 2006.01.08

Symptoms: Varicose vein on the spermatic cord, prostatitis, gastritis. The tongue condition is shown in Photo 28.

Stool/Urine: Stool twice in the morning.

Formula: Pei Lan 17 g, Bai Tou Weng 30 g, Gui Zhi 7 g, Lian Qiao 17 g, Du Huo 30 g.

Photo 28. Tongue 09-#3 (2006.01.08)

PATHOLOGY

Photo 29 shows the details of the tongue diagnosis for the condition of the tongue from Consultation #1. The whole tongue is hard, stagnated and purple. The tongue has curled edges from the Lower Jiao line to the tip of the tongue. The tip itself is red and has a hard lump on it. The middle of the tongue has creases and the root has a greasy coating. The tongue surface is raised from the navel to the diaphragm. The tongue surface has stagnation spots and white blisters, as seen more clearly in Photo 30.

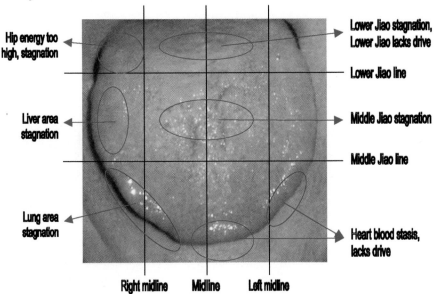

Hip energy too high, stagnation

Lower Jiao stagnation, Lower Jiao lacks drive

Lower Jiao line

Liver area stagnation

Middle Jiao stagnation

Middle Jiao line

Lung area stagnation

Heart blood stasis, lacks drive

Right midline   Midline   Left midline

Photo 29. Analysis of Tongue 09-#1 (2005.12.19)

The curled-up edges of the tongue and in particular the hard lump at the tongue tip can be likened to a fortress with a blocked front exit, which traps matter and energy inside. This results in energy accumulation such that matter in the chest and Upper Jiao area cannot dissipate. Because of this, energy cannot move up so matter and energy from the Middle Jiao (liver, gallbladder, stomach and spleen regions) are also trapped. What follows then is stagnation, fullness, liver *qi* not being distributed and functional imbalance of the spleen and stomach. This in turn leads to imbalance and blockage of matter and energy in the Lower Jiao. In general, all these problems arise because the top part of the body (Upper Jiao) is blocked and the bottom (Lower Jiao) is not accessible. Consequently, lightness cannot rise and turbidity cannot sink, the San Jiao is not smooth and the Gong Zhuan does not circulate normally.

To solve the issues described, the strategy used is similar to blowing up a fortress. Treatment must eliminate the hard lump at the tip of the tongue and the curled edges along the sides. This will open up a pathway for the movement of energy and allow stagnated matter to dissipate. The Upper, Middle and Lower Jiao matter and energy will then flow smoothly. As a result, lightness will naturally ascend and turbidity descend, the San Jiao will flow freely and the Gong Zhuan will circulate normally. This approach will solve the body's health issues and allow the patient to recover health.

Explanation of the Formula

- *Chao Zao Ren* increases the density and pressure of the space around the left atrium and the left ventricle, which increases the output volume of blood from the heart. This causes a corresponding increase in the return flow of blood to the right atrium, which nourishes the liver and gallbladder, thereby enhancing *ying qi* (acquired essence).

- *Jiao San Xian* enhances the flow of matter and energy within and around the organs of the Middle Jiao. It agitates the movement of energy which then drives the movement of matter, enhances the appetite, eliminates indigestion and restores the functions of the Middle Jiao organs.

- *Gui Zhi* adjusts and balances cells inside and out, opens the cell walls and allows matter and energy to freely transform inside and outside the cells.

- *Lian Qiao* dissipates the heat in the Upper Jiao space through the skin pores. It clears the field around the heart, dissipates energy in the lung space, exercises the spleen and stomach and raises spleen *qi*.

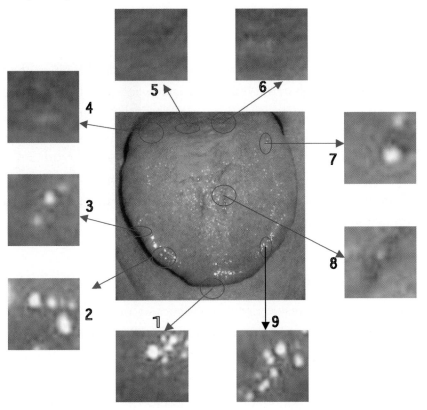

Photo 30. Close-ups of Tongue 09-#1 (2005.12.19)

- *Xiang Fu* enables the energy from the Middle Jiao (below the diaphragm) to pass up through the diaphragm and reach the Shan Zhong via the Gong Zhuan pathway. It lifts spleen *qi* and reduces the pressure in the Middle Jiao space. It can adjust *qi*, stop pain and nourish *qi* and blood.

- *Du Huo* leads the energy in the head downwards to the legs and gives the Lower Jiao a push. This strengthens the Lower Jiao and provides the drive for the movement of matter and energy in the Lower Jiao.

- *Pei Lan* clears the water pathway of the Middle Jiao. It clears dampness and damp turbidity in the Middle Jiao.

CASE 10: HEART PROBLEMS

Consultation #1:

ID: 10   **Sex:** Female   **Age:** 50

Symptoms: Heart problems.

Stool/Urine: Constipation.

Formula: Dang Gui 17 g, Lian Qiao 17 g, Ban Lan Gen 17 g, Gui Zhi 7 g.

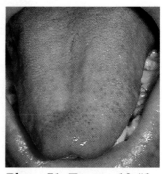

Photo 31. Tongue 10-#1

PATHOLOGY

The details of the tongue diagnosis are shown in Photo 32. The whole tongue is excessively wet and stagnated throughout. There is stagnation in the liver and kidneys, stomach and intestines, the Middle Jiao, the left rib area and the heart area.

Most noticeable is the tip of the tongue, which is raised with a raspberry-like appearance and an indented tip. The raised tip indicates blockage of the Upper Jiao by way of heart blood stagnation. The indentation at the tip indicates inadequate energy and blood in the area of the heart. The blockage in the upper part inhibits the movement of the Middle Jiao, which in turn, causes the Lower Jiao to not flow easily and smoothly. As a result, the Lower Jiao lacks driving force and develops its own blockages and health issues, such as constipation.

The issues described are resolved by first resolving the blockage represented by the raised tip of the tongue. Level the tip by dissipating the stagnation of the heart and lungs. This will open the pathway in the Upper Jiao, which will also allow the matter and energy of the Middle Jiao and the Lower Jiao to dissipate and move, nourish the Lower Jiao and build its drive, and promote the circulation of the Gong Zhuan. Once this occurs, the body's symptoms will disappear and health will be restored.

EXPLANATION OF THE FORMULA

- *Dang Gui* nourishes and promotes energy transformation in the Meng Men area.

- *Gui Zhi* balances the cells inside and outside.

- *Ban Lan Gen* nourishes the heart with matter and energy.

- *Lian Qiao* clears the density around the heart, reduces the energy in the lung space and removes the heat released with the use of Gui Zhi.

- This formula is effective for adjusting the functions of the heart and the lungs, activating the driving force of the Meng Men area, and regaining the body's health.

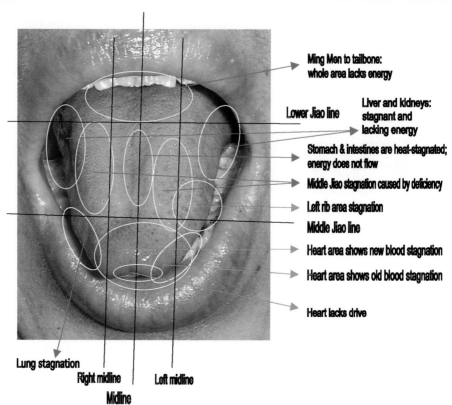

Ming Men to tailbone:
whole area lacks energy

Lower Jiao line

Liver and kidneys:
stagnant and
lacking energy

Stomach & intestines are heat-stagnated;
energy does not flow

Middle Jiao stagnation caused by deficiency

Left rib area stagnation

Middle Jiao line

Heart area shows new blood stagnation

Heart area shows old blood stagnation

Heart lacks drive

Lung stagnation

Right midline   Left midline

Midline

Photo 32. Analysis of Tongue 10-#1

CASE 11: HEAT STAGNATION

Consultation #1:

ID: 11   **Sex:** Female   **Age:** 4

Symptoms: Adjustments sought for general improvement of health; no critical symptoms of note. The tongue is shown in Photos 33 and 34.

Stool/Urine: Stool once a day; no specific times.

Formula: Jiao San Xian 5 g each, Chi Shao 5 g, Shi Chang Pu 7 g, Jin Yin Hua 7 g, Du Huo 4 g

PATHOLOGY

Photo 33 shows the details of the tongue analysis. The first impression of this tongue is that it looks like a stick, so it is called a stick tongue.

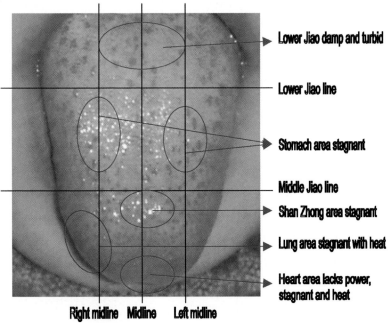

Photo 33. Analysis of Tongue 11-#1

The whole tongue is thick and shows heat stagnation throughout. The Shan Zhong area in the middle of the tongue is raised. The tip of the tongue is indented and the tongue narrows towards the front. If the tongue were a highway, narrowing of the highway would force cars to slow down, causing traffic jams. The root of the tongue is damp and turbid.

The areas of the heart and lungs in the Upper Jiao region of the tongue show heat and stagnation. When the area of the chest is heavy the head will not be clear, which affects the development of intelligence in a young person. Heaviness in the chest also causes discomfort in the stomach and spleen areas because it slows down cell activity and movement of matter in the intestines.

The problems indicated by the tongue can be solved by first removing the raised area at the front part of the tongue (Shan Zhong area). This opens the body's San Jiao pathway allowing the Middle Jiao and Lower Jiao energy and matter to flow through smoothly. If the San Jiao flows, the Gong Zhuan energy circulation will be smooth and health will be restored.

EXPLANATION OF THE FORMULA

- *Jiao San Xian* promotes the flow of the San Jiao.

- *Chi Shao* promotes blood circulation and removes blood stagnation.

- *Shi Chang Pu* dissipates the energy in the head area by promote the downward flow of energy. It removes and dissipates energy in the chest area by removing damp heat from the right side of the heart. This reduces the density and pressure around the right atrium and the right ventricle, which then allows energy to come down from the area of the head.

- *Jin Yin Hua* clears the lung of excessive energy and impurities without affecting the *yuan qi* function of the lung.

- *Du Huo* makes energy move downwards from the head to the toes, opens the Wai Jiao and promotes free flow of the Gong Zhuan.

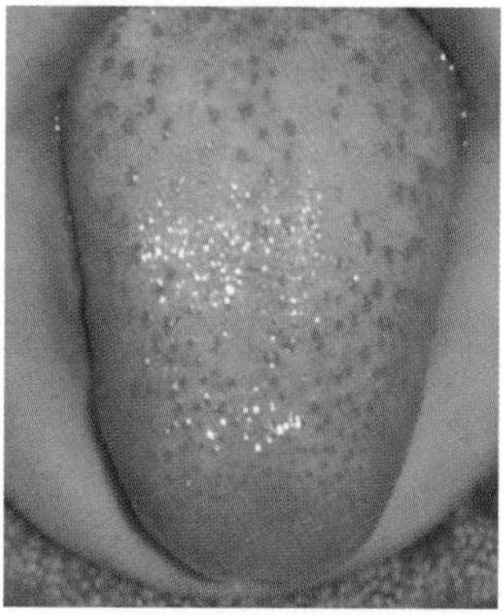

**Photo 34. Tongue 11-#1
(Before Treatment)**

DISCUSSION OF TREATMENT

Photo 34 shows the tongue condition before treatment, Photo 35 after treatment. Changes have obviously occurred in the tongue as a result of treatment.

Before treatment, the tongue shows as a *stick tongue.* The tongue color is purple and the whole tongue shows heat and stagnation. The Shan Zhong area is raised, the tip is indented and the tongue narrows towards the front.

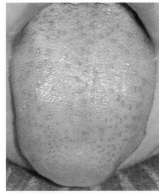

Photo 35. Tongue 11-#2 (After Treatment)

After treatment, the tongue color is lighter, the indentation at the tip is gone, the raised area at the front of the tongue is much smoother, and the whole tongue is flatter, wider and not as rigid. These are all indications that the prescribed formula has reduced the heat stagnation and is working as desired.

CASE 12: HEPATITIS B

Consultation #1:

ID: 12   **Sex:** Male   **Age:** 49

Symptoms: Hepatitis B. Abdomnal pain. The tongue is shown in Photo 36.

Stool/Urine: Stool once a day at noontime.

Formula: Du Huo 30 g, Gong Ying 17 g.

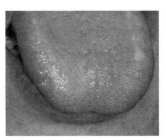

Photo 36. Tongue 12-#1 (2006.02.07)

PATHOLOGY

The details of the tongue analysis are shown in Photo 37. The tongue is large and fills the patient's mouth. The tongue tip is indented and skewed to the left, with the left side being slightly larger than the right. The edges of the tongue are raised on both sides as is the Shan Zhong area in the front part of the tongue. The tongue coating is slightly yellow and there are many white blisters and stagnation spots on the surface of the tongue, as shown more clearly in the photo enlargements in Photo 38.

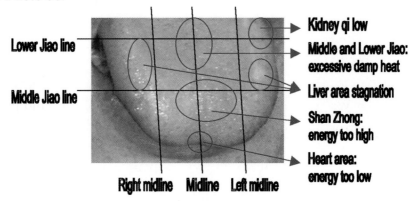

Lower Jiao line

Middle Jiao line

Right midline   Midline   Left midline

Kidney qi low

Middle and Lower Jiao: excessive damp heat

Liver area stagnation

Shan Zhong: energy too high

Heart area: energy too low

Photo 37. Analysis of Tongue 12-#1 (2006.02.07)

The tongue conditions observed are due to stagnation of matter and energy in the Upper Jiao, which blocks the exit and movement of matter for the Middle and Lower Jiao. Consequently, the matter in the area of the tongue tip area cannot be replenished so the energy of the heart is low. At the same time, the Upper Jiao stagnation blocks the energy pathway for the Lower Jiao area.

The situation in the San Jiao is like that of a pond of water. If the inlet and outlet pathways are blocked, the water cannot discharge or refresh appropriately. Over time, the pond turns into a stagnant body of water, eventually contaminating its surroundings. In the body, blockage of the energy and matter pathways in the Upper, Middle and Lower Jiao similarly leads to functional imbalances of the organs and creates a series of health issues.

To resolve the health problems indicated by the tongue, treatment must first target the raised area at the front part of the tongue so as to level it. This allows energy to flow through to the end of the tongue tip, thus clearing the entire Upper Jiao, which will help to fill the indentation at the tip. At the same time, a matter pathway opens for the Middle and Lower Jiao, allowing stagnated matter to quickly dissipate from those areas. Ultimately, the San Jiao will be clear of stagnation, the

Gong Zhuan will circulate normally and the body will quickly return to health.

EXPLANATION OF THE FORMULA

- *Du Huo* leads energy in the head downward to the Lower Jiao via the Wai Jiao space. A dosage of 30 grams of Du Huo pulls energy from the tip of the tongue and dissipates lung area energy. This allows liver energy to also dissipate and the liver to recover. Using 30 grams of Du Huo is important as the dosage must be adequate to dissipate the excess energy in the Upper Jiao and re-plenish the energy deficiency of the Lower Jiao. The abdominal pain experienced by the patient is caused by *qi* and blood block-age. This symptom is relieved by Du Huo, which pulls energy downwards, thereby causing *qi* and blood to flow freely.

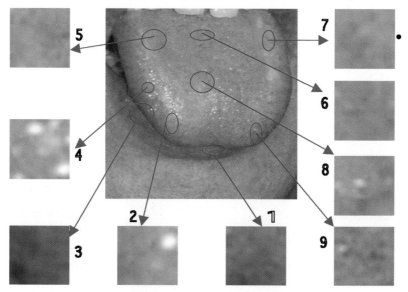

Photo 38. Analysis of Tongue 11-#1

Gong Ying clears the Wai Jiao body space and dissipates energy all around. It reduces the pressure of the space and enables faster transformation of matter to energy. A dosage of 17 grams dissi-pates infections by clearing the excess energy in the space.

- The Body Space Medicine use of just two herbs, Du Huo and Gong Ying, can solve all the symptoms of this patient.

CASE 13: HYPERTENSION (HIGH BLOOD PRESSURE)

Consultation #1: 2006.01.08

ID: 13   **Sex:** Female

Symptoms: Cold feeling around the navel, occasional dizziness, hypertension, fatigue, pain in the legs, anxiety. The tongue is shown in Photo 39.

Stool/Urine: Stool once a day in the morning.

Formula: Chi Shao 17 g, Jin Yin Hua 17 g, Gui Zhi 7 g, Du Huo 30 g, Pei Lan 17 g.

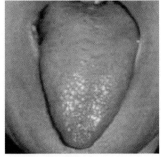

Photo 39. Tongue 13-#1 (2006.01.08)

PATHOLOGY

Photo 40 shows the details of the tongue analysis. This type of tongue looks like a stick, so it is called a *stick tongue*. The tongue is also offset to the right side of the mouth. The whole tongue shows

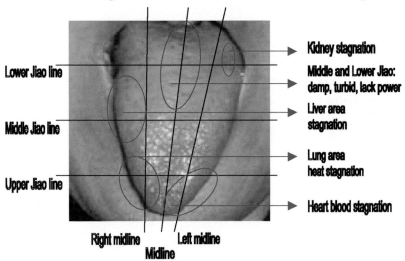

Photo 40. Analysis of Tongue 13-#1 (2006.01.08)

stagnation. From the tip of the tongue to the middle of the tongue are many stagnation spots, as shown in the close-ups in Photo 41.

The tongue is purple in color but the tip is red. The tongue tip has many blood stagnation spots and several prominent blisters.

The tongue narrows from the Middle Jiao line to the tip. This area of the tongue is also very hard and has no coating. However, the middle and the root of the tongue have a sticky yellow coating. The right side of the tongue is also larger than the left side.

The above conditions all result from stagnation. The heat stagnation around the heart and excess energy in the lung area both contribute to the stagnation above the diaphragm (in the Upper Jiao). There is an imbalance in the distribution of water between the right and left sides of the body, as indicated by the right side of the tongue being larger. The narrowing of the tip of the tongue is the result of matter stagnation inside the cells; matter cannot transform and energy cannot dissipate. This blocks the transformation of matter and energy in the Middle and Lower Jiao, with the result that dampness and turbidity collect below the diaphragm. The effect is similar to a six-lane highway suddenly narrowing down to three lanes, with ensuing traffic jams.

To solve the problems described, the first priority is to dissipate the stagnation at the tip of the tongue. This is done by activating the matter in the cells of the Upper Jiao, which provides a path for matter to move up from the lower parts of the body, thereby allowing San Jiao energy to flow freely. Using this treatment approach can resolve all symptoms and allow the patient to recover.

EXPLANATION OF THE FORMULA

- *Chi Shao* promotes blood circulation. It removes blood stagnation in the blood vessels.

- *Jin Yin Hua* dissipates the excess energy and impurities in the space of the lungs. It reduces the pressure of the space and promotes the transformation of matter to energy.

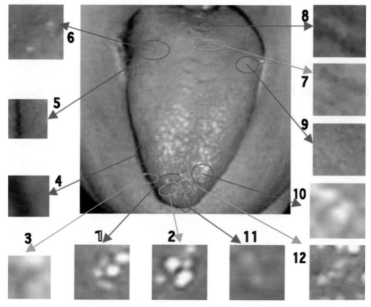

Photo 41. Close-ups of Tongue 13-#1 (2006.01.08)

- *Gui Zhi* balances the transformation between matter inside cells and energy outside cells.

- *Du Huo* promotes the downward movement of energy from the head to the toes, which charges the Lower Jiao, promotes Gong Zhuan circulation and nourishes the kidneys and the brain.

- *Pei Lan* removes the dampness and turbid energy in the Middle Jiao, promotes the flow of water and balances the water in the body.

Case 14: Intestinal Inflammation

Consultation #1: 2006.01.02

ID: 14   **Sex:** Male   **Age:** 33

Symptoms: Itchiness of the whole body, chronic inflammation of the intestines, swollen and painful lymph glands in the right lower jaw. The tongue is shown in Photo 42.

Stool/Urine: Stool once in the morning immediately upon waking, loose in form.

Formula: Gui Zhi 7 g, Jin Yin Hua 17 g, Ma Huang 4 g.

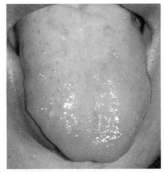

Photo 42. Tongue 14-#1 (Before Treatment)

DISCUSSION OF TREATMENT

Photo 42 shows the condition of the tongue before treatment was given. At the consultation, treatment was promptly given in the form of writing out and chanting the herb formula for less than thirty seconds. Immediately afterwards, Photo 43 of the tongue was taken.

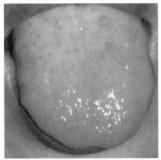

Photo 43. Tongue 14-#2 (After Treatment by Message Healing)

The differences in the tongue conditions before and after treatment are quite clear. After treatment, the tip of the tongue is wider, the coating thinner, and the bump at the front of the tongue flatter. This shows that the prescribed formula is effective. It also shows that writing and chanting the formula without any physical herbs is an effective healing technique (a form of *message healing*).

Post-consultation, the patient's follow-up treatment included taking preparations of the physical herbs and continuing to chant the formula.

PATHOLOGY

Photo 44 shows the details of the tongue analysis. The whole tongue organ is thick, fat, wet and light purple in color. The tip of the tongue is indented, the front section is red, and the left side of the tip is thicker than the right side. Both sides of the tongue are raised in the middle, with the left edge protruding outwards. In particular, the Shan Zhong area is high and raised. There are white blisters on the top of the tongue and the root of the tongue has a thick white coating.

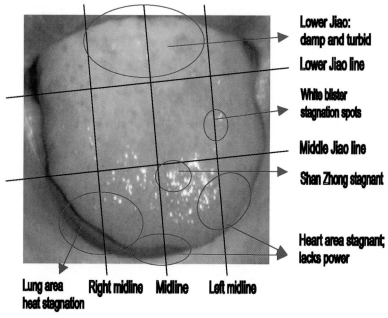

Photo 44. Analysis of Tongue 14-#1 (2006.01.02)

The bump or raised area in the Shan Zhong area of the tongue means matter in the cells is stagnant. Since energy is not dissipating, it blocks the transformation of matter and energy in the Middle Jiao and Lower Jiao. The blockage manifests in the tongue conditions and the observed symptoms.

The itchiness of the whole body is due to heat stagnation in the cells. The chronic inflammation of the intestines is due to Upper Jiao blockage. Dysfunction of the digestive system results when energy cannot move in the Middle and Lower Jiao. Consequently, cell activity is low and movement is very slow in the intestines.

To solve all these issues, treatment must first solve the problem at the front of the tongue — Upper Jiao stagnation and blockage. Treatment should focus on reducing the thickness of the tongue and dissipating the stagnation. Then matter will move and energy flow freely within the Middle and Lower Jiao. Once this is achieved, the body will return to health.

EXPLANATION OF THE FORMULA

- *Gui Zhi* adjusts matter and energy conditions inside and outside the cells.

- *Jin Yin Hua* removes excessive energy in the space of the lungs, thereby reducing the pressure of the space.

- *Ma Huang* opens the cells to dissipate energy and matter.

- This three-herb combination promotes and speeds up the transformation of matter to energy within the cells. The energy generated moves out of the cells into the body space to clear the heat and stagnation of the body.

CASE 15: KIDNEY CANCER, LIVER TUMOR, DIABETES

Consultation #1: 2005.11.08

ID: 15   **Sex:** Male   **Age:** 44

Symptoms: The patient previously received an operation for a cancerous left kidney. Post-operation, there is a tumor in the blood vessels of the liver, pain in the liver area, stuffiness in the chest and diabetes. The tongue is shown in Photo 45.

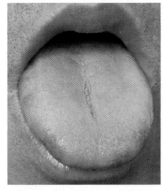

Photo 45. Tongue 15-#1 (2005.11.08)

Stool/Urine: Stool once or twice a day.

Formula: Gui Zhi 12 g, Lian Qiao 17 g, Wu Zei Gu 30 g.

PATHOLOGY

Details of the tongue analysis are shown in Photo 46. The tongue is full, thick, purple and has no coating. The tongue lacks energy. There is a ridge and cracks along the midline of the Middle and Lower Jiao areas of the tongue, indicating water imbalance. The dark coloration in the areas of the liver, kidneys and lungs along the edge of the tongue indicate stagnation in all three areas of the San Jiao — the Upper, Middle and Lower Jiao — as manifested by the liver tumor, diabetes, kidney and water issues. The root problem stems from the lack of driving force for the Ming Men as evidenced by the condition of the tongue in the Lower Jiao.

In traditional Chinese medicine, the Ming Men is considered the source of the San Jiao and is associated with Kidney *yang* (i.e., kidney function). Kidney *yang* provides the driving force for the body's functions. The kidneys in the Lower Jiao regulate water in the body and store the body's congenital essence, *yuan qi*, inherited from the parents. The kidneys work with the San Jiao to transform *qi* and move water. Consequently, improper functioning of the Kidneys depletes *yuan qi* and Ming Men fire.

In this case, the tongue condition shows that *yuan qi* is lacking; kidney *yang* is inadequate. There is not enough drive to properly transform *qi* in the Lower Jiao, digest food and clear the turbid from the light in the Middle Jiao, and distribute fluids in the Upper Jiao. This results in Middle Jiao stagnation, inaction of the stomach and intestines leading to blocked energy and matter, pain in the liver area, etc., which the tongue displayed. Middle Jiao stagnation in turn leads to inaction of the Upper Jiao, where the inactivity of the lung and heart showed on the tongue as heart and lung stagnation, which the patient experienced as stuffiness in the chest.

EXPLANATION OF THE FORMULA

- *Gui Zhi* opens the cell walls, adjusts and balances matter inside and energy outside the cells.

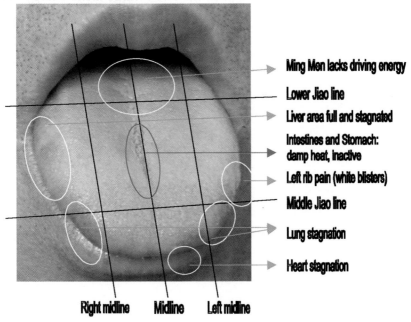

Ming Men lacks driving energy

Lower Jiao line

Liver area full and stagnated

Intestines and Stomach: damp heat, inactive

Left rib pain (white blisters)

Middle Jiao line

Lung stagnation

Heart stagnation

Right midline   Midline   Left midline

Photo 46. Analysis of Tongue 15-#1 (2005.11.08)

- *Lian Qiao* dispels the heat and energy generated from the energy-matter transformation action of Gui Zhi.

- *Wu Zei Gu* acts on the Middle Jiao. It disperses energy stagnation in the liver and stomach, increases the return flow of blood to the spleen and helps the spleen dissipate blood stasis.

- This formula engages and activates the cells of the whole body to restore the body's health.

Consultation #2: 2005.11.15

Symptoms: The patient previously received an operation for a cancerous left kidney. Post-operation, the patient has a tumor in the blood vessels of the liver, pain in the liver area, stuffiness in the chest, diabetes and high blood pressure. The tongue is shown in Photo 47.

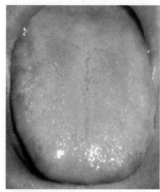

Stool/Urine: Stool once or twice a day in the morning.

Photo 47. Tongue 15-#2
(2005.11.15)

Formula: Chao Zao Ren 7 g, Gui Zhi 7 g, Jie Geng 6 g, Ge Geng 17 g.

DISCUSSION OF TREATMENT

Photo 47 shows the condition of the tongue after one week of Body Space Medicine herb treatment. The tongue shows less stagnation, the dark areas along the edges of the tongue are not as dark, the color of the tongue body is paler and not as purple, the tongue is not as thick and full, the ridge along the median is shallower, and the tongue now has a clear coating. These improvements in the tongue mirror the changes in the body, indicating the formula prescribed in Consultation #1 is effective in improving the body's health.

EXPLANATION OF THE FORMULA

Based on the condition of the tongue presented in Consultation #2, the prescription is changed to strengthen the function of the heart, dissipate the stagnation in the lungs, relieve the pressure on the liver and kidneys, and open the exit for the lungs in the back.

- *Chao Zao Ren* increases the pumping power of the heart to push blood to the four extremities. It increases the density and pressure in the space around the left atrium and the left ventricle, which nourishes the heart, strengthens the bones and tendons, and strengthens the back.

- *Jie Geng* opens the exit for the lungs, allowing turbidity to sink, clears the lungs by reducing lung pressure and lifting lung *qi*, and moves energy up from the level of the ribs.

- *Ge Geng* opens the capillary system in the muscles of the back to eliminate heat and to moisten the muscle cells.

CASE 16: KIDNEY INFECTION

Consultation #1: 2006.02.10

ID: 16   **Sex:** Male   **Age:** 42

Symptoms: Kidney infection, back pain, sore and swollen legs, bloating of the stomach, phlegm. The tongue is shown in Photo 48.

Stool/Urine: Stool once a day in the morning.

Formula: Pei Lan 17 g, Gui Zhi 7 g, Lian Qiao 17 g, Du Zhong 7 g, Du Huo 17 g, Jiao San Xian 15 g each.

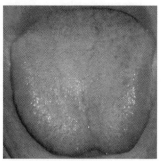

Photo 48. Tongue 16-#1 (Before Treatment)

PATHOLOGY

Photo 49 shows the analysis of the tongue before the patient was treated. The whole tongue is fat, thick and purple; it shows heavy stagnation. The tongue is skewed to the left and the tip is indented. The two sides beside the tip are fat and thick. The Shan Zhong area in the front part of the tongue has a trench and is dark (esophagus area).

The Middle Jiao area is raised, signifying that the Middle Jiao area of the body is blocking the upward movement of matter and energy from the Lower Jiao. Consequently, the Lower Jiao matter is stuck and stagnated. When the cells in the foundation energy center of the Lower Jiao cannot transform and regenerate normally, the Lower Jiao will be weak, the kidneys will not be nourished, and back and leg pain will result.

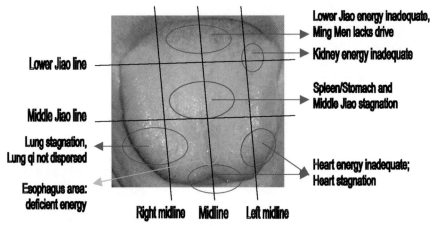

Photo 49. Analysis of Tongue 16-#1 (Before Treatment)

At the same time, energy in the space of the Middle Jiao is too high (raised middle section of the tongue); matter cannot transform and is therefore stagnated. Stomach *qi* cannot rise and lung *qi* cannot sink. The spleen and stomach are weak, the stomach is bloated, the lung *qi* cannot distribute, and the shoulders and back have discomfort.

These problems are solved by first resolving the stagnation issue in the Middle Jiao. The raised area in the Middle Jiao area of the tongue must be leveled through persistent treatment. When the congestion in the Middle Jiao starts moving up, the Shan Zhong area in the front part of the tongue will naturally level. As lung qi begins to distribute, the matter and energy of the San Jiao will have a pathway to move, the body's clearing action of *lightness ascends, turbidity sinks* will be able to function, the Gong Zhuan can circulate freely, and the body will recover its health.

EXPLANATION OF THE FORMULA

- *Pei Lan* clears the Middle Jiao water pathway. It clears dampness and damp turbidity in the Middle Jiao, opens the stomach and nourishes the spleen.

- *Gui Zhi* opens the cell walls, relaxes the cells and softens the tension within the cells. It adjusts the balance and transformation between matter inside cells and energy outside cells.

- *Lian Qiao* instantly clears the energy and heat radiated out of the cells. It clears the field around the heart, disperses the energy in the lung space, exercises the spleen and stomach and raises spleen *qi.* Used with Gui Zhi, it disperses the heat generated from the action of Gui Zhi in the body.

- *Du Zhong* increases the pressure and energy in the Lower Jiao space. Higher space pressure helps energy transfer into cells faster, transforming and enriching matter inside the cells. It replenishes deficient energy inside and outside the cells.

- *Du Huo* leads the energy in the head down to the legs through the Wai Jiao, charging the Lower Jiao with a big push. A dosage of 30 grams can replenish the energy in the Lower Jiao.

- *Jiao San Xian* enhances the flow of matter and energy within and around the organs of the Middle Jiao. It agitates the movement of energy which then drives the movement of matter, enhances the appetite, eliminates indigestion and restores the functions of the Middle Jiao organs.

DISCUSSION

The tongue is compared before and after treatment. Photo 48, Photo 49 and Photo 51 all show the condition of the tongue before treatment was given. Photo 50 and Photo 52 show the condition of the tongue after treatment with Body Space Medicine herbs.

The post-treatment photos show that the trench in the tongue tip region around the Shan Zhong area is shallower. The thickness on the two sides of the tongue is reduced and the tongue color is paler and not as purple. The whole tongue has narrowed and shows less stagnation. The close-up photographs of select areas of the tongue are not as dark, indicating less density and pressure in those

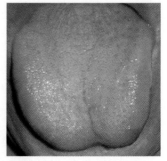

Photo 50. Tongue 19-#2 (After Treatment)

areas. These changes indicate that the Body Space Medicine herb formula is effective. The tongue condition has improved, which reflects the healing changes happening in the body.

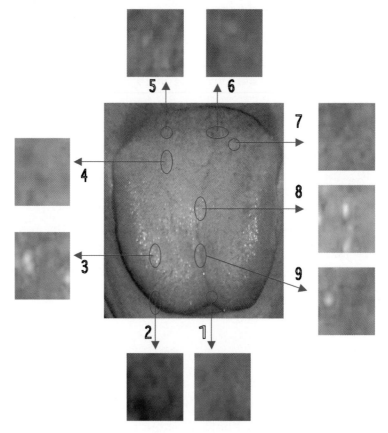

Photo 51. Close-ups of Tongue 16-#1 (Before Treatment)

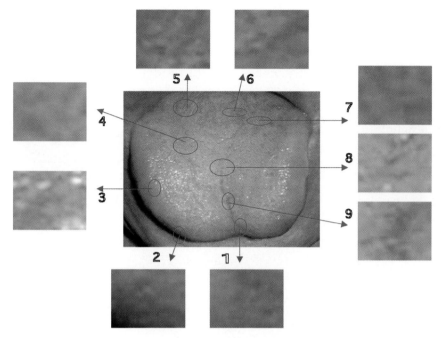

Photo 52. Close-ups of Tongue 16-#2 (After Treatment)

CASE 17: KNEE JOINT DEGENERATION, STOMACH FULLNESS

Consultation #1:

ID: 17 **Sex:** Female

Symptoms: Tight shoulders, feeling of fullness on the right side of the head, degenerative knee joints, fullness in the stomach. The tongue condition is shown in Photo 53.

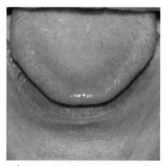

Stool/Urine: Stool twice a day, morning and afternoon; sometimes dry, sometimes loose.

Photo 53. Tongue 17-#1 (Before Treatment)

Formula: Du Huo 30 g, Pei Lan 17 g, Gui Zhi 7 g, Lian Qiao 17 g.

PATHOLOGY

Photo 54 shows the details of the tongue analysis. Overall, the entire tongue is hard and stagnant. It lacks fluid and has no coating. The tongue is raised and curled up at the tip and along the front edges.

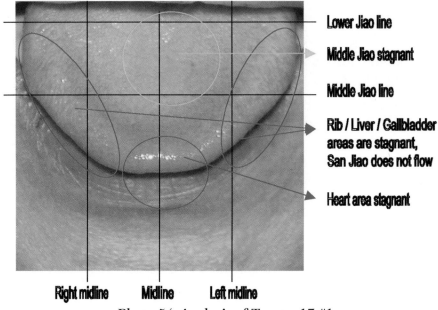

Lower Jiao line

Middle Jiao stagnant

Middle Jiao line

Rib / Liver / Gallbladder areas are stagnant, San Jiao does not flow

Heart area stagnant

Right midline   Midline   Left midline

Photo 54. Analysis of Tongue 17-#1

The purple color of the tongue body and the high raised curl at the front of the tongue indicate the Upper Jiao energy is stagnant and cannot dissipate. This is responsible for the sensations of fullness in the head, heaviness in the chest and heart stagnation symptoms.

The Upper Jiao stagnation not only blocks the movement of matter locally but also blocks the smooth transformation of matter and energy in the Middle Jiao. This causes stagnation of the Middle Jiao and fullness of the stomach.

Treatment to resolve these problems must first flatten the high curl at the front of the tongue so as to allow the cells to vibrate. The stagnated matter can then dissipate from the cells as energy. When energy starts flowing smoothly in the Upper Jiao, it will give the Lower Jiao a big push and drive the Gong Zhuan to circulate normally. The patient's health can then be restored.

Explanation of the Formula

- *Du Huo* promotes Upper Jiao energy to flow downwards. A dosage of 30 grams has the effect of making the energy charge down from the head, boosting the Lower Jiao, nourishing the kidneys and leading Lower Jiao energy upwards. By dissipating Upper Jiao energy, Du Huo activates the energy of the Middle and the Lower Jiao, and normalizes the Gong Zhuan function and circulation.

- *Pei Lan* removes dampness and turbid energy.

- *Gui Zhi* adjusts and balances matter inside the cells and energy outside the cells.

- *Lian Qiao* removes the heat generated by the action of Gui Zhi.

Discussion of Treatment

Photo 55 shows the condition of the tongue after Body Space Medicine herb treatment. The tongue appears completely different after treatment.

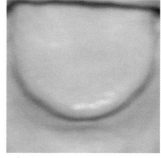

Prior to treatment, the tongue color was purple and the tongue body hard and stagnant. The tongue had no coating and lacked water. The tip and sides of the tongue had bumps and a high curl.

Photo 55. Tongue 17-#2 (After Treatment)

After treatment, the color of the tongue is much lighter, the body is softer and shows much less stagnation, the edge of the tongue is flat and the surface moist. The improvements in the condition of the tongue are evidence that the herb formula prescribed is effective and working well.

CASE 18: LIVER CANCER

Consultation #1: 2005.11.08

ID: 18   **Sex:** Male   **Age:** 52

Symptoms: Liver cancer, cough with phlegm. The tongue is shown in Photo 56.

Stool/Urine: Stool normal, urine yellow.

Formula: Gui Zhi 7 g, Lian Qiao 30 g, Zhe Bei 30 g, Gong Ying 17 g, Dang Gui 7 g.

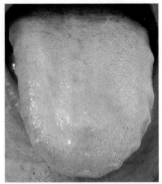

Photo 56. Tongue 18-#1 (2005.11.08)

Pathology

Photo 57 shows the details of the tongue diagnosis. Overall, the tongue is fat and thick, the tip is hard and red, the color is pale and the front and sides are raised, with the right side higher than the left. The middle part has a yellow coating, while the root has a greasy yellow coating.

These conditions indicate the heart has blood stasis; there is accumulated matter which is not moving. The lung energy is high, hot and stagnated. The accumulated matter does not dissipate but stagnates in the lungs, manifesting as a cough.

Lung stagnation also blocks the Five Elements aspect of metal (Lung) generating water (Kidney). Consequently, the kidneys receive no nourishment (lung energy does not descend), which quickly depletes their *yuan qi* (inherited essence).

The damp heat in the Lower Jiao area of the tongue shows inadequate drive in the Lower Jiao, which leads to kidney deficiency and back pain. There is not enough energy in the Lower Jiao to drive the

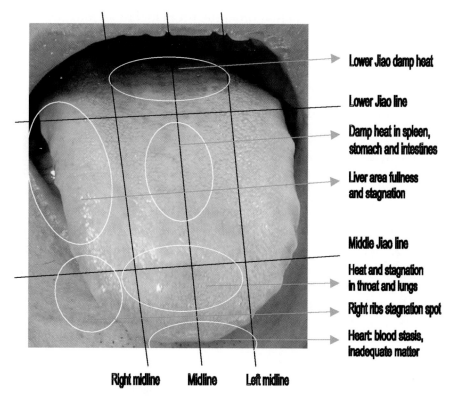

Photo 57. Analysis of Tongue 18-#1 (2005.11.08)

movement of matter and energy in the Middle Jiao, thereby causing swelling and pain in the liver area, and discomfort of the spleen and stomach. Because the Middle Jiao matter is not moving, energy is also not able to radiate and move upwards. The raised area on the right side of the lung region also blocks the energy source of the heart, causing heart blood stasis, matter accumulation and blood deficiency. All these unfavorable conditions of the body are indicated by the tongue analysis, as shown in Photo 57.

EXPLANATION OF THE FORMULA

- *Gui Zhi* opens cells in all parts of the body, coordinates and balances the matter inside the cells and the energy outside the cells.

- *Zhe Bei* dissipates stagnation in the bronchial tubes and air sacs of the lungs, reduces the density of the lung space and nourishes the kidneys. In combination with Lian Qiao and Gong Ying, it clears excess energy and eliminates inflammation in the lung space.

- *Gong Ying* enables the body's energy to be distributed everywhere. This reduces the pressure of the space and stimulates energy in the Wai Jiao space.

- *Dang Gui* increases the density, pressure and energy in the space around the cells, which enriches matter inside the cells and increases the body's stamina. It also improves the flow of blood and qi by increasing the output of arterial blood from the left atrium and left ventricle.

- The use of this formula will adjust and improve the health of the whole body.

Consultation #2: 2005.11.15

Symptoms: Liver cancer, lower abdominal pain. The tongue is shown in Photo 58.

Stool/Urine: Loose stool.

Formula: Dan Shen 17 g, Yin Chen 12 g, Gui Zhi 7 g, Lian Qiao 17 g, Jiao San Xian 15 g each.

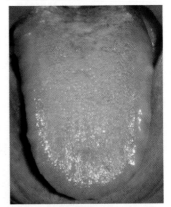

Photo 58. Tongue 18-#2 (2005.11.15)

DISCUSSION OF TREATMENT

Photo 58 shows the change in condition of the tongue after one week of Body Space Medicine herb treatment. The greasy coating is reduced and the tongue is softer, thinner and redder, all of which indicate the efficacy of treatment.

CASE 19: LIVER PAIN, EDEMA, NUMBNESS

Consultation #1: 2006.01.11

ID: 19   **Sex:** Female   **Age:** 48

Symptoms: Edema in the left calf, pain in the area of the liver, soreness in the left toes, numbness on the right side of the body, pressure and pain in the back, apprehension, head discomfort, sore knees. The tongue is shown in Photo 59.

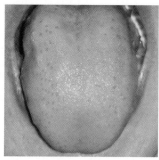

Photo 59. Tongue 19-#1 (2006.01.11)

Stool/Urine: Loose stool once a day in the morning.

Formula: Pei Lan 17 g, Qiang Huo 4 g, Du Huo 30 g.

PATHOLOGY

The tongue analysis is shown in Photo 60. Photo enlargements of selected areas of the same tongue are shown in Photo 61. Overall, the tongue is large and fills the whole mouth. The left side is larger than the right, the edges of both sides are uneven in shape and the tongue tip is slightly indented. The middle part of the tongue is raised, blocking the San Jiao pathway like a hill, with the result that the

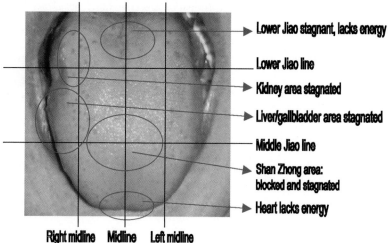

Lower Jiao stagnant, lacks energy

Lower Jiao line

Kidney area stagnated

Liver/gallbladder area stagnated

Middle Jiao line

Shan Zhong area: blocked and stagnated

Heart lacks energy

Right midline   Midline   Left midline

Photo 60. Analysis of Tongue 19-#1 (2006.01.11)

Lower Jiao area is stagnated. The coating is watery and the tongue surface is covered with white blisters and stagnation spots.

The raised area in the middle of the tongue causes matter in the Middle Jiao to accumulate; it cannot dissipate so energy from the lower parts cannot flow up. Consequently, the Upper Jiao does not receive energy from below and the energy from the Lower Jiao cannot exit because of the blockage. As a result, the entire San Jiao (Upper, Middle and Lower Jiao) is stuck, causing the symptoms experienced by the patient.

Treatment must first solve the matter accumulation in the Middle Jiao and dissipate the energy in this area. When the Middle Jiao matter moves, the energy of the chest area follows, clearing the lungs and allowing the heart to be replenished and nourished. This has the effect of filling out the indentation at the tip and leveling the raised area in the middle of the tongue. The Lower Jiao energy will then have a pathway to move up. When this happens, the San Jiao will function normally, the Gong Zhuan will circulate properly and the body will naturally regain its health.

EXPLANATION OF THE FORMULA

- *Pei Lan* clears the water pathway of the Middle Jiao; it clears dampness and turbidity from the energy of the Middle Jiao.

- *Qiang Huo* brings energy upwards, from the toes to the head.

- *Du Huo* leads energy downwards, from the head to the toes.

- *Qiang Huo* and Du Huo create a push-pull action when used together, which promotes circulation of the Gong Zhuan. When these two herbs are used with Pei Lan (which clears damp turbidity), the condition of the body will improve very quickly.

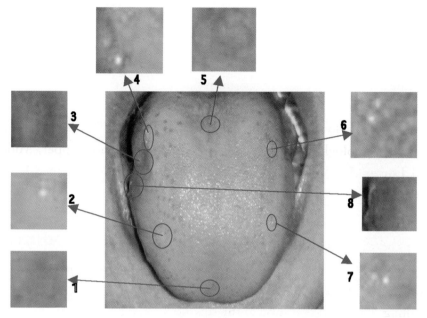

Photo 61. Close-ups of Tongue 19-#1 (2006.01.11)

CASE 20: LUNG CANCER

Consultation #1: 2005.11.06

ID: 20 **Sex:** Male **Age:** 65

Symptoms: Cancer of the right lung, cough with phlegm, heart issues. The tongue is shown in Photo 62.

Stool/Urine: Stool once a day.

Formula: Chao Zao Ren 7 g, Gui Zhi 7 g, Du Zhong 17 g, Fu Shi 17 g.

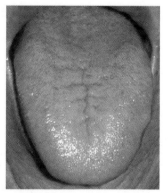

Photo 62. Tongue 20-#1 (2005.11.06)

PATHOLOGY

Photo 63 shows the details of the tongue analysis. Overall, the tongue is dull red in color, lacks moisture and has stagnation spots. There is a greasy yellow coating in the middle and at the root. The front part of the tongue is raised. There are vertical and lateral cracks down the midline, primarily in the Middle Jiao area and the front part of the Lower Jiao area.

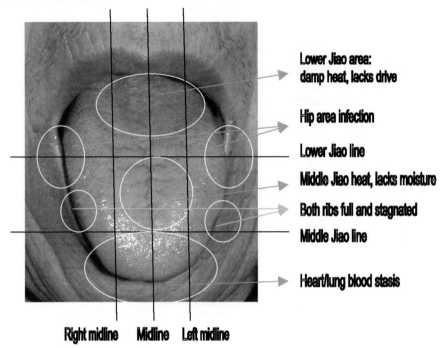

Photo 63. Analysis of Tongue 20-#1 (2005.11.06)

The characteristics of the tongue indicate stagnation in the Upper Jiao (raised front part). The heart area is full and stuffy, showing heat stagnation. The cells are not active enough and matter in the cells cannot dissipate as energy. Consequently, the lung *qi* does not distribute but collects and *takes form*, which causes discomfort and cancer.

Since lung energy cannot descend to nourish the kidneys, it does not generate kidney water, and so the Ming Men drive is inadequate. The stagnation of the Ming Men leads to stagnation in the Lower Jiao, which in turn has inadequate energy to drive or activate the Middle Jiao. Because the San Jiao does not flow, the Gong Zhuan also does not flow. Poor health and dysfunction result.

EXPLANATION OF THE FORMULA

- *Chao Zao Ren* increases the pressure and density of the space around the left atrium, thereby increasing the heart's output flow of blood to the body, which leads to an increase in the return flow of blood to the right atrium. It nourishes the heart, strengthens the bones and tendons, and increases the strength of the back.

- *Gui Zhi* balances matter and energy in and around the cells. When combined with Chao Zao Ren, it nourishes the skin and muscles.

- *Du Zhong* increases the energy and pressure of the Lower Jiao space, which induces the density of matter inside the cells to also increase. It causes energy in the space to quickly return to the cells to enrich the cells with matter. When combined with Gui Zhi and Chao Zao Ren, it resolves issues of matter deficiency in the body.

- *Fu Shi* clears the lung space, dissolves phlegm and clears the water pathway.

- The use of this formula can quickly return the body to a healthy condition.

Consultation #2: 2005.11.11

Symptoms: Cancer of the right lung, cough. The tongue is shown in Photo 64.

Stool/Urine: Stool once a day; normal.

Formula: Lian Qiao 30 g, Gui Zhi 7 g, Zhe Bei 30 g, Du Huo 7 g.

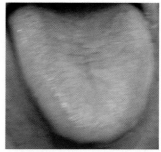

Photo 64. Tongue 20-#2

DISCUSSION

Photo 64 shows the tongue after six days of Body Space Medicine herbal treatment. The coating shows significant improvement, the color of the tongue body is lighter, the body is softer and not as thick. The tongue body shows more moisture and less heat stagnation. These positive changes in the tongue are evidence that the treatment is effective.

For this consultation, the formula is changed to Zhe Bei and Du Huo to increase the activity of the cells in the lungs and the surrounding space. The goal is to lead the lung energy down to the area of the kidneys to strengthen the drive of the Ming Men and Lower Jiao (Metal generates Water), increasing the circulation of the Gong Zhuan.

Consultation #3: 2005.11.19

Symptoms: Less coughing and less phlegm. Tongue tastes salty. Cancer of the right lung; the mediastinum lymph node is swollen. The tongue is shown in Photo 65.

Stool/Urine: Bowel movement in the morning (normal); urine normal.

Formula: Yi Mi Ren 17 g, Xiang Fu 7 g, Gui Zhi 7 g, Fu Shi 17 g.

DISCUSSION

Photo 65 shows the tongue condition after a second week of Body Space Medicine herb treatment. The tongue body is softer, the raised tongue tip is now lower and more level, the cracks in the Middle Jiao are less pronounced, but the Middle Jiao is still full and stuffy, indicating there is not enough movement. The Lower Jiao still shows damp

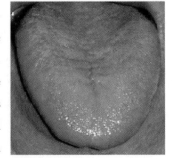

Photo 65. Tongue 20-#3 (2005.11.19)

heat, indicating that the Lower Jiao still does not have enough energy to drive energy upwards to the Middle Jiao.

The new formula uses *Yi Mi Ren* to clear the damp heat around the cells of the Lower Jiao, increase cell stamina, absorb water, nourish *jing qi* and clear the water pathway. *Xiang Fu* opens the spleen door, lifts spleen *qi* up and reduces the pressure in the Middle Jiao space so that the potential for dissipating energy from the cells is stronger. *Gui Zhi* adjusts and balances cells inside and outside by opening cell walls, which speeds the transformation between matter and energy. *Fu Shi* lightens the lungs, removes phlegm and clears dampness from the field and reduces the density of the lung space.

CASE 21: LUNG CANCER, FACIAL NUMBNESS

Consultation #1: 2005.12.12

ID: 21   **Sex:** Male   **Age:** 57

Symptoms: Lung cancer, cough, phlegm clear and sticky or white and bubbled. Fatigue and pain in the left rib area, legs and knees. Transient pain (moves) around the whole body. Numbness on the left side of the forehead, left side of the crown and right side of the lips. The tongue is shown in Photo 66.

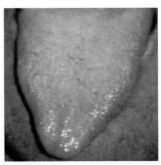

Photo 66. Tongue 21-#1 (2005.12.12)

Stool/Urine: Stool once a day.

Formula: Chi Shao 30 g, Gui Zhi 7 g, Lian Qiao 17 g, Du Huo 17 g, Pei Lan 17 g.

PATHOLOGY

Photo 67 shows the details of the tongue analysis. Overall, the tongue is purple in color, skewed to the right and tapers sharply from the Upper Jiao line forward to the tip of the tongue.

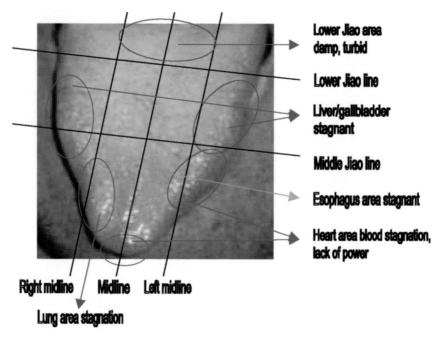

Lower Jiao area damp, turbid

Lower Jiao line

Liver/gallbladder stagnant

Middle Jiao line

Esophagus area stagnant

Heart area blood stagnation, lack of power

Right midline   Midline   Left midline

Lung area stagnation

Photo 67. Analysis of Tongue 21-#1 (2005.12.12)

The whole tongue is hard and stagnant, as indicated by the purple color of the body and the red edges. The entire tongue surface is covered with many white blisters and old blood stagnation spots, which can be seen more clearly in the photo enlargements in Photo 68.

The tip of the tongue has a red bump. Both sides of the Upper Jiao section of the tongue are red (lung and heart stagnation) and there is a slight ridge down the median of this area (esophagus stagnation). The right side of the tongue is bigger and thicker than the left side. There is a sticky yellow coating at the root of the tongue.

The condition of this tongue indicates Upper Jiao stagnation; matter is stagnated in the cells and does not move. This causes blood stagnation in the heart and distension of the lungs as lung *qi* cannot dissipate. Because the Upper Jiao energy does not flow, the energies of the Middle and Lower Jiao have no pathway through which to move up. Consequently, more and more matter and energy accumulate inside the cells. Over time, this ball of congested energy stuck in the body produces many symptoms such as cough, phlegm, fatigue, pain, numbness and even cancerous mutations of cells.

The manifested symptoms associated with the observed problems of this tongue are resolved by tackling the problems at the tongue tip first. Give treatment to eliminate the bump, relax the body and open the tip of the tongue. This activates the matter in the cells so that lung energy can flow smoothly. In so doing, it establishes a path for the transformation of energy and matter for the Middle and Lower Jiao. Once the San Jiao (Upper, Middle and Lower Jiao) energy and matter flow smoothly, the Gong Zhuan function will normalize and the body will return to a healthy condition.

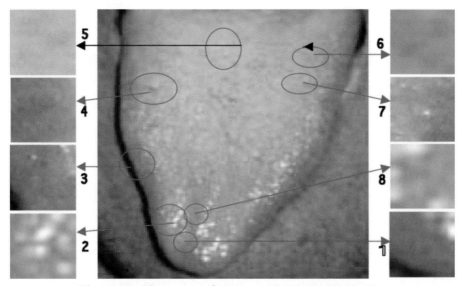

Photo 68. Close-ups of Tongue 21-#1 (2005.12.12)

EXPLANATION OF THE FORMULA

- *Chi Shao* promotes blood circulation and removes blood stagnation in the blood vessels; it opens the path to promote blood flow in the blood vessels.

- *Gui Zhi* balances the transformation between matter inside and energy outside the cells.

- *Lian Qiao* clears the density around the heart by dissipating the energy in the lung space and removes heat from within and around the cells. It lifts spleen *qi* and activates the spleen and the stomach. Lian Qiao also clears the heat generated by the action of Gui Zhi.

- *Du Huo* promotes the downward flow of energy from the head to the toes. This sudden charge of energy gives the Lower Jiao a big push, transforming matter and increasing the energy of the Lower Jiao.

- *Pei Lan* removes dampness and turbidity in the Middle Jiao. It also dissipates dampness and balances the stomach.

Consultation #2: 2005.12.19

Symptoms: Lung cancer (right middle lobe), white phlegm, shortness of breath, fatigue, pain in the extremities, pain in the lower left shoulder blade upon coughing. The tongue is shown in Photo 69.

Stool/Urine: Stool on alternate days, but not dry; urine normal.

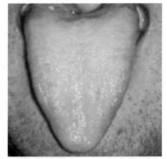

Photo 69. Tongue 21-#2 (2005.12.19)

Formula: Pei Lan 17 g, Gui Zhi 7 g, Lian Qiao 17 g, Chi Shao 7 g, Du Huo 7 g.

Consultation #3: 2005.12.26

Symptoms: Lung cancer (right middle lobe), white phlegm, shortness of breath, fatigue. Pain in the extremities, the lower left lower shoulder blade upon coughing, and in the right rib area. Numbness from the left

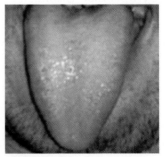

Photo 70. Tongue 21-#3 (2005.12.26)

eyebrow to the crown. Numbness in the area of the right lower lip. The tongue condition is shown in Photo 70.

Stool/Urine: Stool on alternate days.

Formula: Dang Gui 30 g, Chi Shao 17 g, Gui Zhi 7 g, Lian Qiao 17 g, Du Huo 17 g, Bai Tou Weng 30 g.

DISCUSSION OF TREATMENT

Photos 66, 69 and 70 track the changes in the tongue during two successive weeks of Body Space Medicine herb treatments. The coating, shape and color of the tongue show clear changes from week to week. The tongue condition in Consultation #3 (Photo 70) shows that the coating is not as thick or as sticky and has a smaller coverage than before. The shape of the tongue is smoother and the color lighter. The whole tongue is softer and has more vitality. The changes observed in the condition of the tongue indicate that the herb formulas used have been very effective. With continued Body Space Medicine herb treatment, the patient should continue to improve and recover his health.

CASE 22: PANCREATIC CANCER METASTASIZED TO LIVER AND GALLBLADDER

Consultation #1: 2005.11.17

ID: 22   **Sex:** Male   **Age:** 47

Symptoms: Stomach ache after meals or sometimes during the night for the past six months. Cannot tolerate greasy food. The tongue is shown in Photo 71.

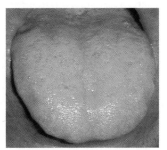

Photo 71. Tongue 22-#1 (2005.11.17)

Stool/Urine: Stool very dry, once every two to three days.

Formula: Zhe Bei 40 g, Bing Lang 30 g, Gui Zhi 7 g, Lian Qiao 17 g, Du Huo 6 g, Da Fu Pi 30 g.

Consultation #2: 2005.11.23

Symptoms: Pancreatic cancer, stomach ache in the morning. Fullness upon eating, therefore not able to eat much. The tongue is shown in Photo 72.

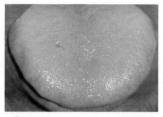

Photo 72. Tongue 22-#2 (2005.11.23)

Stool/Urine: Stool normal but dry, urine yellow.

Formula: Jiao Si Xian 30 g, Pei Lan 17 g, Gui Zhi 7 g, Lian Qiao 17 g.

Consultation #3: 2005.12.07

Symptoms: Pancreatic cancer, stomach ache during the night, pain in the chest area. The tongue is shown in Photo 73.

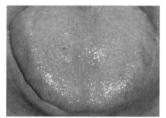

Photo 73. Tongue 22-#3 (2005.12.07)

Stool/Urine: Stool once every two to three days.

Formula: Dang Gui 17 g, Gui Zhi 7 g, Lian Qiao 17 g, Du Huo 7 g, Ma Huang 4 g.

Consultation #4: 2005.12.22

Symptoms: Pancreatic cancer, pain in the area of the liver during the night. Water accumulation in the abdomen, poor appetite. The tongue is shown in Photo 74.

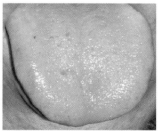

Photo 74. Tongue 22-#4 (2005.12.22)

Stool/Urine: Stool once in the afternoon.

Formula: Chi Shao 17 g, Huo Xiang 12 g, Pei Lan 17 g, Lian Qiao 17 g, Ma Huang 4 g, Du Huo 17 g, Da Fu Pi 30 g, Jiao Si Xian 20 g each.

Consultation #5: 2006.01.01

Symptoms: Pancreatic cancer, pain in the upper abdomen, normal appetite. The tongue is shown in Photo 75.

Stool/Urine: Stool once a day in the morning, normal.

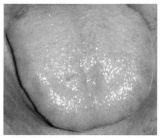

Photo 75. Tongue 22-#5 (2006.01.01)

Formula: Jiao San Xian 15 g each, Dan Shen 17 g, Gui Zhi 7 g, Lian Qiao 17 g, Du Huo 30 g, Da Fu Pi 40 g, Shi Chang Pu 30 g.

Consultation 6: 2006.01.09

Symptoms: Pancreatic cancer, pain in the liver area. The tongue condition is shown in Photo 76.

Stool/Urine: Stool once in two days.

Formula: Pei Lan 17 g, Gui Zhi 7 g, Lian Qiao 17 g, Du Huo 30 g, Da Fu Pi 30 g, Sheng Mai Ya 30 g.

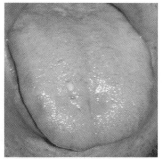

Photo 76. Tongue 22-#6 (2006.01.09)

DISCUSSION OF TREATMENT

After two months of Body Space Medicine herb treatment the cancers of the liver and gallbladder have disappeared; only traces of pancreatic cancer remain. The patient continues to receive ongoing treatment.

PATHOLOGY

Photo 77 shows the details of the tongue analysis from Consultation #6 on January 9, 2006. Close-up details of the same tongue are shown in Photo 78. The general impression of the whole tongue is one of moistness and blood stagnation. The tongue body is thick, big and purple. Its surface is covered with many white blisters. The tip is indented and there is a raised elliptically shaped area in the middle of the tongue. The edges on both sides of the tongue are thick, full and stagnant. The coating at the root of the tongue is yellow and sticky. There is a big white blister surrounded by many stagnation spots in the pancreas area of the tongue.

The condition of this tongue indicates there is too much water in the cells of the body; the cells cannot dissipate the water properly. Because of the stagnated matter in the cells, the energies of the lungs, liver and spleen do not flow smoothly. The Lower Jiao is therefore moist with turbid energy, which prevents the lighter energy from flowing up and the turbid energy from flowing down. The transformation of matter to energy is stagnated inside the body. Therefore, the San Jiao water does not flow well and the Gong Zhuan energy pathway does not circulate

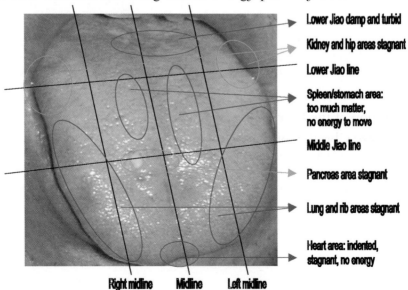

Photo 77. Analysis of Tongue 22-#6 (2006.01.09)

well. These dysfunctions lead to dizziness, irritation and a feeling of heaviness in the chest. The patient lacks energy, has no desire to talk and experiences pain in the areas of the liver, gallbladder, spleen and stomach. The stool is dry and abnormal.

To solve these issues, treatment must first focus on removing the excess water from the cells. Next, the San Jiao space must be fully opened so that the Gong Zhuan can flow freely. Then the body can return to normal health.

EXPLANATION OF THE FORMULA

The herb formula prescribed at Consultation #6 is explained as follows:

- *Pei Lan* dissipates the moist and turbid energy from the Middle Jiao.

- *Da Fu Pi* stimulates the energy of the Middle Jiao in the Wai Jiao body space so that energy can move better. As the Middle Jiao energy moves, it dissipates excess water through the large and small intestines, which remove it as urine. This promotes the movement of energy and matter downward. When *qi* and blood flow easily, it promotes the transformation of energy to matter.

- *Sheng Mai Ya* moves energy in the liver area to the left side of the Middle Jiao (below the diaphragm), which stimulates cellular vibration of the heart, strengthens heart function and balances the energy vibration of the liver and the stomach.

- *Gui Zhi* opens cell walls. It balances the transformation between matter inside the cells and energy outside the cells.

- *Lian Qiao* clears dense energy around the heart, promotes the energy of the spleen and stomach, stimulates spleen *qi* and removes the heat produced by action of Gui Zhi.

- *Du Huo* promotes the sudden downward movement of energy from the head to the feet, pushing strongly on the Lower Jiao to replenish its driving force. This stimulates the transformation of energy and matter in the Lower Jiao and promotes the Gong Zhuan flow in the body.

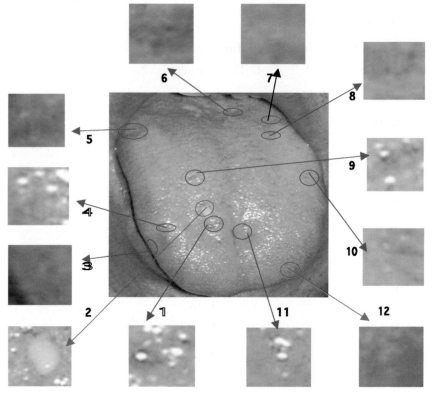

Photo 78. Close-ups of Tongue 22-#6 (2006.01.09)

CASE 23: PROSTATITIS, JOINT PAIN

Consultation #1: 2005.11.13

ID: 23   **Sex:** Male   **Age:** 39

Symptoms: Skin problems, pain in the area of the liver, back and knees, prostatitis, abdominal bloating, apprehension and nervousness at times, high blood pressure. The tongue is shown in Photo 79.

Stool/Urine: Stool once a day in the morning.

Formula: Yi Mi Ren 17 g, Jiao San Xian 15 g each, Gui Zhi 7 g, Lian Qiao 17 g.

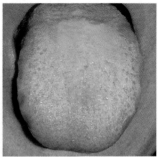

Photo 79. Tongue 23-#1 (2005.11.13)

Consultation #2: 2005.11.27

Symptoms: Prostatitis. Back fatigue. Pain and swelling in the left heel. The tongue is shown in Photo 80.

Stool/Urine: Stool once a day.

Formula: Huo Xiang 12 g, Pei Lan 17 g, Gui Zhi 7 g, Jie Gen 6 g.

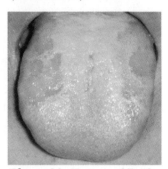

Photo 80. Tongue 23-#2 (2005.11.27)

Consultation #3: 2006.01.11

Symptoms: Prostatitis. Back fatigue and back pain. Rapid heartbeat. Intermittent pain in both heels, knee pain, poor sleep, skin problems. The tongue is shown in Photo 81.

Stool/Urine: Stool 1 to 2 times per day; urine flow incomplete.

Formula: Pei Lan 17 g, Qiang Huo 4 g, Du Huo 30 g.

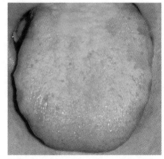

Photo 81. Tongue 23-#3 (2006.01.11)

PATHOLOGY

Details of the tongue analysis from Consultation #1 are shown in Photo 82. The entire tongue has a wet, watery coating. The tongue is large, fills the mouth and is slightly skewed towards the right. From the navel up to the tip, the tongue body is fat, thick, soft and lacks energy.

The tip is red and indented; the surface has white blisters and blood stasis spots. The edges of the two sides and the Shan Zhong area are raised. The coating in the Lower Jiao is thick and greasy.

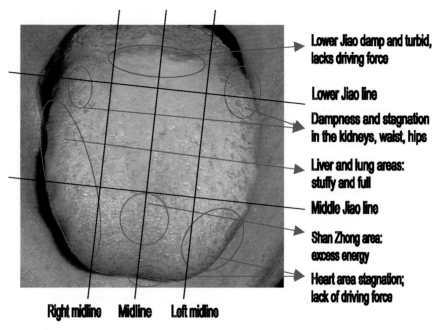

Right midline   Midline   Left midline

Photo 82. Analysis of Tongue 23-#1 (2005.11.13)

These tongue characteristics indicate there is too much water in the cells blocking the exit of energy. In particular, lung *qi* cannot be distributed and the lung cells remain inactive. Matter accumulates as it cannot move or dissipate properly. The matter-energy inside the lungs does not clear properly, with the result that the areas of the chest, ribs, liver and gallbladder in the Middle Jiao feel bloated and stuffy. Middle Jiao fullness also blocks the movement of the Lower Jiao energy. Traditional Chinese Medicine understands this pathological symptom with the teaching: *Qi accumulates into form; qi dissolves into wind.*

To treat the symptoms displayed, first solve the water issue inside the cells by providing an exit for the water. When the water in the cells starts to flow, matter will dissolve and the lung *qi* will open, allowing the energy above the diaphragm to move up. At the same time, the matter in the Middle Jiao region of the liver, gallbladder, spleen and stomach now has an exit. Areas with energy accumulation will begin to dissipate and Lower Jiao matter and energy will also begin moving smoothly. When the body attains normal flow in the San Jiao, the Gong Zhuan will circulate normally, recovery will occur and good health will prevail.

EXPLANATION OF THE FORMULA

- *Yi Mi Ren* absorbs excess water in the body from the cells and passes it out as urine. It clears the damp heat in the space surrounding the cells, absorbs water, nourishes *jing qi* (reproductive energy stored in the kidneys) and clears the water pathways.

- *Jiao San Xian* enhances the flow of matter and energy within and around every organ of the Middle Jiao. It allows energy to move up and down, driving the movement of matter, restoring the functions of the Middle Jiao organs, enhancing appetite and eliminating indigestion.

- *Gui Zhi* balances cells inside and out. It opens the cell walls, allowing matter and energy to transform freely inside and outside the cells, and adjusts imbalances.

- *Lian Qiao* reduces the heat in the Upper Jiao space by dissipating it through the skin pores, clears the field around the heart, dissipates energy in the lung space, exercises the spleen and stomach, and increases spleen *qi.*

- *Lian Qiao* (in combination with Gui Zhi) reduces the heat released by the action and adjustments of Gui Zhi.

DISCUSSION OF TREATMENT

This case study shows the changes in tongue condition after two months of Body Space Medicine treatment. Photo 83 compares the condition of the patient's tongue at three consultations. The pictures clearly show the changes in the tongue before and after taking herbs. The image on the left shows the tongue condition before treatment at the patient's first consultation (November 13, 2005). The tongue color is purple, there is heavy dampness, there is a fog-like white coating that covers the entire tongue surface, and the tongue tip and the sides of the tongue have heavy stagnation. The center image shows the tongue after two weeks of treatment (November 27, 2005) and the image on the right shows the tongue condition after two months of treatment (January 11, 2006). Continued improvement was observed each time.

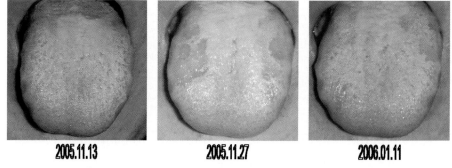

2005.11.13   **2005.11.27**   **2006.01.11**

Photo 83. Analysis of Tongue 23-#1 (2005.11.13)

Overall, the tongue color is paler; it is not as purple or red as before. The indented area at the tongue tip is not as pronounced and the thick greasy coating has started to dissipate. There are fewer stagnation spots and white blisters. The whole tongue body has stretched and relaxed as a result of better San Jiao and Gong Zhuan flow. As of January 11, 2006, the patient had undergone two months of Body Space Medicine treatment and was advised to continue treatment.

CASE 24: PSORIASIS

Consultation #1: 2005.11.06

ID: 24   **Sex:** Male   **Age:** 23

Symptoms: Psoriasis. The tongue is shown in Photo 84.

Stool/Urine: Stool 1 to 2 times per day.

Formula: Pei Lan 17 g, Bai Zhu 7 g, Gui Zhi 7 g, Du Zhong 12gm.

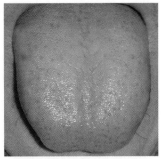

Photo 84. Tongue 24-#1 (2005.11.06)

Consultation #2: 2005.11.13

Symptoms: Psoriasis. The tongue is shown in Photo 85.

Stool/Urine: Stool 1 to 2 times per day.

Formula: Pei Lan 17 g, Bai Zhu 7 g, Gui Zhi 7 g, Du Zhong 12 g.

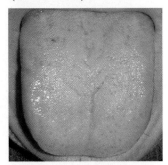

Photo 85. Tongue 24-#2 (2005.11.13)

Consultation #3: 2006.01.01

Symptoms: Psoriasis all over; itchiness. The tongue is shown in Photo 86.

Stool/Urine: Stool twice per day, dry; urine yellow.

Formula: Chi Shao 17 g, Gui Zhi 7 g, Lian Qiao 17 g, Chan Tui 6 g, Dang Gui 17 g, Chao Si Xian 15 g each, Du Huo 17 g.

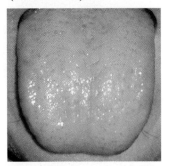

Photo 86. Tongue 24-#3 (2006.01.01)

PATHOLOGY

The following discussion is based on the analysis of the tongue first shown in Photo 84 of Consultation #1, and detailed in Photo 87 and Photo 88. The whole tongue is big, thick and full and has no coating. It is purple in color, has an indentation at the tip and a gully down the midline. The surface has stagnation spots and white blisters. The two sides are raised.

These conditions indicate excessive water in the cells; water is trapped inside the cells and not moving. The situation is analogous to farm land that is flooded; the land is soaked with water, and nothing can grow. Similarly, the excess water trapped inside the cells affects a person's health. Without proper passageways to dissipate, the excess water accumulates inside the body, causing fullness in the chest and lungs.

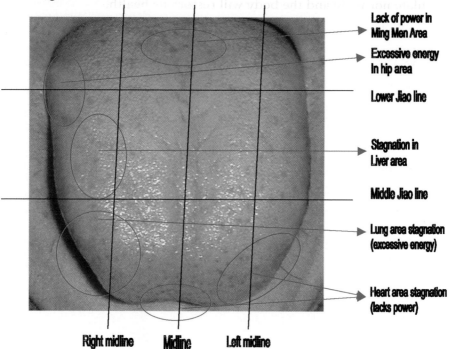

Photo 87. Analysis of Tongue 24-#1 (2005.11.06)

Too much energy in the chest and Upper Jiao prevents the lung *qi* from distributing and blocks the movement of matter in its pathway like a wall. As a result, Lower Jiao matter and energy also cannot move properly, with the result that there is inadequate drive for the Lower Jiao energy to move up.

To solve the situation, the water issue must be tackled first — provide an exit for the water to quickly flow out.

Once the accumulated water inside the cells disperses, the lung pressure will reduce and the blocked matter in the Middle Jiao will start moving and dispersing.

The Middle Jiao will then have space to allow Lower Jiao matter and energy to move up. The Meng Men will activate and the San Jiao will flow smoothly. The outcome is that the Gong Zhuan will start to circulate normally and the body will restore its health.

EXPLANATION OF THE FORMULA

- *Pei Lan* dissipates water and removes dampness and turbidity in the Middle Jiao.

- *Bai Zhu* increases energy in the space of the Middle Jiao, increases the density inside and outside the cells, increases the pressure in the space and promotes the transformation of energy to matter.

- *Gui Zhi* balances cells internally and externally, opens cell walls and promotes the free transformation between matter and energy inside and outside the cells.

- *Du Zhong* increases energy and increases the pressure in the Lower Jiao. It increases the density both within and around the cells and enables the energy in the space to enter the cells, thus quickly enriching the cells with matter (as energy transforms into matter). This nourishes energy deficiency inside the cells as well as the *Du* meridian and the kidneys.

- Du Zhong, Bai Zhu and Gui Zhi work together to resolve the matter blockage and energy deficiency problem in the body.

The three photos taken of the tongue show the condition of the tongue before and after treatments. Photos 84, 87 and 88 show the condition of the tongue at Consultation #1 before treatment, Photo 85 at

Consultation #2 after one week of treatment, and Photo 86 at Consultation #3 after almost two months of treatment.

Clearly, the tongue can be seen to have undergone key changes between consultations. The tongue coating showed significant changes and the body color lightened. The original raised areas on both sides of the tongue have been reduced and the cracks on the midline are smaller and less pronounced. The indentation at the tip of the tongue is also smaller. The symptoms of stagnation are much reduced for the whole tongue — the tongue is less tense, the stagnation spots and white blisters are reduced — evidence that the treatment is effective.

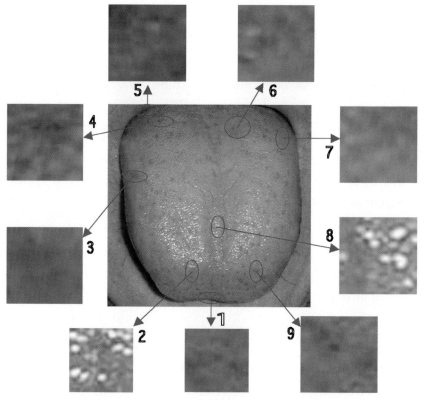

Photo 88. Close-ups of Tongue 24-#1 (2005.11.06)

CASE 25: RHEUMATOID ARTHRITIS, AMENORRHEA

Consultation #1: 2005.11.28

ID: 25   **Sex:** Female   **Age:** 28

Symptoms: Rheumatoid arthritis. The tongue is shown in Photo 89.

Stool/Urine: Normal.

Formula: Dan Pi 30 g, Jin Yin Hua 17 g, Bo He 10 g, Jiao San Xian 15 g each, Du Huo 6 g.

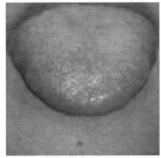

Photo 89. Tongue 25-#1 (2005.11.28)

Consultation #2: 2005.12.25

Symptoms: Rheumatoid arthritis. Pain throughout the whole body, particularly at the cervix. Blood deficiency. No menstruation for over one year (amenorrhea). The tongue is shown in Photo 90.

Stool/Urine: Stool once a day in the morning, urine normal.

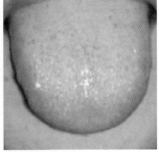

Photo 90. Tongue 25-#2 ((2005.12.25)

Formula: Chi Shao 17 g, Gong Ying 30 g, Gui Zhi 7 g, Lian Qiao 17 g, Du Huo 17 g.

Consultation #3: 2006.01.16

Symptoms: Rheumatoid arthritis, pain in the cervix. No menstruation for a year and a half (amenorrhea). Blood deficiency, headache, edema in the legs and soreness in the back. The tongue is shown in Photo 91.

Stool/Urine: Stool once a day, loose.

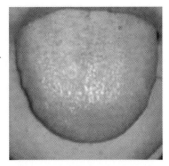

Photo 91. Tongue 25-#3 (2006.01.16)

Formula: Jin Yin Hua 17 g, Du Huo 17 g, Gui Zhi 7 g, Lian Qiao 17 g, Shi Chang Pu 30 g.

PATHOLOGY

Photo 92 shows the tongue analysis for the tongue condition presented in Consultation #1 on November 28, 2005 prior to treatment. Photo 93 shows photo enlargements for selected areas of the same tongue. The darker areas of the tongue generally indicate greater density, identifying more serious conditions and areas of focus for treatment.

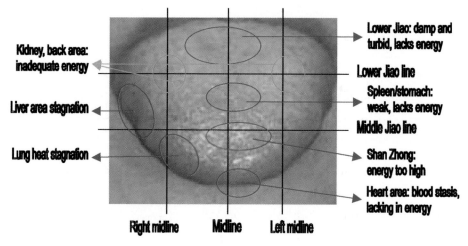

Photo 92. Analysis of Tongue 25-#1 (2005.11.28)

The tongue has three raised areas and three dented areas. The three raised areas are (a) the edges along the tip of the tongue, (b) the Shan Zhong area and (c) the spleen and stomach area in the Middle Jiao. The three dented areas are (a) the tongue tip, (b) below the chest and the diaphragm and (c) the Ming Men area below the navel.

The tongue is purple; its surface has blood stasis and is covered with many white blisters. Behind the Middle Jiao area, the coating is yellow and greasy. The whole tongue is fat, thick, soft and lacks energy. This is due to the tongue tip being raised, which indicates matter and energy accumulating, becoming immobile and forming an obstacle.

The situation is like having a gate in the middle of a water channel; the gate blocks the channel so water cannot flow. In the case of the tongue, the Upper Jiao is stagnated and cannot move; it is the gate that blocks the Lower Jiao exits and causes matter to accumulate. This leads to headache, chest distension, edema, sore back, and so on.

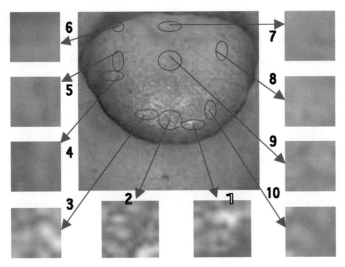

Photo 93. Close-up of Tongue 25-#1 (2005.11.28)

Continuing the analogy of the body as a channel of water, these observed problems can be solved by opening the gate to release the water in the channel so that it can flow normally and unimpeded. In the body, this means opening the exit for the Upper Jiao, which then provides an exit for the flow of energy and matter in the Middle and Lower Jiao. Then the San Jiao will clear and the Gong Zhuan will function normally, with the effect that the body will return to health.

EXPLANATION OF THE FORMULA

- *Dan Pi* clears the stagnated heat in the blood inside the cells; it also adjusts the *qi* in the blood.

- *Jin Yin Hua* reduces the excess energy in the lungs without affecting the lung function of producing and distributing *yuan qi* (acquired *qi* from food and air). It turns damp heat in the cells to energy and matter.

- *Bo He* transforms matter in the cells to energy and dissipates this energy outward and up through the layers of the body to the skin. In so doing, the energy moves through every space of the body, colliding and interacting with them, eventually reaching the surface to relieve surface conditions. It also enables stagnated energy in the liver region to dissipate through the Wai Jiao space to the surface of the body.

- *Jiao San Xian* clears the energy of the Middle Jiao, enabling energy to move up and down. The resulting activity of the Middle Jiao cells increases appetite and restores the function of the Middle Jiao organs.

- *Du Huo* leads energy downwards from the head to the feet, giving the Lower Jiao a turbo boost. This provides driving force for the Lower Jiao energy and matter to move upward and stimulates the normal circulation of the Gong Zhuan.

DISCUSSION OF TREATMENT

Photo 89 shows the condition of the patient's tongue at Consultation #1 before treatment. Photos 90 and 91 show the follow-up condition of the tongue at Consultations #2 and #3, respectively. The color variations and density of selected regions for each tongue can be seen in the photo enlargements of Photo 93, Photo 94 and Photo 95, respectively. The photographs show the change in condition, color, shape and density of the tongue over six weeks of Body Space Medicine herb treatment.

Photos 89, 92 and 93 have already been discussed under Pathology.

Photo 90 and Photo 94 show the tongue condition at Consultation #2 on Dec 25, 2005. This tongue is the result of taking the herb formula given in Consultation #1 for four weeks. The color is paler, the internal heat stagnation inside the cells has dissipated and the shape of the tongue is more elongated (particularly in the stagnated areas). The dents on the tongue midline in the Lower Jiao Ming Men area and the Middle Jiao area have flattened but the two sides along the midline are still somewhat raised and retain a greasy yellow coating.

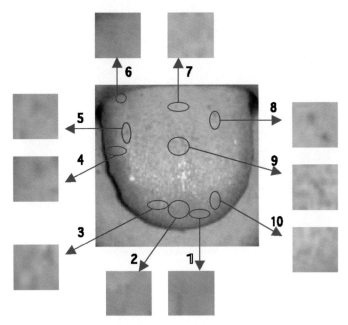

Photo 94. Close-up of Tongue 25-#2 (2005.12.25)

Photo 91 and Photo 95 show the tongue condition at Consultation #3 on January 16, 2006. This tongue is the result of taking the herb formula given on December 25, 2005 for three weeks. The color of the tongue is actually darker than the tongue of the previous consultation, as shown in Photo 90.

However, a darker tongue color after herb treatment is not necessarily cause for alarm as the whole tongue must be analyzed to determine the body's overall condition. On further analysis, it can be seen that the proportion of flat area in the Upper Jiao area of the tongue tip has actually increased (as if the tongue was preparing a foundation). The white blisters in the Shan Zhong area in the front part of the tongue are now less clustered than before, which indicates that the accumulated matter and energy inside the cells are separating and moving. The blockage in the Upper Jiao is indeed dissipating, showing that the prescription is working as intended.

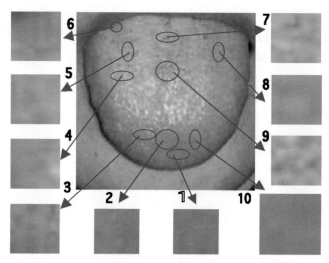

Photo 95. Close-up of Tongue 25-#3 (2006.01.16)

CASE 26: RICKETS (OSTEOMALACIA)

Consultation #1: 2006.01.18

ID: 26   **Sex:** Male   **Age:** 16

Symptoms: Rickets (osteomalacia). Discomfort in the left hip, spinal column and sides. The tongue is shown in Photo 96.

Stool/Urine: Stool once or twice a day.

Formula: Pei Lan 17 g, Gui Zhi 7 g, Lian Qiao 17 g, Du Huo 17 g.

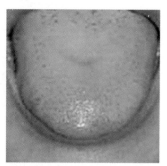

Photo 96. Tongue 26-#1 (2006.01.18)

Consultation #2: 2006.01.24

Symptoms: Rickets (osteomalacia). Pain throughout the body, left hip bone is soft, eye issues. The tongue is shown in Photo 97.

Stool/Urine: Stool once or twice a day.

Formula: Pei Lan 17 g, Gui Zhi 7 g, Lian Qiao 17 g, Du Huo 30 g, Ma Huang 4 g.

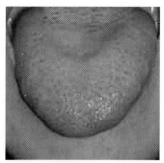

Photo 97. Tongue 26-#2 (2006.01.24)

PATHOLOGY

Photo 96 shows the tongue before treatment. Photo 97 shows the condition of the tongue after one week of Body Space Medicine herb treatment. The herb formula prescribed in Consultation #1 was based on the tongue analysis shown in Photo 98. Photo enlargements of the same tongue are shown in Photo 99.

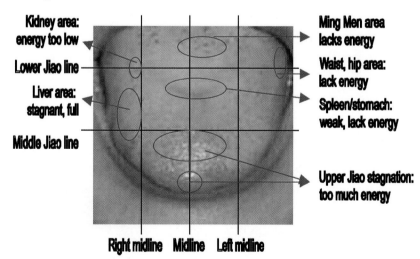

Photo 98. Analysis of Tongue 26-#1 (2006.01.18)

Overall, the tongue is wet, watery and turbid. The tip of the tongue is red with white blisters, the middle is raised, thick and full, and the root is high in turbidity. There is a thick greasy white coating in the

Middle and Lower Jiao areas of the tongue. The surface has stagnation spots and the middle part of the tongue has a dent.

The tongue is very high in damp turbidity, indicating that water is stagnated and immobile in the space around the cells. As a result, the matter energy is inadequate in the spleen, stomach and Lower Jiao, and the chest space is full. This condition manifests as discomfort, tightness in the back, deficiency of the spleen and stomach, inadequate kidney *qi* and a feeling of fullness in the areas of the ribs.

When the body space is blocked by damp turbidity, all cell activity slows down. The damp turbidity trapped in the Lower Jiao attacks the spinal column. In time, the joints become affected which will lead to immune system issues. If left untreated, the situation will also lead to heart problems.

The problems described can be solved by first clearing the damp turbidity and leveling the raised area in the front part of the tongue. The strategy is to clear the blockage and let traffic of matter and energy flow. In other words, make the San Jiao flow freely so that energy can circulate normally in the Gong Zhuan, enabling the body to recover its health.

Explanation of the Formula

- *Pei Lan* clears the San Jiao water pathway. It clears damp turbidity in the Middle and Lower Jiao, balances the water in the body and opens a pathway for cell movement.

- *Gui Zhi* opens the cell walls, allowing the free transformation between matter and energy, and adjusts imbalances of matter inside cells and energy outside cells.

- *Lian Qiao* instantly clears the energy and heat generated by the cells in response to Gui Zhi. It dissipates the lung space energy, exercises the spleen and stomach, lifts spleen *qi*, and clears the field by clearing accumulated matter in the space.

- *Du Huo* instantly leads energy downwards from the head to the feet, which charges the Lower Jiao and stimulates the Lower Jiao cells into action. The dosage of Du Huo was increased in the second consultation (30 g) at the same time Ma Huang was added. The higher dosage increases the downward driving force on the movement of energy and also implements the Five Elements application of Metal (lungs) generating Water (kidneys). In other words, Du Huo causes lung energy to charge down, nourishing the kidneys and increasing the stamina of the Ming Men area.

- *Ma Huang* opens all the cells in the body so that the matter inside the cells can be dissipated as energy. It enhances the effect of Gui Zhi to further increase the openness of all cells in the body.

- In summary, the formula clears damp turbidity in the body, opens cell walls to allow for free exchange of matter and energy, and treats the main issues.

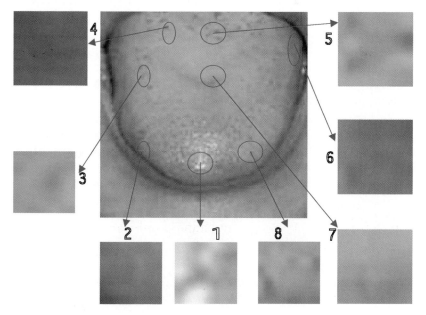

Photo 99. Close-ups of Tongue 26-#1 (2006.01.18)

CASE 27: STOMACH CANCER, ULCER

Consultation #1: 2005.11.01

ID: 27   **Sex:** Male   **Age:** 63

Symptoms: Stomach cancer, ulcer, distension of the stomach. The tongue is shown in Photo 100.

Photo 100. Tongue 27-#1 (2005.11.01)

Stool/Urine: Stool once a day, but small in amount.

Formula: Dang Gui 7 g, Huang Qi 17 g, Bai Zhu 7 g.

PATHOLOGY

Photo 101 shows details of the tongue diagnosis. The tongue is thick with cracks down the midline. The tip of the tongue is thin; the sides are raised and thick. The right side of the tongue is thicker than the left side. The tongue is red in color. There is no coating on the tongue.

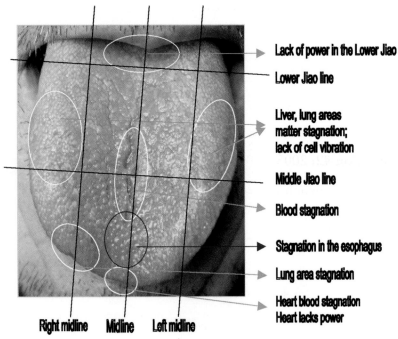

Lack of power in the Lower Jiao

Lower Jiao line

Liver, lung areas matter stagnation; lack of cell vibration

Middle Jiao line

Blood stagnation

Stagnation in the esophagus

Lung area stagnation

Heart blood stagnation
Heart lacks power

Right midline   Midline   Left midline

Photo 101. Analysis of Tongue 27-#1 (2005.11.01)

The tongue observations and body symptoms all indicate energy and blood stagnation in the body. There is excessive energy in the lungs such that the body cannot retain energy, resulting in inadequate power in the Meng Men area and poor functioning of the stomach and intestines. The Lower Jiao has insufficient driving force to move its energy up to the Middle Jiao. Consequently, the energy in the Middle Jiao is immobile, resulting in blocked energy in the Upper Jiao.

EXPLANATION OF THE FORMULA

- *Dang Gui* adjusts *qi* and blood.

- *Huang Qi* activates the energy in the space of the Hui Yin area (above the perineum). This in turn stimulates and radiates energy to the spleen, stomach and lungs.

- *Bai Zhu* increases the moisture in the Lower Jiao, which allows the energy in the Lower Jiao to move upward. This enables the action of "lightness ascending and turbidity descending" and aids the free flow of the Gong Zhuan.

- This three-herb formula increases the energy in the Lower Jiao and stimulates cell vibration in the Middle Jiao, which reaches the lung area. When the lung cells activate, the accumulated lung energy can then dissipate and all symptoms will resolve.

Consultation #2: 2005.11.07

Symptoms: Stomach cancer. The tongue is shown in Photo 102.

Stool/Urine: Loose stool 1 to 2 times in the evening.

Formula: Yun Ling 4 g, Zi Hua Di Ding 12 g, Qiang Huo 7 g, Gui Zhi 7 g.

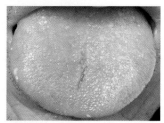

Photo 102. Tongue 27-#2 (2005.11.07)

CASE 28: STOMACH ULCER, BREAST LUMP

Consultation #1: 2006.01.19

ID: 28   **Sex:** Female   **Age:** 60

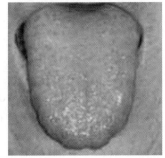

Symptoms: Stomach has blood stagnation, edema and a serious ulcer. Hot chest, hard lump in the lower left breast, hiccups, heaviness in the back, dry mouth. The tongue is shown in Photo 103.

Photo 103. Tongue 28-#1 (2006.01.19)

Stool/Urine: Stool once every two days.

Formula: Dang Gui 17 g, Lian Qiao 17 g, Du Huo 30 g, Zhi Mu 7 g, Zhe Bei 30 g.

PATHOLOGY

Details of the tongue analysis are shown in Photo 104. The tip of the tongue is raised, indented and has a red and hard stagnation spot. Both areas on either side of the midline are raised and there is a crack along the midline. There is a large blister in each rib area. The root of the tongue has a thick and sticky coating. The tongue surface has various stagnation spots and white blisters, with the color being grayish around the white blisters, as seen more clearly in Photo 105.

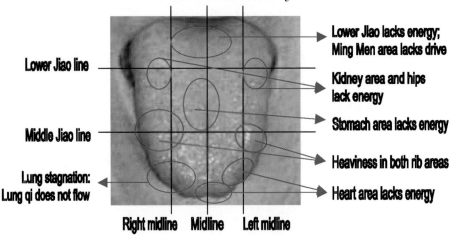

Lower Jiao line

Middle Jiao line

Lung stagnation: Lung qi does not flow

Lower Jiao lacks energy; Ming Men area lacks drive

Kidney area and hips lack energy

Stomach area lacks energy

Heaviness in both rib areas

Heart area lacks energy

Right midline   Midline   Left midline

Photo 104. Analysis of Tongue 28-#1 (2006.01.19)

The bump at the tip of the tongue indicates energy is stuck in the Upper Jiao, which means energy in turn is also stuck in the Middle Jiao and Lower Jiao. When energy cannot move in the Upper Jiao, it accumulates and becomes damp and hot, which prevents lung *qi* from flowing freely and slows digestion.

To solve the issues described, treatment must first focus on removing the bump at the tip of the tongue. Once this bump is leveled, the Upper Jiao energy will be able to flow like water released from a dam. When energy moves, the San Jiao will flow freely and the Gong Zhuan will circulate normally. Then the body will recover its health very quickly.

EXPLANATION OF THE FORMULA

- *Dang Gui* accelerates the microcirculation of the body, promotes the movement of matter and increases the body's driving force.

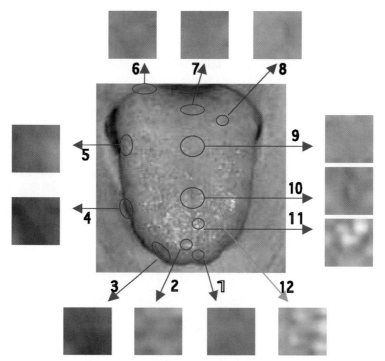

Photo 105. Close-ups of Tongue 28-#1 (2006.01.19)

A dosage of 17 grams makes energy flow and stimulates bowel movement. It also increases the output volume of blood from the left atrium and the left ventricle and nourishes the blood.

- *Lian Qiao* removes the heat and energy in the space of the Upper Jiao and clears the field around the heart, dissipating the energy in the lung space, activates the spleen and the stomach, and lifts spleen *qi.*

- *Du Huo* promotes the downward flow of energy from the head to the toes, charging and energizing the Lower Jiao to lead the circulation of the Gong Zhuan.

- *Zhi Mu* cools the lungs and the stomach, increases the moisture of the stomach and the Du meridian, cools lung heat and removes kidney heat. It also removes dampness from the back of the bladder area, increases fluid in the kidneys to bring heat down from the heart and promotes the upward movement of water from the kidneys.

- *Zhe Bei* reduces pressure and heat, dissipating the energy in the space of the Upper Jiao. A dosage of 30 grams can quickly dissipate lung heat and nourish the kidneys (activating and stimulating energy collision in the kidney area). By clearing the lungs, Zhe Bei enhances the circulation of energy in the Gong Zhuan.

- The combination of these herbs reduces lung heat quickly, nourishes heart and kidney energy and promotes San Jiao flow. As a result, the Gong Zhuan will circulate normally and many health issues will be resolved.

CASE 29: TONGUE – UPPER JIAO BLOCKAGE

Consultation #1:

ID: 29   **Sex:** Female   **Age:** 43

Symptoms: Tightness in the chest, hiccups, lassitude and weakness in the lower limbs, dizziness, poor appetite. The tongue is shown in Photo 106.

Formula: Mao Gou 12 g, Pei Lan 17 g, Gui Zhi 7 g.

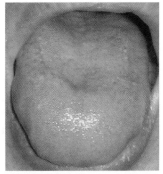

Photo 106. Tongue 29-#1

PATHOLOGY

Details of the tongue analysis are shown in Photo 107. The front part of the tongue is raised and without coating; the Upper Jiao is swollen and large. The middle of the tongue has a deep dent indicating *zhong qi*[4] is insufficient.

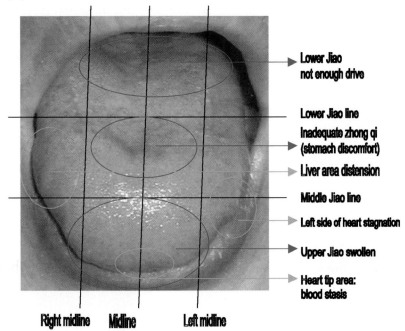

Photo 107. Analysis of Tongue 29-#1

Stomach issues develop because of the raised front part of the tongue; the Upper Jiao is swollen and blocked, so Middle Jiao energy cannot move up. If the Middle Jiao is blocked, then the Lower Jiao is also blocked. The Lower Jiao energy cannot move up nor receive nourishment; it therefore lacks drive, which is the cause of the fatigue in the lower limbs and the lack of appetite. The swelling at the front part of tongue (Upper Jiao blockage) is responsible for all these issues.

The goal for treatment is to reduce the swelling and size of the raised area in the front part of the tongue. Once the blockage in the Upper Jiao dissipates, the energy of the Middle Jiao and Lower Jiao can move. The Gong Zhuan can then circulate normally about the body, rectifying health conditions. Symptoms will disappear and the body will return to health.

EXPLANATION OF THE FORMULA

- *Mao Gou* dissipates the energy in the Wai Jiao space so that the energy in the space around the cells can replenish the strength and vigor inside the cells. It enhances the drive of the cells and also nourishes the liver and kidneys.

- *Pei Lan* clears dampness and turbid energy in the Middle Jiao.

- *Gui Zhi* opens cell walls and balances the transformation between matter in the cells and energy around the cells.

CASE 30: UTERINE FIBROID TUMOR (UTERINE LEIOMYOMATA)

Consultation #1

ID: 30   **Sex:** Female   **Age:** 40

Symptoms: Benign fibroid tumor in the uterus (uterine leiomyomata); distension of the lower abdomen. The tongue is shown in Photo 108.

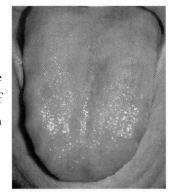

Photo 108. Tongue 30-#1

Stool/Urine: Stool once a day, small amount and not formed; frequent urine.

Formula: Chao Zao Ren 7 g, Gui Zhi 7 g, Du Zhong 17 g, Xiang Fu 17 g.

PATHOLOGY

Photo 109 shows the details of the tongue analysis.

Overall, the whole tongue is stagnated, pale and soft, lacks energy and has no coating. The front of the tongue has no wall to block *wind*. The heart lacks driving force. The energy radiation from the upper part of the body to the back is low, so the energy does not reach the Lower Jiao to nourish and energize it. Consequently, the upper parts are stagnated and the Lower Jiao has no driving force, which leads to issues with the uterus and other organs.

EXPLANATION OF THE FORMULA

- *Chao Zao Ren* increases the energy to the left side of the heart. This energy re-enters the heart cells, energizing and increasing the blood output of the heart. This causes a corresponding increase in the volume of venous blood returning to the right atrium. The result is increased arterial circulation and a stronger heart.

- *Gui Zhi* adjusts and balances the transformation between matter inside cells and energy in the space around the cells. When combined with Chao Zao Ren, it loosens muscles and nourishes the skin.

- *Du Zhong* increases the pressure of the Lower Jiao space. It increases the density of the space and replenishes energy deficient conditions within and around the cells so that the cells are enriched with matter.

- *Xiang Fu* lifts spleen *qi*, exercises matter and adjusts *qi* in the Middle Jiao, alleviates pain, and helps to adjust both *qi* and blood. These properties are helpful in treating gynecological issues.

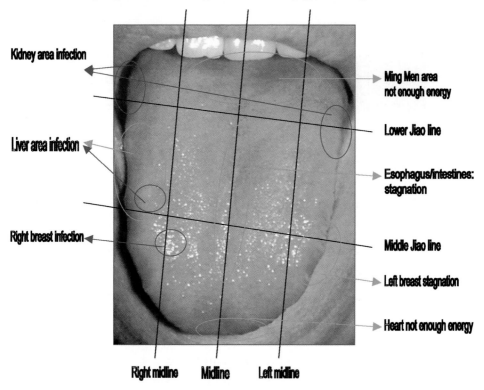

Kidney area infection

Liver area infection

Right breast infection

Ming Men area not enough energy

Lower Jiao line

Esophagus/intestines: stagnation

Middle Jiao line

Left breast stagnation

Heart not enough energy

Right midline   Midline   Left midline

Photo 109. Analysis of Tongue 30-#1

CASE 31: UTERINE TUMOR, FATIGUE

Consultation #1: 2006.01.22

ID: 31   **Sex:** Female   **Age:** 39

Symptoms: Uterine tumor. The whole body lacks energy. The tongue is shown in Photo 110.

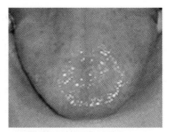

Photo 110. Tongue 31-#1 (2006.01.22)

Formula: Jiao San Xian 15 g each, Gui Zhi 7 g, Lian Qiao 17 g, Dang Gui 17 g, Du Zhong 7 g.

PATHOLOGY

Photo 111 shows details of the tongue diagnosis. Additional details such as color variations and the density for different sections of the tongue can be seen in Photo 112.

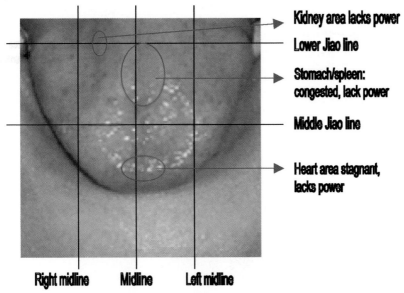

Photo 111. Analysis of Tongue 31-#1 (2006.01.22)

The tip of the tongue is red, raised and stagnated. The Middle Jiao region of the tongue is raised and high. There are also many stagnation spots and white blisters on the surface of the tongue.

From the center of the Middle Jiao area to the tip of the tongue is a large circular depression, somewhat like a basin surrounded by mountains. The depression represents dry heat and stagnation.

The basin at the front of tongue and the raised area surrounding it in the middle causes energy and matter to accumulate, which blocks the passageway. Unable to dissipate, the energy in the Lower Jiao does not move and subsequently lacks drive, with the consequence that matter stagnates and the San Jiao does not flow freely. Therefore, the whole body feels weak and suffers from stagnation. In particular, the chest and back feel heavy, the spleen is weak and distended, the kidneys are weak, the back is sore and the uterus has a tumor (i.e., excess matter and energy).

To resolve these conditions, treatment must first focus on leveling the raised area on the midline of the tongue to disperse the stagnation in the Middle Jiao. When the Middle Jiao is activated, it can disperse energy and matter properly. The San Jiao will then activate and move excess energy to nourish the organs and areas low in energy. The Gong Zhuan pathway will then follow suit and be able to flow smoothly, which will return the body to health.

EXPLANATION OF THE FORMULA

- *Jiao San Xian* clears stagnation in the Middle Jiao, allows energy to flow up and down freely, activates the cellular vibration of the Middle Jiao and promotes the movement of matter.

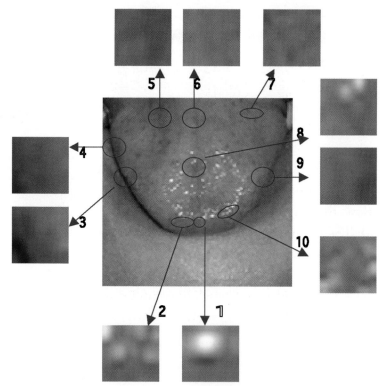

Photo 112. Close-ups of Tongue 31-#1 (2006.01.22)

- *Gui Zhi* opens the cell walls, balances and promotes the transformation between matter and energy in and around the cells.

- *Lian Qiao* removes the heat and energy in the space of the Upper Jiao and dissipates heat through the skin pores. It clears the density of the heart space dissipating it as energy in the lung space, activates the spleen and the stomach; and lifts spleen *qi*. When used with Gui Zhi, it clears the heat generated by the action of Gui Zhi.

- *Dang Gui* increases the circulation of blood in the capillaries, promotes the movement of matter and increases water content in the cells.

- *Du Zhong* promotes faster transformation of energy into matter, thereby increasing matter in the cells and the energy in the space.

CASE 32: UTERINE TUMOR, HYPOMENORRHEA

Consultation #1: 2006.02.08

ID: 32   **Sex:** Female   **Age:** 43

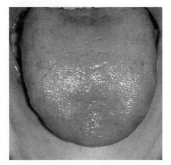

Symptoms: Dark spots on the face, headaches, dizziness, lack of energy throughout the whole body, uterine tumor. Both breasts feel distended during menstruation. Low blood flow during menstruation (hypomenorrhea). The tongue is shown in Photo 113.

Photo 113. Tongue 32-#1 (2006.02.08)

Stool/Urine: Stool once every two days, dry.

Formula: Jiao Si Xian 20 g each, Gui Zhi 7 g, Lian Qiao 17 g, Du Huo 30 g, Gong Ying 17 g.

Pathology

Photo 114 shows details of the tongue analysis and Photo 115 shows close-ups of the tongue. The tongue is thick, very big and has no coating. This tongue is typical of a person who has matter issues in the body. There is a large depression at the tip and another at the root of the tongue. In contrast, the Middle Jiao area in the middle of the tongue is raised especially high.

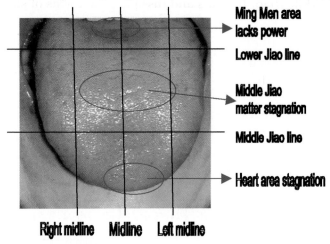

Photo 114. Analysis of Tongue 32-#1 (2006.02.08)

Imagine an irrigation trench on a farm. The channel down the midline of the tongue can be likened to a trench used for watering crops. However, a hill in the middle of the trench blocks water flow such that the land cannot receive the water nourishment. Without water flow, the soil dries up and crops die. Over time the stagnant water rusts the water pipe, eventually corroding and destroying the whole pipe.

The analogy of the farm trench applies to the body. In this case, the matter stagnation in the Middle Jiao causes problems above the diaphragm. The middle of the tongue is big and raised; its blockage causes the lower abdomen to develop problems. The matter in the Middle Jiao is stagnant and does not move.

The solution for the tongue conditions shown is to solve the Middle Jiao problem by dissipating the accumulated energy and matter and promoting the San Jiao flow and Gong Zhuan circulation. When the Gong Zhuan circulates normally, all the other problems will be resolved.

EXPLANATION OF THE FORMULA

- *Jiao Si Xian* balances the transformation of energy and matter in the Middle Jiao. It treats and dissipates all forms of stagnation in the Middle Jiao.

- *Gui Zhi* opens the cell walls, dissipates and reduces the tension of the cells, and promotes the transformation between matter and energy.

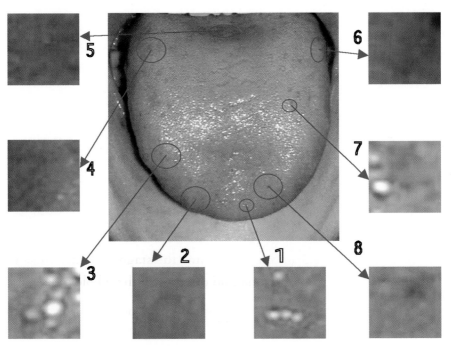

Photo 115. Close-ups of Tongue 32-#1 (2006.02.08)

- *Lian Qiao* dissipates the water path in the Middle Jiao, removes the dampness and turbid energy in the Middle Jiao, and improves the appetite. When used with Gui Zhi, it removes the heat generated by the action of Gui Zhi.

- *Du Huo* promotes the downward flow of energy from the head to the toes, giving the Lower Jiao a big push in the process. A dosage of 30 grams can energize the Lower Jiao.

- *Gong Ying* promotes energy dissipation in all areas of the body, reduces pressure in the space and promotes quicker matter to energy transformation. A dosage of 17 grams works well as an anti-inflammatory agent by removing excess energy in the space.

6

The Mission of
Body Space Medicine

I have given you the essence of Body Space Medicine. This healing system offers an entirely new way to use Chinese herbs. Traditional Chinese medicine practitioners, other medical professionals and healers of all modalities can use Body Space Medicine and its unique theories and methods. The most important new theories that I have revealed include the Message Energy Matter theory and the Gong Zhuan/Zi Zhuan theory. The tongue diagnosis of Body Space Medicine is also new. It greatly simplifies the historical approach of traditional Chinese medicine. I humbly believe that Body Space Medicine is a new medicine for the twenty-first century.

The new wisdom, theory, knowledge, diagnosis and application of herbs in Body Space Medicine will be of great interest to medical professionals. But the essence of Body Space Medicine — the quantum herb formulas — is so simple that anyone can learn this system. I reveal these secrets that I have studied, researched, practiced and refined for my entire life because I want everyone worldwide to benefit from this new medicine.

Millions of people worldwide are suffering. They need practical treasures and tools to self-heal. You have the power to heal yourself. What I can do, you can do. Body Space Medicine is very simple, practical and effective. It can serve all healing needs — at the physical, emotional, mental and spiritual levels. It can serve healing for chronic and life-threatening conditions. In particular, Body Space Medicine serves cancer patients with extraordinary results. Moreover, if physical herbs are not available, Body Space Medicine teaches you to use the message of the herbs to adjust and regulate the body for better health. The use of soul herbs in this way is another breakthrough of this quantum medicine.

Body Space Medicine teaches you how to treat and prevent illness, cultivate and purify your soul, develop the latent capabilities of your body, mind, heart and soul, and elevate your soul's standing. This book has focused on the tongue diagnosis and herbs of Body Space Medicine. My next book on Body Space Medicine will focus on its soul aspects. For now, let me say that widespread practice of Body Space Medicine will help all souls to join as one to create a harmonious world.

The scope of the practice and application of Body Space Medicine is broad. The techniques of Body Space Medicine are effective both within the minute universe of the human body and within the larger universe of nature, the planets, stars and galaxies. Purifying and cleansing the energy in the space inside the body is a breakthrough healing method for humanity's optimum health. Similarly, purifying and cleansing the energy in the space of nature will create a pure and beautiful environment for the world and the universe.

Be forewarned however. Before the halcyon days of the twenty-first century arrive, there will be great winds of change and great washes of tide, obstacles and difficulties. The current societal and political climate, the global mood, the health of populations and Mother Nature herself will change. On the other shore of this transition of Mother Earth, all souls will unite and all thoughts will harmonize. Follow this guidance: use your boundless kindness, love, forgiveness and compassion to serve humanity, Mother Earth and the universe.

I share my life experience with all medical professionals, practitioners of all healing modalities and all of humanity. I wish you will learn and apply this healing system to benefit yourself, your loved ones and all of humanity. I wish Body Space Medicine to be a service of healing, prevention of illness, rejuvenation and prolonging life for humanity.

I call upon all of humanity and all souls to unite. Let us give our utmost to create a beautiful twenty-first century. This is the ultimate goal of Body Space Medicine — to bring health, longevity, fulfillment, stability and harmony to humanity. May we all be successful!

This is my love and contribution of service to all of you. I am dedicated to serve you all.

Appendix 1

LIST OF FIGURES

LIST OF TABLES

Appendix 2
Color Illustrations

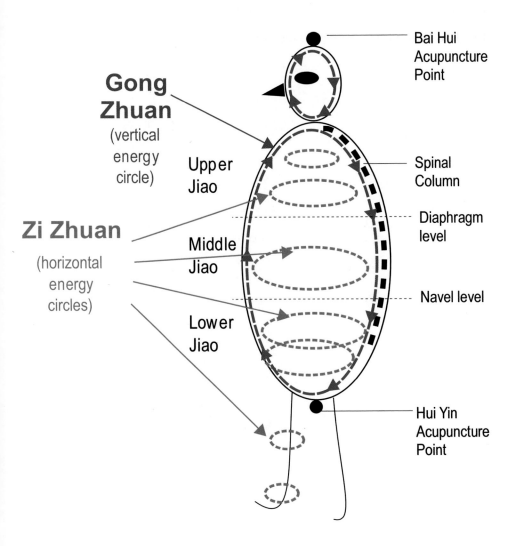

Figure 1. Gong Zhuan and Zi Zhuan Energy Circles of the Body

Tongue Map of the Body

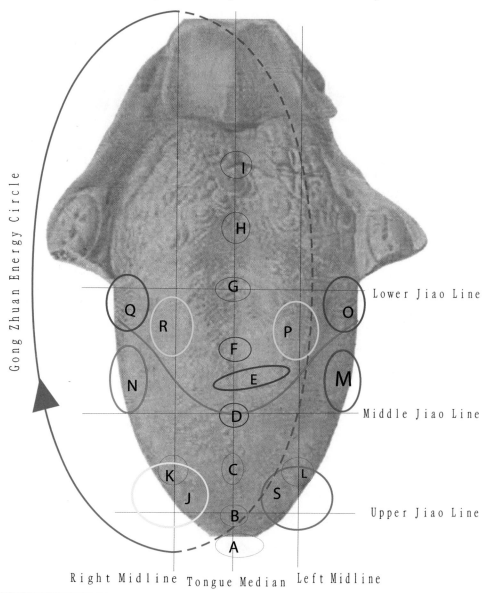

Figure 2. Tongue Map of the Body

A: The tip of the Heart   B: Tian Tu   C: Shan Zhong   D: Ju Que
E: Pancreas   F: Zhong Wan   G: Navel   H: Dan Tian
I: Coccyx   J: Lungs   K: Right Breast   L: Left Breast   Q: Right Kidney
O: Left Kidney S: Heart   P: Stomach   R: Stomach Function
N: Liver/Gall Bladder   M: Liver/Gall Bladder Function

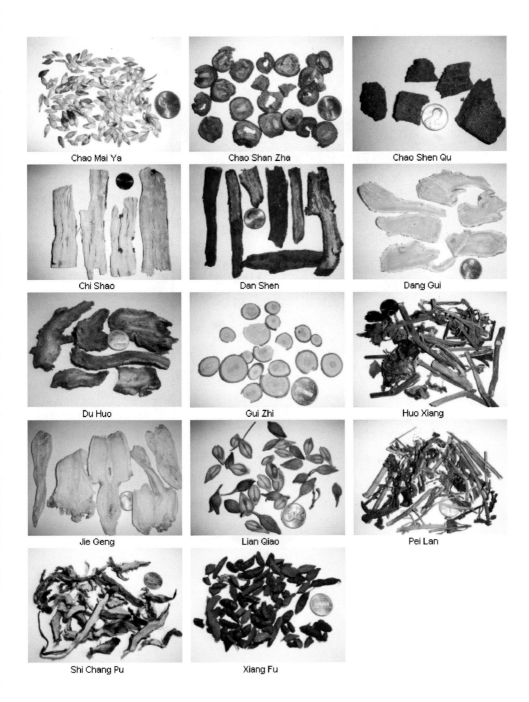

Figure 3. Key Herbs of Body Space Medicine

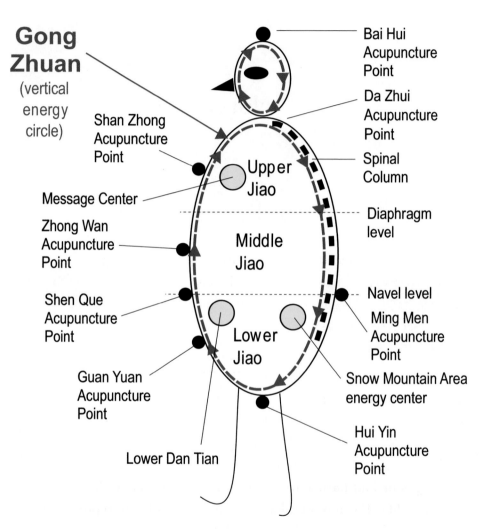

Gong Zhuan

(vertical energy circle)

Bai Hui Acupuncture Point

Da Zhui Acupuncture Point

Shan Zhong Acupuncture Point

Spinal Column

Upper Jiao

Message Center

Diaphragm level

Zhong Wan Acupuncture Point

Middle Jiao

Shen Que Acupuncture Point

Navel level

Ming Men Acupuncture Point

Lower Jiao

Guan Yuan Acupuncture Point

Snow Mountain Area energy center

Hui Yin Acupuncture Point

Lower Dan Tian

Figure 4. Gong Zhuan Energy Circle

Notes

CHAPTER 1. KEY THEORIES AND CONCEPTS

1. Tao, pronounced "dao," also known as The Way, is an ancient Chinese philosophy that credits Tao as the origin of all things. Tao is the universal laws and principles, so is omnipotent and infallible. Lao Zi wrote in the *Tao Te Jing*, "The Tao begets one. One begets two. Two begets three. Three begets all things."

2. Spiritual blockages are the results of mistakes you have made in previous lives and in your current life. These mistakes are recorded in the spiritual world as bad karma, also known as bad te (pronounced "duh"), which means "virtue" or "deeds." Any harmful acts, behaviors and even thoughts that you create will add to your bad karma. Spiritual law clearly states: a person with bad karma will pay a price and learn lessons. Spiritual blockages or bad karma are the root of blockages and disasters in every aspect of life. For more on karma, see my worldwide representative Zhi Gang Sha's books, *Soul Study: A Guide to Accessing Your Highest Powers* (Zhi Neng Press, 1997) and *Soul Mind Body Medicine: A Complete Soul Healing System for Optimum Health and Vitality* (New World Library, 2006).

3. Jiu Tian literally translates as "the nine Heavens," while Tian Wai Tian literally means "the Heaven outside Heaven."

CHAPTER 2. TONGUE READING

1. My next book will focus on the Xiu Lian aspects of Body Space Medicine.

2. The *cun*, pronounced "chuen," is a personal unit of measurement used in traditional Chinese medicine. One *cun* is defined as the width of the top joint of the thumb at its widest part. Although the absolute measurement of one *cun* varies from person to person, it is roughly equivalent to one inch.

CHAPTER 3. HERBS IN BODY SPACE MEDICINE

1. *Zang Fu* refers to the internal organs of traditional Chinese medicine. The six *zang* (yin) organs are the liver, heart, spleen, lungs, kidneys and pericardium. The six *fu* (yang) organs are the gallbladder, small intestine, stomach, large intestine, urinary bladder and San Jiao.

2. The Shan Zhong acupuncture point is located midway between the nipples in the area of the Message Center, which is also known as the Middle Dan Tian or heart chakra. The Message Center is where *zong qi* (ancestral *qi*), the energy formed from breath and food essence, gathers.

3. The portal vein drains blood into the liver. After the blood is cleaned by the liver, it flows through the hepatic veins into the inferior vena cava which is a large vein that carries the oxygen-depleted blood from the lower parts of the body, including the liver, to the heart.

CHAPTER 4.
THE FOUR QUANTUM HERB FORMULAS OF BODY SPACE MEDICINE

1. Chao Bing Lang is added to the three-herb combination called Jiao San Xian (comprised of Chao Mai Ya, Chao Shan Zha and Chao Shen Qu) to form the four-herb combination called Jiao Si Xian.

Chapter 5. Case Studies

1. *Jing qi* is prenatal *qi* or ancestral *qi*, one's inherited life essence. *Jing qi* is stored in the Snow Mountain or Ming Men Area.

2. *Yuan qi* is the body's driving force. Its source is the Hui Yin area above the perineum.

3. Wind, one of the six external factors causing illness according to traditional Chinese medicine, can arise from liver dysfunction and is the leading factor responsible for diseases. Pathogenic wind can move about and change as it attacks the body (just like the wind), resulting in changing symptoms and locations.

4. *Zhong qi* or pectoral *qi* is produced in the lungs from air and water. It serves as the dynamic force of respiration.